1 MONTH OF FREE READING

at

www.ForgottenBooks.com

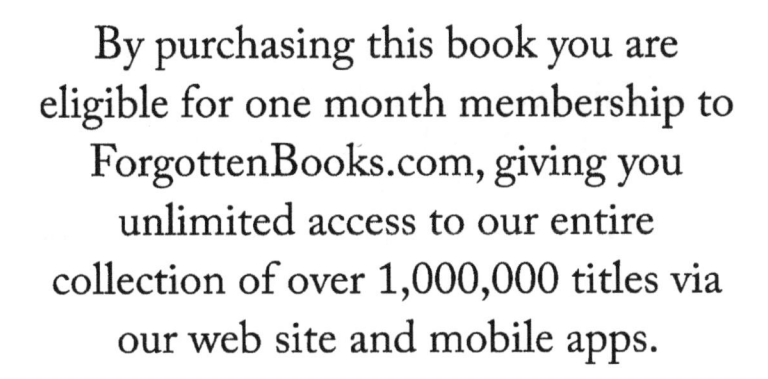

By purchasing this book you are eligible for one month membership to ForgottenBooks.com, giving you unlimited access to our entire collection of over 1,000,000 titles via our web site and mobile apps.

To claim your free month visit:
www.forgottenbooks.com/free74912

* Offer is valid for 45 days from date of purchase. Terms and conditions apply.

English
Français
Deutsche
Italiano
Español
Português

www.forgottenbooks.com

Mythology Photography **Fiction** Fishing Christianity **Art** Cooking Essays Buddhism Freemasonry Medicine **Biology** Music **Ancient Egypt** Evolution Carpentry Physics Dance Geology **Mathematics** Fitness Shakespeare **Folklore** Yoga Marketing **Confidence** Immortality Biographies Poetry **Psychology** Witchcraft Electronics Chemistry History **Law** Accounting **Philosophy** Anthropology Alchemy Drama Quantum Mechanics Atheism Sexual Health **Ancient History** **Entrepreneurship** Languages Sport Paleontology Needlework Islam **Metaphysics** Investment Archaeology Parenting Statistics Criminology **Motivational**

THE HUMAN FACTOR IN EDUCATION

BY

JAMES PHINNEY MUNROE, S.B., Litt.D.

VICE-CHAIRMAN FEDERAL BOARD FOR VOCATIONAL EDUCATION;
SECRETARY OF THE CORPORATION, MASSACHUSETTS INSTITUTE OF TECHNOLOGY; PRESIDENT (1910–11) NATIONAL SOCIETY FOR VOCATIONAL EDUCATION;
CHAIRMAN (1908–18) MASSACHUSETTS COMMISSION FOR THE BLIND
AUTHOR OF "THE EDUCATIONAL IDEAL," "NEW DEMANDS IN EDUCATION," "THE NEW ENGLAND CONSCIENCE," ETC.

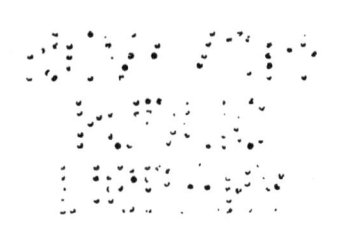

New York
THE MACMILLAN COMPANY
1920

All rights reserved

COPYRIGHT, 1920,
By THE MACMILLAN COMPANY.

Set up and electrotyped. Published January, 1920.

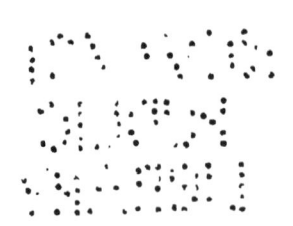

PREFACE

The extraordinary conditions surrounding social and economic life to-day have forced even the most indifferent to consider some of the fundamental questions which lie at the root of real national efficiency. Abnormal profits in certain industries, serious stagnation in others, the cost of living mounting by leaps and bounds, wages following after with a rapidity never before experienced, and the man on a salary distracted in his effort to make both ends meet: these and other untoward things have brought about a state of unstable equilibrium pregnant with danger.

While the United States is infinitely richer than in 1870, while, moreover, its currency system and its business credits are on a much firmer foundation than they were fifty years ago, there is nevertheless so close a parallel between the conditions of to-day and those immediately following the Civil War as to call up to older men uncomfortable recollections of what was perhaps the most far-reaching of American panics, that of 1873.

At that period, moreover, the United States was practically self-contained industrially, politically and socially; whereas to-day it is not only a member, but for the moment the dominant member, of a vast interrelated industrial and financial organism in which a country that in 1873 thought locally in terms of thousands, is now thinking internationally and in terms of millions of dollars.

Some of the leading questions which industry, witnessing such devastation as never before was possible, asks itself, are these:

(1) Will the after-peace period bring an unprecedented rush of men and women fleeing from militarism, or will it bring a further depletion of an already insufficient labor supply, in order to build up the wrecked industries of Europe?

(2) Will the cessation of hostilities find the great nations of Europe so occupied in meeting their own long suspended industrial demands that, for several years at least, they will care little for foreign trade; or, on the contrary, will they at once flood the markets of other countries with vast quantities of goods?

(3) Will this country remain on its present comparatively low tariff basis; or will it, under the fear of this flooding, return to high tariff?

(4) Will the war have so intensified the industrial training of the European nations that they will outstrip us even in fields formerly our own; or will their people be so unnerved and unsettled by the strain of war as to require another generation for the recovery of even normal efficiency?

(5) Will the United States be wise enough to mobilize its intellectual and industrial forces in such a way as to make science and education effective servants of

civilization; or will it go muddling on in the wasteful ways of *laissez-faire?*

(6) Will New York remain the financial centre of the world, retaining a dominant share of the gold supply; or will that supply rapidly make its way back to London, Paris and Berlin, restoring the London " square mile " to its old commanding position?

(7) Will the hoped-for fall of prices be rapid or slow; and, in either case, how can the necessary reductions in the present wage-scale be made without inducing widespread labor troubles?

Whatever may prove to be the answers to these grave questions, those answers will bring with them complicated problems of finance, of manufacturing, of legislation, of education, of the relations between employer and employee, that can be solved only by meeting them in the spirit in which modern science meets complex problems of engineering or of public health. The day of dealing with such matters by rule of thumb has forever passed; and the attitude of mind of the trained engineer, applying the teachings of pure and applied science to specific problems, must be that in which these hard questions of the next ten or twenty years should be resolutely faced.

It is significant that these great problems are, in the final analysis, almost purely human ones. Questions of immigration, of industrial relations, of labor efficiency, even of the tariff and of finance, can be solved only through crowd psychology, through sound education, through improving the relations between man and man, through permanently influencing the composite point of view of thousands, and indeed millions, of human beings. Consequently, in far greater measure than ever before, the welfare of the United States during the crucial time following the Great War will depend upon the efficiency with which are handled the infinitely complex problems of modern human relations.

If the United States is to maintain the financial and industrial leadership which has been thrust upon it by the extraordinary conditions in Europe, it must, among other things, handle the immigration question as a scientific problem, not as one to be treated without thought or system; it must establish relations between employer and employee based, not upon the self-seeking of both, but upon their common needs and upon their loyalty the one to the other; it must develop its public education in such a way as to make efficient workmen and men competent to lead; it must deal with the tariff question not, as heretofore, at the behest of selfish interests, but on grounds of sound social economy; and it must seek out and give authority to men big enough to handle complicated financial questions as statesmen, not as tools either of those who, though equally greedy, are forever denouncing Wall Street greed, or of Wall Street itself.

Immigrants are badly needed in this country, but they should be of the right sort, they should be distributed where they are needed, and they should be systematically trained to become true citizens of the United States. Capital cannot exist without labor and labor cannot exist without capital; therefore neither can long maintain itself in enmity: their common salvation depends upön wise coöperation and mutual loyalty. Efficient workmen cannot be developed without a widespread education in efficiency, beginning with the primary school. Foreign competition cannot be successfully met unless those efficient workmen are officered, from the lowest foreman up to the company's president, by men who know how to buy, how to manufacture and how to market, and who appreciate what team work really means. And even attainment of these ideal conditions will not save the country, industrially and socially, unless we see to it that the intricate questions of legislation and of foreign relations are handled by educated men determined to serve, not themselves or their party, but above all else, their country. The crucial problems of the next twenty-five years depend for their solution upon the strength, the integrity and the wise patience of every human factor; and this means that each of those human factors must be sanely educated for his particular responsibility towards the common task.

CONTENTS

CHAPTER		PAGE
I.	IN SOCIETY	
	The Real Superman	1
	The World of the Penny Wise	11
	Socialism	35
	The "Political Animal"	54
	The Workaday World	63
	The Human Home	80
	The Human Family	91
	The Human Community	104
II.	IN INDUSTRY	
	The Boy in Business	115
	The Human Factor in Business	131
	Art in Human Life	141
	Industrial Art in Human Leadership . . .	156
	The School and the Manufacturer . . .	168
III.	IN TEACHING	
	Education: the Common Human Task . .	182
	Education for Earning	191
	Standardization	212
	Child Idleness	217
	College Trustees and College Faculties . .	221
	Science and the University	235
IV.	IN RECONSTRUCTION	
	The Main Objectives	254
	A National Service Year	265
	Saving Human Waste	281
	The War's Crippled	293
	Employing the Handicapped	309

xi

I. IN SOCIETY

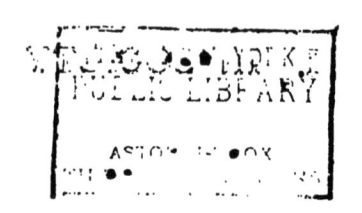

THE HUMAN FACTOR IN EDUCATION

THE REAL SUPERMAN

The old world passed out of existence in the tragic August of 1914. The world in which the rising generation will play its part is one as different from that into which men born in the "sixties" entered as theirs differed from that of the eighteenth century. The last thirty-five years have seen changes in the scale of American social, business and intellectual life vast in their magnitude; and now, with the ending of this greatest of wars, there will be a new leap forward, not only on the side of industry and commerce, but still more in those things which affect the social, emotional and educational life of the people.

Meanwhile we live in the midst of paradox. We are seeing, on the one hand, such national expenditure as, five years ago, was declared impossible. On the other hand, we have just experienced an absorption in economies and a cheerfulness in deprivations of which we believed ourselves incapable. We have witnessed preparations for the taking of human life on a scale which it was asserted this people would never countenance or bring themselves to pay for. On the other hand, we are developing such an interest in the safeguarding of human life as seemed beyond the powers of this happy-go-lucky people. We have just gone through the greatest proportional depletion of our schools and colleges since the Civil War; yet never before has the public interest in and concern for education been so acute as now.

These apparent paradoxes are, in fact, not such at all. They are merely the two sides of a single shield and one is, in fact, the inevitable corollary of the other. In order that the good things involved in economy of living, in care for human life and in sound education, might be realized and worked for, it seemingly was necessary for the nation to be brought face to face with the awful facts of reckless expenditure, of waste of human life, of threatening disaster through ignorance or through lack of a due reserve of highly skilled and highly educated men. And the silver lining to this hideous cloud of devastating war is found in the fact that out of its dreadful sufferings and wastes and long-enduring evils will come, in time, a thrift, a regard for individual life and a confidence in the power of real education that will not only be new to this country, but, in its effect upon coming generations, will be so beneficial as almost to offset the manifold evils of the war.

The education of the late nineteenth century, owing to tradition, inertia and a general ignorance as to what education means, was largely one of waste. We wasted well-intentioned effort upon perfectly fruitless things. We wasted the time of child and youth upon work that meant as little to us as it did to them. We shrank from wasting money in experimentation, but delighted in spending ten times as much upon traditional teaching the very source of whose tradition had for generations been forgotten. We wasted our natural resources and taught coming generations how to continue that waste in exaggerated forms. And, worst of all, we wasted that most precious of all national assets, human ability and human energy, with almost drunken prodigality. And none of us felt any immediate responsibility. That we survived this national orgy, that we are to-day richer and more powerful than ever before, is testimony to the soundness not of our methods, but of our national birthright and of mother nature.

To have gone on with this social and educational waste, however, for another generation or two would have brought us unfailingly to the brink of national bankruptcy. Already we were getting disturbed about the shrinkage in our forests, our coal and our many other national endowments. Already we were beginning to measure and weigh the oncoming generation and to find alarming portents in its diminishing vitality. Already we were asking ourselves why we should protect our vegetable, and not our human growths; why we should have elaborate laws for the preservation of hogs, and none for the preservation of boys and girls. And some of us were even daring to question the sacredness of our educational traditions and to wonder if it were really ordained of Heaven that the child should be fitted to the educational process rather than that the educational process should be fitted to the child.

Upon this shadowland of questioning and doubt, burst the great war. As is the habit of catastrophes, it brought us face to face with naked and appalling facts. That we found ourselves unprepared to deal with such an enemy as Germany, who has made war a supreme business for half a century, is perhaps to our credit; but it is greatly to our discredit that we could not rise quickly to a vast emergency, whatever might be its origin or character. We found ourselves to have become, through great riches and much absorption in them, slothful and self-indulgent. We found that our sons and daughters knew more about motor-cars than about creative work. We learned that our governmental machinery was rusty with age and circumlocution. We discovered that, far from having unlimited agricultural and mineral resources, a few months, or even a few weeks, might bring us to national starvation and death from cold. And we found ourselves compelled to take exact stock of our human energy, to count it out, individual by individual, for service in battle, in the factory and on the farm; and, to our increasing alarm, we are discovering that those human resources have a very definite limitation both in numbers and in fitness for the tasks that they must do. So, practically for the first time in our haphazard American life, we are facing the inexorable fact that we have been a nation wasteful beyond all others and that this waste must stop. And that stopping can come only through an education which is no longer wasteful, and through a focusing of that education to a large degree upon the problems of preventing wastes.

Education, after the great war, will cease to be, there is reason to believe, a spendthrift in itself and a praiser and promoter of extravagance. It will be, on the contrary, an education conserving the pupil's time, his individuality and his special aptitudes and talents; it will be one that, directly and indirectly, will fix attention upon certain great fundamental wastes which must no longer be permitted, and the prevention of which is a thing worthy of the best efforts of mankind.

The supreme acquisitive years are those between birth and majority, and in those years the physical and mental health, the character, the aims and practically the life career of the individual are for all time determined. Yet a large proportion of those precious twenty-one years are now thrown away, because of the ignorance of parents as to what education means; because of the adherence of schools to traditions which have meant nothing since medieval days; because of our fear of teaching immediately practical and useful things; because of our queer notions that work is a curse and that play has no training value; because we create vast educational plants and then use them to one fifth of their capacity; because, in short, we do not take a human being seriously until he becomes a man, until the precious period in which he might have been made a real man and an effective citizen has irrevocably passed.

The first lesson that education itself must learn is that it is a serious business: serious, because it deals with the prime asset of mankind; a business because it has a certain definite task to do and a limited time in which to do it, and should conserve every minute and every resource of that short training period. Most current education cannot presume to call itself, however, either serious or businesslike; for it leaves four fifths of its task to be performed haphazard, upon the streets and in by-ways; because it still regards the child as a mechanism to be fitted into its stereotyped machinery, not as a human intellect and soul to be individually developed; because it sublimely ignores all the experience and teaching of other businesses; because, while spending a great proportion of the national revenue, it feels no obligation to render any specific returns for those expenditures, and makes no study of the efficiency of the output of its vast and costly mechanism.

The war will almost have been worth while if, through the lessons it has taught, our complex educational systems come to realize that they must make themselves really efficient, by using their plants to capacity; by supervising the whole training of the child, in school and out; by making use of the immense educative power of both real work and real play; by teaching those who are to be the fathers and mothers of the future how to make homes and how to fulfill their obligations to society; by developing children into self-respecting citizens not only by training them for democratic citizenship, but by carefully helping them to make for themselves a real place in the social and economic world.

More than this, education in the United States after the war will utilize to a degree quite beyond present experience numerous aids and forces outside the school. The home is far more interested in educating the child than is the school; yet at scarcely a single point do these chief elements in the upbringing of the boy and girl come into coöperation or even into contact. The community has everything at stake in this matter of education, for upon the quality of its citizenship its happiness and prosperity depend; yet, except through a school board or an occasional interested citizen, the community is as remote from the inside of the schoolhouse as it is from the steppes of Turkestan. Industry must depend for its welfare wholly upon the kind of youth who come to it as workers; yet only in extremely rare instances does the school, which is training the coming generation and the industries, whose future lies in the hands of that new supply of workers, come together for the common end of making youth competent for this vast business of producing and distributing goods essential to human well-being. Outside every schoolroom and every college hall is a great field of nature, of agriculture, of manufacturing, of political and of social experience. Associated with all those human activities are thousands of men and women, not only competent, but eager to share effectively in the work of the schools. Yet they and the school and college faculties are as far apart as the antipodes. In every city are huge collections, libraries and other fountains of knowledge which are being used only by a few institutions. Those citizens, those industries, those vast storehouses of knowledge should be made essential elements in the educational system of the whole United States, and we should regard as clearly defrauded that child who, as a part of his elementary education, that youth who, as a part of his secondary and college training, that student who, as a part of his professional preparation, has not had every opportunity to get the use of some or all of these almost untouched sources of true learning. The term " social education " is still a strange one to most of us; but in it lies the whole economic, intellectual and moral future of this country. If the coming generation is to be educated to take its proper and effective place in the vast complex of modern society, it must have as its teachers, not merely some few men and women paid to hear lessons and to give formal lectures; it must have the teaching of all the varied forces of modern social and industrial life, it must be brought, as far as possible, into real contact with all the elements which are building, out of the resources of nature and of man, an ever more complicated, ever more efficient and ever more spiritual world.

By the cataclysm of this great war, the forces of industrial and social life, the intellectual activities and, above all, the spiritual emotions of human society have been stirred to their uttermost limits. Before, we skated on the surfaces of things; now we are looking into their illimitable depths. Before, we regarded industry as a means for making money; now we perceive it to be one of the essential formatives of human society. Before, we looked upon human beings as automata and their education as a sort of hocus-pocus with little relation to mental or spiritual life; now we know that every individual is precious and that his personality and its right development are essential elements in the Divine scheme. Out of this welter of battle and preparation for battle is to come to all the world, and especially to this new part of it, teeming with wealth of body and mind and soul, widespread self-searchings and profound self-revelations. From those will be born, in the proximate generations, such poets, such artists, such men of science, such philosophers, such great intellectual and moral leaders, as will make this materially great country of ours enduringly great. For the vast stores of grains and minerals, the wealth of cities, the labor and the striving of mankind exist, not for the heaping up of gold and the creating of things and more things; they exist as the rich source and fruitful menstruum out of which, in each succeeding generation, emerge a few master minds, a few discoverers, a few real poets, a few high spiritual leaders, who, by their work, their inspiration and their compelling example, raise their generation one step higher in the great, continuous uplift of the world. And the time will almost surely come, after the hurts and sorrows of this great war have been in some measure healed, when we in the United States will, to use Lincoln's fine phrase, "solemnly rejoice" that by this cataclysm we were shaken to our very foundations and that out of those deep and catastrophic national emotions were born the supreme men and women who will issue, directly or indirectly, from this world-wide conflict, and who will make this great nation of composite races not only the leader, but also the exemplar of mankind.

THE WORLD OF THE PENNY WISE

The usage of the great war, which dated events from "Somewhere in France," gives precedent for saying that "Somewhere in New England" the following conversation may (or may not) have taken place. The scene is a picturesque village, ten miles from a railroad. Its wide, grass-grown street is lined with a double row of elms, its untrimmed fruit trees bear infrequent and weazened apples, its houses, for the most part unpainted, are falling into decay. The windows of its one store are filled with fly-specked rubbish, its three or four churches advertise the poverty of their congregations: yet over it all is an air of exquisite peace.

The only person visible is an elderly farmer leaning against a lop-sided post and chewing, ruminatingly, a bit of straw. Having, with neither animation nor interest, and with an acid economy of words, indicated the way to the railroad, he seems disposed to relapse into the prevailing somnolence. The motorist, however, with the jarring alertness of his kind, wonders if even this ancient model of humanity may not be cranked into some sort of verbal speed.

"Don't you find it inconvenient to be so far from the railroad?"

"Naw. Could ha' had the railroad here when I was a little shaver, but none on us didn't want it."

"How's that?"

"Waal, they had it fixed fer to take some of our bes' farm land and to soak us fer betterments; so father an' some o' the rest on 'em fit it tooth and nail, and made 'em go through Hog Holler, ten miles further down."

"Aren't you sorry now?"

"Naw. Wife's brother lives down to Hog Holler (though they don't call it that naow; got some highfalutin' name like Rainbow Falls;) and when I see him last, 'bout ten years ago, he said he was kep' awake terribul by the trains an' the fact'ries, an' thet they warn't no more comfort settin' roun' the hotel, it's so darn full o' strangers."

"Have pretty good crops?"

"Tolerbul. Them fool perfessors from the Agercult'al College tried ter tell us our fields needed suthin' stronger'n caow manure; but when we found out what them new-fangled fert'lizers cost, we see through their game. Guess they git consideble of a rake-off."

"Your houses here are mighty picturesque; but don't you think a little paint would do them good?"

"Gosh A'mighty, man, I guess you don't know what paint costs. You city fellers may want ter throw yore money away on sech foolishness as paint; we don't."

"You have such a fine air here I suppose you don't need a doctor?"

"No sirree; yarb tea an' petent medicines is good enough for us. Don't ketch me payin' no fifty cents to no dandified young cuss fer looking' at my tongue. Kin see it myself in the lookin' glass fer nawthin'."

" Don't have many deaths, then? "

" Wall, no, 'cep'in fum quinsy sore throat an' scarlet fever and sich like. An' the wimmen nowadays don't seem ter be able ter raise the'r young uns. Why, my mother had fifteen, an' they didn't but ten on 'em die young. Wimmen these days think they've done well if they raise one."

" That's why you have so many graveyards, I suppose."

" Waal, didn't strike me as they wus tu many, when I think er some er the folks here as orter be in 'em. 'Tenny rate, this lan' up here araoun' the churches ain't good for nawthin'; jest as well ter put it ter some use. Don't cost nawthin' ter git berried here neither; taown pays fer it."

" How do you happen to have so many churches in so small a place? "

" Waal, they ain't much er anythin' in the way of amusement 'cep' goin' ter church; an' country ministers is dirt cheap."

" I suppose your moral conditions must be exceptionally good."

" Hey? Oh, morals: I guess they ain't no more moral taown in this here state. Why, we don't drink nawthin' 'cep' hard cider, which don't cost nawthin'; an' we don't swear 'cep' when none o' the ministers ain't 'raound; an' they ain't a soul in this taown but what kin lead in prayer to beat the band."

"I suppose your young people are all happily married?"

"Waal, it's funny about that. See them boys an' gals comin' out er skule? Waal, I guess quite a lot of 'em would hev kinder hard work to prove in a court er law jest who they belonged ter."

"Oh, that's the schoolhouse, is it?"

"Yaas; used ter be Bill Jones' barn, but his crops shrunk so he heddn't no use fer it, an' it didn't cost much ter fix it fer schoolin'."

"Have a good teacher?"

"Waal, Mandy Jones ain't no great shakes fer book larnin', but she's gosh-all-fired on lickins. She hedden't brains enough ter keep store, so she's glad to teach fer almost nawthin'."

"But your boys and girls don't learn much, do they?"

"She larns 'em as much as is good fer 'em. Why, over ter the next taown they got a high-price college cuss ter teach the skule, an' what d'ye think come uv it? The boys an' gals all got ressless an' most on 'em wus fer leavin' home. None on our young folks hain't wanted to git out er here sence I kin remember."

"Thank you very much for your information. Could I have a drink of water?"

"Glad ter git it for yer, but I warn yer yer may not like it. We think it's fust class, but some city folks we've giv it to, said it tasted o' the sink drain. They're both reel handy ter the back door. — Ye think yer better not wait? Waal, all right; come agin."

And as we glided out from the farther end of the

glorious double arch of elms we saw him re-settle himself against the post, resuming his straw.

Looking back, however, at that lovely village, with its absolute peace, its freedom from "problems," its ignorance of cankering ambitions, the "honk" of the motor-car seemed the despairing cry of a lost soul, driven from Paradise into the arid desert of money-making, money-spending, politics, social ambition and the ceaseless game of grab. In that calm backwater of the world, there are no self-questionings, no making for the sake of spending, no unsatisfiable wants, no moral conflicts; simply a peaceful acceptance of things as they are, with the firm conviction that in such contentment lies the beginning and end of wisdom. How delightful, for example, must have been the self-satisfaction of the old Nantucketers, who used to refer to the rest of the United States as "off-island."

Thoreau, who retired to the woods to live upon nothing (and immediately came out again to borrow Emerson's axe); Bronson Alcott, who meditated on the unknowable, while his wife did the washing; David Grayson, who, in his "back-to-nature" books, lives without thought of the morrow, sure of concocting some suitable adventure: certainly all such men as these have reached the pinnacle of true happiness, whence they can look down with genuine pity upon us poor, unenlightened "materialists," bargaining in our stores and offices, banging along, some in the over-capitalized trolley-car and some in the under-capitalized motor-car, all of us working and smirking for our daily bread, all of us hanging desperately to the skirts of Fortune who, sooner or later, whisks around the corner, leaving us ruefully staring at a bit of moonshine torn from her vanished robe!

Followers of the so-called "simple life" have certainly learned the wisdom of saving, not only their pennies, but their nerves. They have succeeded in reducing life to its lowest terms, and have put into actual practice all the smug copybook maxims, such as "Waste not, want not," "A penny saved is a penny earned," etc. But — the early Christians tried this living-upon-nothing policy, as a means of saving their souls, and they brought on the hideous miseries of the Dark Ages. The people of India have for generations saved themselves from vulgar, materialistic activity, and famine and pestilence are their never-ceasing reward. In short, the naked savage basking under the bread-fruit tree, and the hobo, kicked and "moved on," are the only truly logical exponents of the simple life; but the unfettered ease which they and the more sophisticated loafers have certainly secured is paid for, many times over, by the rest of the social organism which must carry its own burdens and these drones besides.

The Greatest of Teachers crystallized the whole philosophy of living in the parable of the talents. He who buried even his one small talent was "wicked and slothful"; and only to those who used and multiplied their opportunities was there given promise of abundant life.

The accomplished idler is charming, the hermit is

sincerely pious, the social recluse is surely harmless, the decaying village is picturesque, the reducing of life to its lowest terms sounds innocent and praiseworthy; but the hard fact is that all those persons and all those communities that do not put themselves, their one talent or their ten talents, to strenuous use, are, in the vivid English slang, mere " slackers." With mankind always fighting to preserve what of good it has achieved and to reach even higher standards of achievement, the man or group of men that refuses to struggle, that is willing to enjoy the advantages of civilization without working for them, is no better than the coward who lets the other fellow do the defending of his home and property.

We abhor the outcome — if it is the outcome — of the teachings of that more or less insane Mephistopheles who whispered dreams of world-conquest into the too-willing ears of William-the-Second-to-nobody, but we must agree that Nietzsche's fundamental doctrine is sound. That thesis upon which his whole grim teaching rests is that Life is given us to live, and that we should live it to the very full. " No," Nietzsche says, "life has not disappointed me! On the contrary, every year . . . I find it richer, more desirable, more enigmatical — And knowledge itself . . . for me it is a world of perils and triumphs." "Life as a means for gaining knowledge — with this principle in one's heart," he continues, "one can . . . live joyfully and laugh gaily." And later in this treatise of his on " The Gay Science," he says: " Believe me, the secret of gathering the fertilest harvest and the greatest enjoyment from existence is . . . to live dangerously," by which he means: to live out of the common rut, to live, not as one of a herd, but as a pioneer.

The responsibility of the individual — not selfishly to himself, but generously to his group and to the future — that was Nietzsche's ceaseless contention; and it is that responsibility and its resulting glory which most of us timid mortals are every day sacrificing to the dullness, the cowardice, the sloth, the conventionality of the unenterprising, unimaginative crowd. We are always patting ourselves on the back for being prudent; and we cannot, or will not, see that in saving the penny of stupid ease to-day we are wasting the pound of glorious accomplishment to-morrow. Grubbing in the muck for the coveted ha'pennies that the little world around us has decided to be safe and sane, we never look up and never realize, therefore, the golden fortune of real achievement that a life lived, as Nietzsche says, "dangerously" would have been glad to give.

Only simpletons believe in the life which is called "simple," but which is really rudimentary; only fools hide their earnings, actually or metaphorically, in an old stocking. There is nothing so expensive as misplaced economy, whether in material or in spiritual things, whether of our money, of our minds or of ourselves. A most significant remark was made by Cameron Forbes just after he came back from his service as Governor-General of the Philippines. Speaking of the government roads out there, he said, "They cost about seven times as much as yours, for we couldn't possibly afford to build such cheap roads as you do."

The most important lesson that the efficiency engineers — and they are in number as the locusts of Scripture — have taught us, is that the secret of business prosperity is not to save, but to spend. The owner who thinks he is making money by cutting wages, sticking to antiquated machinery and starving his salesmen is on the rapid road to ruin. True economy lies not in cheese-paring, but in liberal spending, in wise outlay for men, for machinery, and for keeping both at their maximum efficiency. What is true of the factory is doubly true of the household, the city and the State. Every cent not spent now in warding off evils, in preventing wastes, in promoting real, sound progress, means dollars spent in the future in trying, usually in vain, to repair the resulting, and wholly needless, damage. The heavy taxes, the high cost of living, the civic burden and the personal sorrow that follow in the wake of crime, drunkenness, insanity, pauperism, feeblemindedness, etc., all represent the "pound foolishness" that is being relentlessly wrung from us now to make amends for our "penny wisdom" and that of our forebears in the past, in not having spent liberally money and thought and time in destroying the causes of these blighting evils.

It costs a little less to erect wooden houses than fire-resisting ones; so we build acres and acres of them, and our " national ash-pile " represents every year almost as large a sum as that expended on new buildings. And so long as it is Chicago or Chelsea or Salem that burns up, we, living elsewhere, are cheerfully resigned.

We flatter ourselves, of course, that the insurance

companies shoulder this great waste; but they do not and they cannot. The expense of this colossal burning and the huge cost, too, of supporting fire departments that attempt, in vain, to prevent it, comes entirely out of the pockets of the citizens. This is a kind of civic " penny wisdom " of which we Americans are especially fond; and the result is that the builders of wooden shacks and three-deckers make a quick profit, and we, the poor public, with our huge bills for fire protection and fire waste, pay that profit and millions of dollars of loss besides. If the building laws were made adequate and were enforced, it would cost the real estate promoters more and their returns would be slower in coming; but in the end the owners would make much more money and the rest of us would find the taxes and the high cost of living rapidly coming down.

One might present unnumbered examples of what our unwillingness to spend a few dollars to-day costs us in thousands to-morrow. Indeed, the main purpose of city and town planning is to try to save our descendants from paying some of the huge sums to remedy our short-sightedness that we are every day expending in a seemingly vain attempt to repair the stupidity or the niggardliness of our near-sighted predecessors. And it is to be hoped that we shall celebrate the 300th anniversary of the landing of the Pilgrim Fathers, not by thanking God that there are still a few of us left whose humble progenitors came over in the hold of the " Mayflower " rather than in the steerage of the " Saxonia "; but that, on the contrary, we shall make this date really notable by so bestirring ourselves in regard to town planning and boy and girl planning, that in 2220, our many times great-grandchildren shall have reason to give hearty thanks that they had, in us, far-seeing and liberal-minded ancestors.

For, after all, it is the human being, not the wide or narrow street, that really counts, and it is in connection with human life and human happiness that our narrow-minded economies exhibit their most lamentable results. Take, for example, the blind. There are at least 4,000 of them in the State of Massachusetts alone; and while, considering what they lose, they are remarkably cheerful, and while, remembering their handicap, an astonishingly large proportion of them take care of themselves, they are an economic drag upon the community, and they are, too often, a heavy burden to themselves and to their families. And the worst of it is that great numbers of them are conspicuous examples of the far-reaching and melancholy effects of an ignorant, or niggardly, "penny wisdom." Here is a little girl who must go through life in darkness and dependence because her parents were too poor, or too untaught, to employ a competent person at her birth. Consequently, when, a few days old, her eyes grew red and swollen, none knew enough to put a drop of silver solution to kill the destroying germ; and, for want of two cents' worth of prevention, she, guilty of nothing, must yet pay life-long, costly penalty. There is a boy whose eyes are rapidly being extinguished by a form of tuberculosis; but, because there is no one who will spend the comparatively few dollars necessary to get him to fresh air and good food, he must pass his life in blindness, and the community must lose his productive labor. This man lost his sight because somebody saved a few cents by substituting wood alcohol for grain alcohol; and that paltry economy is paid for by years of darkness borne by the innocent user of this poisonous fraud. That man was blinded by a chip from a tool that he was grinding, his employers having saved something by not guarding the emery-wheel with an inexpensive shield. Huge areas are scourged with trachoma, a disease inducing blindness, because, when the infection first came to this country, it was thought too costly a task to try to stamp it out. And hundreds are going through life with half-vision, or quarter-vision, or no vision at all, because somebody, or some corporation, or some school-board, thought it good economy to cut down the window area, or to use a poor, flickering gas jet, or to subject the employees or the children to other bad conditions destructive to the human eye.

Probably the greatest existing menace to civilization is feeblemindedness, an incurable malady that transmits itself from generation to generation according to fairly well understood laws, that takes many insidious forms, and that is one of the chief, if not the chief source of crime, sexual immorality, drunkenness, beggary and general misery. To stamp it practically out in two or three generations, and thus to relieve the world of its heaviest burdens, would be entirely possible by segregating all the recognized feebleminded so as to prevent their having children and by so educating the community and especially those concerned, that they who are what may be called "carriers" of feeblemindedness, who have within them, that is, a definite tendency to produce feebleminded offspring, shall refrain from parenthood.

To segregate and educate in this way, however, costs much money, almost as much, for the whole United States, as it cost to maintain the war in Europe for one day. Moreover, it costs frankness and a disregard of Mrs. Grundy to set forth the plain facts concerning feeblemindedness. Consequently we are dealing with this vital problem with the utmost "penny wisdom," segregating less than ten per cent. of the known feebleminded and doing almost nothing in the way of education. Every year, therefore, the problem, its menace and its hideous results, are getting more and more expensive and more and more unmanageable.

"Thrift, thrift, Horatio." Sometimes one grows as pessimistic as Hamlet at seeing the crimes committed every minute in the blessed name of economy. How careful we New Englanders are, how we pile dollar upon dollar until we have a lot to invest in mortgages and stocks and far-away, dubious mines; how we always look on all sides of a proposition before we waste a single cent; how we watch the market to see when to buy and when to sell; how we keep our blooded cattle free from taint, our horses carefully physicked, even our pigs in the clover of perfect sanitary conditions; and, on the other hand, how we throw away ourselves and our children and our children's children, because we cannot see the world-wide difference between wise spending and silly extravagance, because we think that every kind of saving is always true economy, because we cannot comprehend that we are here not to serve ourselves, but, through ourselves, to serve civilization.

So far as we can read the riddle of the universe, this great, rich earth of ours exists mainly, if not solely, for the purpose of breeding men and women, of making them strong, thoughtful and genuinely religious, of creating out of them, in the ages to come, a super-race (to use Nietzsche's term) that shall be perfect physically, wise mentally and God-like morally. Yet, with this inconceivably high mission, with this inexhaustible earth subjected to our use in order that we may fulfill that mission, we slaughter babies by the thousands, — why? To save a few cents in the price of milk, to save a few dollars in the cost of training youth for fatherhood and motherhood. We maim and stunt and blind our boys and girls, we send them down to the uttermost hell of moral degradation, — why? To save fifty cents in guarding machinery, to get a few more dollars out of the rent of tenements, to keep the school budget low, to protect the vested interests of some fat old dowager or some gilded fool. We utterly squander our God-given lives by cultivating that futile thing, society, instead of that noble thing, our minds; by filling our houses with furniture instead of friends, with servants rather than mutual service; by surrounding ourselves with possessions and obligations that feed the senses while they starve the soul; by rearing to ourselves monuments of money and obsequiousness and flattery that fall, when we die, like a house of cards; instead of digging deep the foundations of lives — our own and our children's lives — whose influence shall endure forever, supporting, in the ages to come, that race of supermen and superwomen which should be the glorious goal of all our earthly endeavor. Who knows or cares anything about the gay butterflies of the French court who made sport of Franklin in his sober garb; and who does not know of that plain son of Massachusetts who saved money on his stockings to spend it on his mind? Who can remember the name of one of the panic-stricken millionaires who rushed to Washington upon the news of the ravages of the "Merrimac" and virtually ordered Lincoln to provide a vessel to stop her depredations? After patiently listening to them, Lincoln replied: "If I were as rich as you say you are, if I were as wise as you think you are, and if I were as scared as I see you are, I would provide that vessel myself;" and turned on his heel. They, in every sense of the word, are dead; but the poor, unfashionable Kentuckian grows more living every day.

Even New Englanders, with the inherited thrift of generations in their blood, spend and spend and spend, upon things that are worse than useless; and, hoping to make the balance even, pinch and save and scrimp on undertakings which, even from the purely material standpoint, would bring vast returns, and which, from the point of view of God, are exactly what we men and women are put here to carry through. They may sometimes — remembering their prudent forebears — show a little shame about, and make a feeble apology for, their comparatively harmless extravagance; but of their niggardliness, often colossally far-reaching in its harmfulness, they are always vastly proud.

Take, as a sort of composite example, the conscientious father in what, for want of a better term, we call a good, middle-class New England family. When his children were born he economized, with the full approbation of everyone, on doctor and nurse; with the result that his wife is a semi-invalid, and most of his children have congenital malformations or weaknesses that reduce materially their happiness and strength. By an economy in food for which her neighbors all commend her, the wife has made permanent her own semi-invalidism, which might have been cured by proper nutrition, has kept at a low point the vitality of all her family, and has ruined the digestions of the weaker children. Finding that it can save a few dollars by going into crowded quarters, this estimable family does so, thus cutting itself out of sunshine and fresh air worth many times the difference in rent. Since the furniture and carpets must be kept looking well for the eyes of censorious callers, the children are rarely allowed to play at home or to invite their friends; so those growing boys and girls get their physical and moral education on the street. The carpets remain unspotted; the children do not.

The father being too busy making dollars, and the mother being too busy saving them on essentials and spending them on non-essentials, no one has time to form the children's characters, to study their individualities, or to give them anything but the most haphazard steering through the puzzling and terrifying intricacies of adolescent life. Consequently these young people enter upon the responsibilities of fatherhood and motherhood, of creating homes, or assuming citizenship, almost totally ignorant of what these responsibilities mean and of how they should be met; and they are fortunate if, through an ignorance for which they were in no way to blame, they have not already unfitted themselves for the transmission of clean life and the custody of growing souls.

Penny wisdom as it concerns the hygiene of feeding, clothing and housing of children and youth is bad enough; but infinitely more damage comes from penny wisdom in matters that concern their minds and souls. The false economies that affect their material welfare are mainly savings of money; the false economies that react disastrously upon their mental and spiritual welfare are mainly savings of ourselves, a grudging and shirking of the effort, the discomfort, the ceaseless planning and watchfulness, that the proper rearing of boys and girls entails. The bodies of our sons and daughters we feed (as a rule unhygienically), we clothe (in slavish imitation of the fashions), we shelter (during the comparatively unimportant hours of sleep); but the real, enduring part of them: their intellects, their souls, their characters, we leave to ignorant servants, to more ignorant street companions, to zealous, but untrained, Sunday school teachers, and to the grievously overburdened schools.

Ah, now we have it! There is certainly no "penny wisdom" in the schools; we fairly pour out public moneys on public education, for its support is usually the largest item in the budget. But, as President Eliot and many other wise men and women have pointed out, we spend, but we spend unwisely, we spend, but we spend not nearly enough. Here, as in many other things, we are cursed with a love of superficiality and of making a show. Hence we put up magnificent school buildings expensively equipped, we try to teach everything under the sun except how to live, and we take the cost of all this elaboration out of the wages of the teachers, out of the future efficiency of the boys and girls. What more melancholy spectacle than that seen in so many Western, and some Eastern, towns, where the schoolhouses loom like mountains above a squalid plain of mean, one-story houses, the home, where the child should get seven eighths of his education, wholly subordinated to the schoolhouse where, at the best, he can get but about one eighth. Having "splurged" in the matter of bricks and mortar and curriculum, we must economize on human beings; and female labor being cheaper than male, and untrained labor being cheaper than trained, we are filling our schoolhouses all over the United States with poorly-paid, unskilled women, many of whom regard teaching, not as a high profession, but as a stopgap until the happy day when they may be released by marriage. There are, of course, thousands of women in our schools who know how to teach, who understand what their profession involves, and who are giving unsparingly of themselves year after year to secure to their pupils the best possible education. But the fact must be squarely faced that this exalted type of teacher is in the minority. On the other hand, through our false economy in offering beggarly pay, in failing to provide adequate training, and in requiring one teacher to " educate " — think of it! — forty, fifty or even sixty children at a time, we are putting our sons and daughters, — we are putting even adolescent boys and young men, who need above all things a strong masculine hand during these decisive, formative years, into the care of well-meaning but untrained and utterly overburdened spinsters who have no time to find out what their pupils ought to be taught, no time to study or strengthen character, no time to get the boys or girls started right on that double task — the most difficult and complicated in life — of preparing to make a decent living while at the same time developing a sterling character. An inquiry recently addressed to a great number of eminent engineers, asking them to name the things most important to success in engineering, resulted in their placing first, by an overwhelming majority, the one word " character."

The very fact, however, that it will take years to persuade the public to spend wisely and really generously upon education, makes it the more incumbent upon fathers and mothers to spend themselves, not on mint and anise and cummin (which, being interpreted, is movies and pool and gossip and bridge and shopping), but on the weightier and worth-while activities involved in making sound, ambitious, self-respecting men and women out of their boys and girls. Because the average school works against the health of our sons and daughters, we must strive all the harder to upbuild that health. Because the school tends to stunt the body and mind and even the soul of the child, we must all the more work to expand those. Because the school still depends upon the old, bad stimulus of competition, we must emphasize all the more the beauty of coöperation, of each working for all and all for each. Because the school puts most of its emphasis upon using the head, we must do everything we can to provide occupation for the body and the hands. Because the whole school system tends to make the child a mere cog in a wheel, we must do all in our power to strengthen his individuality. Because the school grounds teach smuttiness and evil curiosity, we must feel the greater responsibility for training in purity and reverence. And it is our responsibility to see that the youth is headed early and headed right for some vocation that will give him, not a mere living, but, what is far more important, real joy in living, the keen pleasure that comes from doing a thing easily, effectively and with ever-growing power.

To consider the problem merely on that pecuniary basis which the term " penny wisdom " implies, we and our neighbors, their children and ours, are without question the most valuable commodities in the world. Weight for weight, and from the purely material standpoint, gold itself is not more precious; for, by the time a boy or girl is ready to enter the high school, the community, including his parents, have spent on him, at the very least, $4,000. On the assumption that he should have forty good working years ahead, and that his average annual earnings will be at least $800, he should contribute, after paying back the $4,000 which he has cost it, $28,000 to the world. Multiply this by the hundreds of thousands of healthy boys and girls who are reaching fourteen every year, and it appears that the world has a human capital almost beyond reckoning. Sometimes the nations, going stark mad as in the fateful year 1914, destroy this potential human capital by a slaughtering more hideous than any shambles. But always those nations are impairing this human treasure — fortunately on a far less terrible scale, — by such penny wisdom as already suggested: by preventable disease, by avoidable accidents, by vices that never should have been allowed to get root, by failure to fit the boy or girl for the work suited to his or her capacity, and by a hundred smug measures through which, in order to save a few barren dollars, we throw away many fruitful lives. One does not need to follow Hood into the garret of the needlewoman to exclaim:

"Oh, God, that bread should be so dear,
And flesh and blood so cheap!"

Yet, startling as is this material aspect of the waste caused by penny wisdom, it is as nothing compared with the spiritual significance of our complacent, false economies. Here is every one of us made sole custodian for at least half a century of an image, an incarnation, a veritable portion, — I speak with reverence, — of God Himself. Here are most of us given, in addition, the custodianship of one or three or more younger incarnations of that ineffable Majesty. Thus honored and thus trusted, is it for us to haggle and question and doubt about the wisdom of spending ourselves and our capacities, to say nothing of our material earnings, for the highest possible service to these God-born tenants of our own and our children's bodies? Every one of us is given some talent, be it only that of turning handsprings, as in the charming story of "Our Lady's Mountebank," and shall we bury that talent, wrapping it in the napkin of timidity, of idleness or of pessimism, because it is unconventional or fatiguing or not worth while to put it to active use? Never again, so far as we know, shall we have the incredibly flattering opportunity to show what we can do with this great gift of life; and shall we fling away this single chance by harnessing ourselves to stupid, petty economies and to penny-wise evasions of the risks of living, as Nietzsche calls it, "dangerously"?

To save money is wholly commendable, so long as one's mind is fixed, not on the pennies saved, but on the dollars to be later spent. To conserve one's health is praiseworthy, so long as one's thoughts are centred, not on one's pulse and breathing and digestion, but on the longer and more effective service that a sound body can give to the world. Economies in household and town and State are at the very basis of human welfare, provided they have as their unvarying object the conservation of social good and the destruction of social evil. But to save money on things that make for health, — physical, mental and moral; to save money when to spend is to secure the sound education of boys and girls for their highest usefulness as citizens, parents and human beings; to save money on those city and town improvements which make for the efficiency and wellbeing of all the people; to save money on measures that safeguard the young and the weak against temptation; to economize on anything which, if maintained and encouraged, would lift boys and girls, men and women, one single step nearer to the high and, as yet, far-off ideals of civilization, is to sow dragon's teeth that are certain to breed a vast army of prolific physical and moral evils requiring incalculable future struggle to subdue.

The hourly distinctions and choosings that must be made between productive economy and destructive niggardliness, between wise spending and foolish squandering, are among the most difficult that confront us. But these things we do actually know: that for an individual to save his money (no matter how little), his strength (no matter how frail), or his time (no matter how limited), when it is a question of measures that affect physical, mental or moral health, that concern sound education, that promote self-development or child development, is to sell his birthright for a mess of pottage. We are certain, too, that for a community

D

to economize on matters that make for the good morals, right training, efficiency as producers and consumers, and the general, genuine happiness of all its citizens, is to surrender every right and duty of democracy. And we know, also, for history is ceaselessly proving it, that all real progress, all sound achievement, all lasting advance in civilization, has come from and through those men and women, those communities, those states and those nations that have freely spent themselves, their resources, their physical, intellectual and moral strength, in multiplying material wealth, in widening mental horizons, in uplifting spiritual understanding, in seeing and pursuing splendid, and expensive, visions. In living " dangerously," — dangerously to the outlook of mole-eyed prudence, dangerously from the point of view of the timid and slothful, dangerously according to the understanding of the crab-like conservative, dangerously from the view-point of Mrs. Grundy, — these men and these women, these cities and these states, have always found life by spending life, and it is they, and they only, who send life on to the next generation a richer, a nobler and a more glorious thing.

SOCIALISM

To-day, with the world in flux, men are asking themselves, as never before, Is our social system right? Or are we, as the socialists say, in a state of anarchy, with the rich growing richer, the poor, poorer, and all becoming more Godless and more hopeless? What are the signs of the times that we must heed for our safety and how shall we interpret that word, " Socialism," which threatens as never before?

Socialism is more than a rallying-cry, more than a passing delusion; it is a tremendous human force, partly wrong, partly right, with which Europe is contending, with which America soon must reckon. Moreover, there are two socialisms: the " Utopian," which is the fruit of the political revolutions of the eighteenth century, and the " scientific," which sprang from the industrial revolutions of the nineteenth. The former did an immense work in compelling reform legislation, it gave birth to a glorious literature, it was an essential phase of progress out of materialism; but it was and must always be impossible because it aims to reform men through human institutions, to secure ethical reaction without first arousing moral action. While this aurora of Utopianism was fading from the upper ether in which it had flamed so brilliantly, the stern conditions of industrial growth were producing, on the earth, a socialism of far other aspect, a socialism without romance, without illusions, without faith, almost without hope.

After the collapse of Utopian socialism, in 1848, there followed a period of nearly twenty years during which the socialists made no demonstration and their existence was almost forgotten. But the tremendous industrial changes, the conversion of hand-labor into machine-labor, had given rise, inevitably, to a new socialism. This first took definite shape in the "International," an alliance of continental workingmen, formed in 1864, carried rapidly into prominence, and killed, in 1871, by its complicity in the horrors of the Paris Commune. The second and permanent organization of modern, or scientific, socialism may be said to have grown out of the famous book, "Capital," published by Karl Marx in 1867. Marx is already out of date, so fast has the movement progressed; but the fundamental principles of his book are still those of that large and growing body of men and women who, under different names and with different details of organization and belief, constitute the social-democratic party. Clinging to this party and hopelessly confused with it, is an immense fringe of anarchists, nihilists, communists, believers in coöperation, nationalists, Georgists, socialists of the chair, progressists, Christian socialists, and others who, without very definite principles or with partial ideas, believe that society is wrong and propose all sorts of ways, good and bad, wise and foolish, for setting it right. Social democracy alone has a definite belief, a positive aim and a well-marked, though varied means of reaching that aim. The first, or radical, wing of social democracy believes in revolution and seizure of capital, with bloodshed if necessary; the second believes in political agitation and in the reform of society through gradual capture of the governments; the third wing maintains that capital itself, by concentration in huge factories, by the formation of joint stock companies and trusts, is rapidly preparing for socialistic organization, and that, by the exercise of a little patience, the great social revolution will take place almost of its own accord.

The social democrats, and all socialists, indeed, believe that for the old tyranny of kings, priests and nobles there has been substituted a new and worse tyranny, that of the *bourgeoisie,* of the manufacturers, merchants and factors who have originated and absorbed an enormous capital and whose trade interests provoked the conflicts and created that top-heavy military system of the late nineteenth century which brought about the great war. It is really against these money-breeders that modern socialism has taken up arms, and, in truth, the injustices against which it fights had their origin in purely industrial conditions. The remedies which it proposes are, therefore, for the most part, along industrial lines.

The social democrats declare that the workman is now nothing more than a slave; that he is the slave not even of man but of a machine. He is, they maintain, a wholly wretched and helpless dependent of our complicated factory system, and the miserable living that he now gains as a servant of steam or electricity is being taken away from him by the ever greater perfection of machinery, so that the body of unemployed is always increasing and, if it is not provided for, will in time destroy the employed, the capitalists and society itself. Karl Marx explains this alleged slavery of the laborer by his theory of surplus value, and he argues that this surplus value can be done away with only by putting the instruments of labor into the possession of the laborers themselves. He contends that every workman, under our present system (and by workman he means a man who does not control or own the machinery and tools with which he works), gives more hours of labor every day than are necessary for the subsistence of himself and those depending upon him, and it is this surplus labor which the capitalist seizes and coins into a fortune. Since Marx believes that the capitalist has no function in society which the laborer could not equally well perform, he regards the property-holder simply as a legalized robber who, by luck, cunning or fraud, has obtained control of the instruments of labor and, through possessing them, is able to drive an unfair bargain with the laborer. By this bargain the toiling workman receives only enough for a bare living while the useless capitalist is supported in luxury.

The capitalist, in his defence, may point out the important part he plays in originating, building up and maintaining the enterprises which furnish work to the laborer, he may show that were it not for his constant watchfulness, his seeking of markets, his advancing of money to pay the workmen, his warehousing of goods months before he can hope to receive any return from them, these enterprises, supporting thousands of families, would fail. He may urge the brain-work, the anxiety, the discouragements that are his; the tact, the foresight, the courage that are essential to success; finally, he may show that, despite these qualities and notwithstanding ceaseless endeavor, capital in nine cases out of ten comes, sooner or later, to shipwreck. He may point, too, to the almost universal dispersion of great fortunes in two or three generations, and to the great moral, educational and sanitary good that has been done by rich men. Such arguments are vain. The true socialist sees only the marked inequalities of fortune, the conspicuous instances of pure "luck," the many idle and vicious rich, the many hopeless and degraded poor; and he declares that the whole system is wrong, that so long as the present conditions prevail, the non-possessing laborer must be the helpless slave of the possessing capitalist. This wrong state of society the social-democrat proposes to remedy by a single but far-reaching step: the abolishing of private ownership in capital. This is the fundamental doctrine of the modern "scientific" school; its definite aim is the "socialization," as it is called, of capital. That is, the social-democrats propose to take out of private hands all tools, machinery, land, food supplies, means of transportation and other things constituting capital and to make them the property of the state, to be used for the good of all. The income from this "socialized" capital is not to be divided equally, — that would be communism, and they repudiate communism even more fiercely than anarchism — but it is to be divided equitably, *i.e.*, every man is to be rewarded according to his capacity and his industry. His daily labor, in other words, is to be appraised and put to his credit; and against this labor fund of his he is to be allowed to draw such supplies of food, clothing, furniture, amusements, etc., as he may wish. Money is to be abolished as unnecessary, and with it will vanish interest, banking and all forms of credit. A man may spend his labor fund as he pleases, he may hoard it and he may bequeath his savings; but he cannot invest the labor that is credited to him nor can he in any way increase it except by addition. His only business dealings will be with the government which, through elected officials and committees, will wholly control production and distribution. Shops and, to a large extent, freight transportation will disappear and every citizen, so far as is possible, will have his wants supplied from his immediate neighborhood. The local officials or committees will establish warehouses for the storage of commodities and will determine what shall be raised and what manufactured in their district, what commodities shall be exported, so to speak, from their district and what goods shall be imported. These or other local officials will determine the worth of everyone's labor and fix its exchange value in terms of the commodities contained in the public warehouses.

Under this system, the socialists believe, idlers, paupers and the unemployed will disappear, since he who would eat must work and he who works may eat. The state will provide, of course, for the aged, the defective and the sick, but these dependents will be supported by right, not, as now, by charity. Courts of civil law, whose existence rests upon property, will vanish; and the criminal courts will soon fall into disuse, so great, they believe, will be the decrease in crime, its three chief sources: poverty, ignorance (education being absolutely compulsory) and drunkenness (the liquor traffic being suppressed or strictly limited) having been taken away. These are but a few of the benefits that, in the eyes of the socialists, will follow this single step: the abolition of private ownership in capital.

But what may be said on the other side? First, what are some of the practical difficulties in the way of the "socialization" of capital? Only extreme socialists advocate the forcible seizure of private property. The majority agree that the present owners either should be directly paid or should receive a fair life income on their capital. But how are these plans for compensation to be carried out? The state cannot borrow, since credit is abolished, and its only available resources consist in the property which it has just seized. It must pay for this confiscated property, then, by means of that very property itself, which is, of course, absurd. If, choosing the other horn of the dilemma, the state should compensate the capitalists by giving them a fair income for 25, 50 or 75 years, it would, seemingly, continue them as a favored class, able to save and leave comparative fortunes to their children. The socialists, however, say No; that these capitalists are to be given an income in perishable goods, in food, drink and amusements, so that the millionaires will be overwhelmed with things that they can neither use nor sell. Still it is not likely that these dispossessed property-holders, now so grasping, will give up even this useless and embarrassing income and as, presumably, their capital now produces almost to its fullest capacity, it cannot be made to yield, under the new system, much more than enough to provide for these ex-capitalists. Therefore, for one generation at least, the workingman must labor chiefly to heap up perishable goods for his former masters. Plainly compensation is not feasible, and those radical socialists who echo Proudhon's cry: " Property is robbery," and demand its seizure without payment are in the right.

Let us suppose, however, that in some way, with or without bloodshed, the state has dispossessed the property-owners, what then? Who is to manage this immense capital, these factories and railroads, these shops and other thousand enterprises? Elected committees? And, if so, who or what will insure their efficiency, their faithfulness, their freedom from corruption? How will it be certain that the state gets the full income from its capital? Have we been so fortunate in our present socialistic enterprises, in our post-office, for example, that we can look forward trustingly to a time when every enterprise shall be in the hands of political committees? But, say the socialists, corruption, self-seeking and incompetence will disappear from the socialistic state, because the best men will rise to the top and neither they nor the lesser men will do wrong, since it will be to their greater interest to do right. The man who cheats or falsifies or adulterates or slights his work will suffer with the rest and, therefore, will have no temptation to do wrong. Will the best men rise to the top and burden themselves with inconceivably hard tasks of administration when they can be comfortable and happy by remaining near the bottom and performing simpler duties? Will the mere fact that they suffer with the rest deter men from stealing, from putting up political "jobs," from tyrannizing and, in a hundred ways, abusing their power? It is difficult to conceive of any transformation that in one year, or in fifty years, will eliminate the ward-politician and will free men in authority from the temptations that come with power and with the handling of large capital in which their ownership is only indirect.

Let us grant, however, that the confiscation of property is happily accomplished and that the state is in the hands of perfectly honest and fully competent men and women. How are these officials to settle questions of demand and supply for a hundred million people or even for an average community? We have now a wonderfully responsive, though crude, regulator of production in the fluctuation of prices. If a commodity is falling short, the price rises, a stimulus is given to its production and, when the temporary shortage is made up, the price falls again, production slackens, not to increase until a rise in price again arouses it. But under the socialistic state, prices are to remain fixed, this commercial thermometer will be lacking, and the government will have little more than guess work to help its agents in determining what shall be produced, when and by whom. In view of this difficulty, the tendency will be to force men to limit their wants and by so doing, a sameness of life, full of harm to human progress, will be brought about. Furthermore, the government will have to reckon with that very uncertain factor, the weather. The million acres of wheat ordered to be sown in the spring may be reduced by blight to 500,000 acres. An unusually mild winter may curtail immensely the demand for the woolens manufactured in advance, and, in many ways, the weather, as well as the fickleness of human wants and fashions, will confuse and upset the government's calculations. A further disturbing element is the fact that the value of commodities in use fluctuates greatly and is often wholly out of proportion to the value of the labor that has been spent upon them. This is a point with which Marx deals in a very unsatisfactory way. He acknowledges the uncertainties and fluctuations of values, but apparently does not look upon them as fatal to that axiom which, using his favorite rule of three, he states as follows: " The value of one commodity is to the value of any other, as the labor-time necessary for the production of the one is to that necessary for the production of the other." Later socialists, led by Schæffle, have brought out very clearly this flaw in Marx's reasoning, and there has long been a bitter war among the social-democrats over this weak point in his triumphant doctrine.

But these practical difficulties in the way of socialism ought not to discredit it. No effort in overcoming them would be too great provided the results were to be such as its friends predict. To the mind of the non-socialist, however, the moral effect of socialism, as it is preached by the social-democrats, would be so bad, the social condition that would be brought about by it would be so infinitely worse than our present tolerable, though imperfect status, that the practical obstacles fade, by comparison, into insignificance.

It is maintained by the socialists that the hard industrial conditions of which they so bitterly complain are due, first, to the private ownership of capital and, secondly, to the competition which the existence of private capital and its struggle for gain make necessary. Many of their writers, indeed, do not blame the capitalist for his alleged tyranny, but grant that he, too, is a victim of circumstances by which he is compelled to lower wages, multiply machinery, increase his output and adulterate his goods, merely that he may keep up in that struggle for existence whose horrors the socialists paint in darkest colors. Is private capital, however, a totally unnecessary factor in civilization and is this competition which it arouses such a hideous nightmare as the socialists would have us believe? The would-be abolisher of capital becomes rather hysterical when he describes the crimes of competition. The industrial world is not a jungle filled with cunning and bloodthirsty beasts; and the individual capitalist does a work in society that can never be satisfactorily performed by the state; for self-interest and the force of competition, by their very nature, compel him to promote the general industrial welfare by cheapening and perfecting processes of manufacture, by multiplying and quickening means of transportation, by extending commerce and by making his products more finished and more artistic. His interest forces him to respond instantly to the fluctuations of demand and to create and stimulate new wants. By this selfish stimulation he exerts a steady upward pressure upon the standard of good living and becomes not only a great industrial but, still more, a mighty moral force. The workman often suffers, without doubt, through bad adjustment of the commercial machinery, from greed, fraud and other vices of which capital has its full share; but, on the other hand, he gains vastly more than he could possibly lose through the competition of trade. With rare exceptions, wages are steadily rising, the working day is shortening, work itself is growing easier. Machinery and competition have done this by cheapening products, by multiplying through mechanism the producing capacity of men, by putting the drudgery of production into the patient hands of steam. If the rich are growing richer, which, in view of the rapid fall in rates of interest, is very doubtful, the poor are growing richer, too, not only, as the savings-banks show, by what they save but, far better, by what they spend; by the inclination and the opportunity they have, every day more freely, to share in those comforts, conveniences and public improvements that are the fruit of competition and are the property of rich and poor alike.

Abstractly it does seem wrong that A should be rich while B, more worthy and intelligent, is poor; but it seems quite as wrong that the Hottentot should be born in South Africa rather than in New York City. Chance plays a tremendous part in life and the overcoming of its disadvantages is an important element in human growth. The immediate and passing effects of the law of chance are often bad, but the law itself is at the very foundation of human progress. The inequalities that men must strive against to overcome, the uncertainty of subsistence, the hardships and difficulties that must be surmounted, the never-ending fight for life, the disappointments and sorrows that make that life doubly hard, — these are the very things that, in the past, have impelled men to make life as tolerable as it is and, in the future, will force them to make it still more worth living. "Difficulties," says Epictetus, "are things that show what men are . . . Remember that God, like a gymnastic trainer, has pitted you against a rough antagonist. For what end? That you may be an Olympic conqueror; and this cannot be without toil." Since the dawn of the race man has been compelled to struggle against the outward forces that tried to keep him cold, naked, hungry and a prey to circumstance, against the inward forces that tended to make a beast of him. But by this struggling, he has practically abolished cold, famine and pestilence, he has annihilated time and space, he has converted the destructive forces of nature into willing servants, he has made a decent, companionable creature of himself. Through struggle, in short, he has evolved civilization out of savagery. But the struggle has not been limited to a fight with nature; that would have brought man only to a state of barbarism. Civilization and its benefits have been reached through the struggle of man with man, that is, through competition. It is the desire to excel — to be first, in war, in love, in industry, that has brought man to his present comparative ease of life. Every step forward out of barbarism has been made through the desire of someone to be a little stronger, a little more respected, a little richer, a little more luxurious than his neighbor. From the collective selfishness of individuals has resulted the good of society. But is external nature so tame, are we so raised above our old savage selves, that we now may say: " let struggle cease; let us rest and enjoy the fruits of the battles that our fathers fought"? Surely not. We know too well how little transforms men into animals. how quickly the unopposed forces of nature take advantage of us, to dare to cease struggling. Socialism, however, would inevitably allow man to relax in his fight for human progress and, soon, not only would humanity be stagnant, but it would have lost much of that which has been so hardly earned. Sane men do nothing without a motive. Their motives for progress thus far have been self-preservation, love and rivalry. What are the motives that will govern the new, socialistic state? Simply abstract goodness and the spirit of philanthropy.

The general love of mankind is to take the place, not only of self-love, but of that stronger motive, family love, which now is the spur to most of us. To-day, in general, men struggle and save and do their best because of the wife and children, the father and mother, the brothers and sisters who depend upon them. By working and saving and doing his duty a man gives his family security, happiness and perhaps comfort; he educates his children and assures them a fairer start than he had; he makes himself and his little group of some consequence in the narrow circle of his neighborhood. The harder the struggle, — unless it kill him, and the proportion of such deaths is small, — the greater his satisfaction in its success. We have not yet reached a point, it will be centuries before we do, where abstract love and general duty can be made so strong a motive for us to do right, to work, to improve ourselves, as are these hard, concrete duties and, if you please, these selfish affections that now centre in the family group. What Pestalozzi called the Trinity of love: father, mother, child, has been the slow growth of centuries, and it is the nucleus of civilization. This nucleus the socialistic state will inevitably destroy. While few of the better sort of socialists actually propose to disintegrate the family group, hardly one of them but scoffs at it as a selfish, outgrown relation, and all look forward to merging it into their ideal social group whose ties are not of blood but of human brotherhood. All socialists claim that the family is a creation of property and that with the abolition of property the tie will weaken and men and women will move out of the narrow circle of household interests into the free air of human brotherhood. They are right in maintaining that socialism will dissolve the family, for it will destroy the sense of responsibility upon which, chiefly, the family rests; they are right, too, in asserting that the family group is based largely upon property; but they are criminally wrong in viewing lightly the destruction of the household and in demanding that its basis, property, be taken away. For the home-property is not, as they would have us believe, the spoil that one group has captured from another; it is not the selfish hoarding which the family must fight for. The home-property represents obligation, it represents the work of the father, the saving of the mother, joined to provide proper education, — using the word in its widest sense — for their children. It is the stern "ought" of duty made tangible. It is the unit of society which, without it, would be a herding of cattle having no higher motives than the satisfaction of hunger and desire.

Finally, the agitation for socialism, especially by men of influence, has the increasingly bad result of befogging the real issues in human progress, of turning attention away from true and pressing evils towards remote and semi-visionary ones. Society suffers to-day not from the sins of government or the greed of capital, but from the ignorance and vice of the individual. We have poverty and disease and anguish all about us, not because a few are too rich and many are too poor, but because all, rich and poor, are, through ignorance or indifference, disobeying the moral law. The problem of to-day is not how to reform society but how to reform the individuals who compose it. The offenders against social order are not alone the idle rich who have stolen the land and the grasping capitalists who grind the faces of the poor; the real destroyers of the state are those men and women who, knowing the right, do wrong; those who, heedlessly or wrongly, enter into marriage; those parents who, bringing children into the world, feel no responsibility for their physical and moral growth; those citizens who, having votes, use them carelessly or dishonestly or throw them away; those young men and women who, having minds and consciences, waste the first and smother the second; those hundreds of thousands who, with all civilization before them, are content to vegetate. Only those rich are guilty who fail to make good use of their greater opportunities, and set examples of folly, selfishness and vice for the poor to imitate. No man, rich or poor, owes anything to the state except to do his duty as a citizen and to live an honest, self-improving life. But this is a very large debt. If everyone who could, paid this obligation, the " submerged tenth," who are so steeped in misery that they cannot do their duty and live honest lives, would soon be so reduced that there would be no social problem left.

In bringing about this result, in teaching duty and right living to the poor as well as to the rich, socialism has its great work to do. It is vain for it to attempt to upset those laws of human progress that are rooted not only in history but in man's very nature. It wastes its strength, it perverts its power. The aid of socialism, of the unselfish union of men, is needed, not in regulating industry, but in solving the moral problems that industrial and social life create; in uplifting the individual by the force of helpful association; in destroying abuses by the power of united action; in showing the beauty and economy of the golden rule.

The greatest need of to-day is to educate the public conscience; but, to do so, the individual consciences, of which public opinion is the sum, must be aroused and taught. Acts of moral legislation, public agitation for reform, aid greatly in this direction. Every wise reform-law that is enforced not only is educational in itself but makes the public conscience more sensitive to other abuses, more ready to correct them. Nothing, indeed, is outside the scope of socialistic legislation; but a sharp distinction must always be made between law-making and law-meddling, between a temporary melioration of individuals and the ultimate good of society. Within these absolute bounds education, health, morals, all are fit subjects for regulation; and in many additional directions the state may properly limit the individual. But not all legislation, even though it be flawless in theory, is good in practice. It may be unwise merely because it cannot be enforced; it may be really bad because its final effect will be worse than that of the abuse it has tried to correct. The test questions regarding a socialistic act are: "Is it class legislation? Is there a strong and stubborn public sentiment that will resist its enforcement? Does it interfere with the proper liberty of the good citizen? Finally, and most important, does it deaden or weaken the sense of individual responsibility?" Hard questions, not always soluble except in the light of dearly bought experience; but, if asked regarding much of the proposed legislation of the socialists, of many acts of our own and the European governments, the answer is too plainly, "Yes." Social democracy, were it realized, would benefit the few lazy and incompetent at the expense of the many industrious; it would interfere with the inalienable and lawful right of the individual to be the chooser, within the narrow bounds that God has placed, of his own destiny; it would be not only contrary, but fatal, to that public conscience, still so feeble, which civilization has nursed into conscious being; in short, it would confuse or take from men and women what slight sense of duty, what incomplete self-reliance they now possess, persuading them that their industrial and moral welfare does not rest mainly with themselves, but with some outward power upon which they may lean and shift all responsibility for their mistakes and sins.

Under socialism there would be for a time, without doubt, greater enjoyment for a greater number of individuals. But this temporary ease and pleasure would be bought at the cost of courage, ambition, self-reliance and those more divine qualities which now impel us, we scarcely know how or why, to moral action, and force the majority of us to carry out the eternal scheme by leaving the world a little better than we found it. A fearful price to pay!

THE "POLITICAL ANIMAL"

AMERICANS are good-natured, quick to see the humor rather than the hurt of lawlessness, fond of euphemistic names for ugly things. The greatest of political needs, therefore, is that of plain speaking. American democracy is in danger, not from the "masses" and not from the European "hordes," but from native, well-educated and socially respected sinners. Consequently the duty of every good citizen is to call these malefactors, not statesmen, not financiers, not magnates, not captains of industry, not honorable senators, but just common thieves. The result, if persisted in, would be as electrical as was the plain speaking of the child in Andersen's story of "The Emperor's New Clothes." The whole court had been humoring his majesty in the preposterous notion that he possessed a magic suit of clothes which made him invisible, and they would have pretended endlessly had not a small boy cried out: "The Emperor is naked," as in truth he was.

For selfish reasons, for partisan reasons, for minor reasons which we cannot analyze, but mainly for the reason that we lack moral courage to say impolite things about men who have power and authority, we go on pretending that Governor A's iniquities, that Mayor B's thievery, that Senator C's oppression of the widow and orphan are all invisible; and we smirk and toady and salaam to these magnates until some person or newspaper with the courage of simple truth points to the great man and declares not only that he is naked, but that he is tattooed from head to foot with the ineradicable record of his miserable deeds. Thereupon some of us stand aghast, others run for the whitewash brush, while still others declare that the word "naked" is in shocking bad taste; but the plain people, if only the truth-teller be sufficiently persistent, will finally see the humbug and hypocrisy of the whole business and will drive the criminal from his power and plundering.

Moreover, when we do try to improve the political situation we follow, as a rule, the example of Mrs. Peterkin who, finding that she had salted instead of sugared her tea, rather than to brew a fresh cup, sought in every conceivable way to neutralize the salt. We eagerly try all manner of legislation-nostrums, corrective ordinances and systems of checks and balances, rather than to go straight to the root of the matter and to demand plain honesty and ordinary efficiency in all branches of the public service. There are, of course, political failures due to the fact that we are still experimenting with the complex problems of democracy; but those are insignificant in comparison with the inefficiencies and losses due solely to corruption, perjury and theft. Do we of moderate means suffer from unjust taxes? It is partly, of course, because of the difficulty of establishing any equitable system of taxation; but it is mainly because a considerable share of the tax-levy is either squandered or stolen, and because, by perjury, many millionaires — individual or corporate — escape contributing their just portion of the public revenues. Do we see great national and state improvements halting in the legislative chambers? It is most often because they are being harnessed to or are standing aside for outrageous " jobs." Do we see our city halls filled with men whom we blush to call our representatives? It is because the " machine " has stolen the political machinery in order that it may misapply the public funds. Do we see our public schools inadequate to the task they have to do? It is because, in many cases, the education, the health, the very lives of our boys and girls are a prey to officialdom that seeks only its own selfish ends.

And shall the millions of American voters who are decent, intelligent and really patriotic announce themselves helpless to stop these thefts, perjuries and malfeasances in office? As well might Gulliver have declared himself conquered by the pack-thread fetters of the Lilliputians. The vast majority of Americans are honest; shall they sit supine while a handful of rascals plunder the public treasury? The great run of men are efficient in their own business; shall they tolerate a less efficiency in governmental affairs? The immense majority are patriotic with that true patriotism which wants the government really to be the protector of the humble, the ally of the morally strong, the teacher of a higher civilization; shall they then countenance an exploitation of the weak and a triumph of the dishonest which, if unchecked, will make our nation a by-word for inefficiency. The evil forces in politics have the advantage of organization, of self-interest, of that hanging-together which is the stern alternative to hanging separately; but the good forces have on their side not only overwhelming numbers, but also the eternal fact that, as Wendell Phillips said, "One on God's side is a majority."

There is no Goliath of political greed so huge that the little stone of truth hurled by the sling of moral courage will not lay it low. There is no Jericho of machine politics so well entrenched that the blast of brave revolt will not level its humbug walls. There is no evil monopoly so fabulously rich that a lighted match of naked fact thrown by a resolute hand will not send it flaming to its own destruction. The pulpits themselves, armed with scriptural texts, upheld slavery; but a handful of men with courage — Brown, Garrison, Lovejoy, Parker — raised a whirlwind that swept it to destruction. The city of New York trembled before Boss Tweed and even the "best citizens" declared that no power could overthrow him; but a few men like Nast and Jennings, with no weapons but pen and pencil, pulled him to pieces like a thing of straw.

Again and again has history shown that when a growing political evil reaches a certain point it becomes a moral evil, and that then some leader arises to champion the right. Over and over again it has been proved that when such leadership appears the people are certain and are glad to follow. So long as there are moral leaders, then, we need have no fear for the ultimate safety of the republic. Only the nation which can no longer breed such captains is on the road to decay. But must we always wait for political wrongs to swell into moral evils before we are to begin their destruction? What a wasteful process! What a cumbersome method of reform! What millions of money and thousands of lives may be sacrificed during the slow years while wickedness is developing to its own destruction! And meanwhile what confusion and error are being instilled into the minds of men, and especially into those of boys and girls, who see the wicked flourishing while the good suffer, and who have neither experience nor imagination to foresee the ultimate triumph of the moral law!

To save this waste, to dispel this moral confusion and doubt, to recognize political evils while they are young and to strangle them while they are still feeble, to make politics clean and businesslike, is the self-appointed and appalling task of the political reformer. What wonder that he sometimes becomes disheartened and half believes the jibes of the spoilsmen who picture him as a mixture of Don Quixote tilting at windmills and of Mrs. Partington with her protesting mop! The final question with him, however, as with every other man who fights the devil, is not: Is the work worth doing? but How can it be most effectually done?

Obviously it is a waste of time to exhort the practical politicians to mend their ways. It is almost equally a waste of time to work with men of middle life; for either they have convictions which have become as a species of religion, or else, having gone so many years without personal convictions, they are as putty in the hands of party managers. But young men, even in these days of youthful sophistication, still have enthusiasm, still cherish moral ambitions, still believe in Utopia; and participation in politics, as the outward sign of the inward grace of new manhood, is to them a welcome and absorbing avocation. Find some way of bringing young men to the ballot-box with higher standards of morality, and of making them see that political morality pays, and the battle for political reform is won. Who is to do this and how is it to be done?

It is a commonplace that political morality depends, not on the politicians, not on the form of government, but on a high general standard of virtue and its application in political affairs. For that standard we must look of course to the home, the church, the school and such voluntary organizations as boys' clubs, settlement houses and Christian associations. They are the only uplifting forces with which youth comes in contact, since the tendency of all other factors in his education (such as the streets, his boy companions, the newspapers, the sights and sounds of daily life) are either neutral or distinctly bad. Beyond their general tendency towards good, what can these several educational forces accomplish specifically in the direction of a higher political morality?

So far as concerns politics, the usual home influence makes mainly for partisanship by transmitting to the son, without reasoning or even argument, the political faith of the father. In so far, however, as his home has taught the boy physical and moral cleanliness, obedience, reverence, kindness, thrift and the other home virtues — which, unhappily, so many homes fail to instill — it has elevated his moral plane and so has helped him to understand the immorality and unthrift of many things in our political life. The schools, to a degree, teach political procedure; but, as a rule, they can do little towards instilling political ethics: first, because they are so completely in the hands of women whose influence along political lines must necessarily be small; and, secondly, because political morality presupposes independence of thought; and our schools, unfortunately, tend strongly to emphasize that surrendering of the judgment, that herding of minds as well as of bodies which is the working-capital of the machine politician. The majority of formal churches, unless they show more independence of their rich and influential parishioners than has been their wont, are not likely to point out many political sins excepting such as are a long distance from their own congregations; and to make politics vital, the subject must be brought close to the daily lives and interests of the young voters. There remain, then, the voluntary organizations; and upon such bodies — already existing or to be created — the political reformer must eventually depend for that special training in political honor, decency and independence of thought which, for the sake of himself and of his country, every youth should have.

There is a great and growing body of young men, between eighteen and thirty years of age, who are intensely and unselfishly interested in politics, who would be glad to understand it rightly, to take part in its battles, to rally round the champions of decency, order, economy and efficiency. The machine politicians recognize this keen interest of early manhood and are prompt to enlist these young men. From them they recruit their battalions of ward-workers to keep in political subservience the hordes of the unthinking. But many of these young fellows who, finding no other opening, take service under the " machine," have no real allegiance to it and would gladly enlist themselves, were there easy opportunity, under the banner of reform. And there are still more who, perceiving no chance for political work except with the " machine," and discovering in those selfish organizations everything revolting to their young ideals and fresh enthusiasms, turn away entirely from politics, disgusted with it and determined to take no share in what, so far as they can see, is but a matter of sordid barter and unfair sale. Devise some rational, business-like, really democratic method of enlisting these eager young fellows in the cause of clean politics, and of so protecting the organization thus formed that it cannot be stolen by any of the " machines," and the political power of the city and of the state will in the end be theirs.

Such organizations, however, cannot hold together upon the unsteady foundations of widely separated elections. Neither can they succeed upon the general and rather vague platform of " purifying " politics. Young men, unless disillusioned, have large ideals and demand a comprehensive battle-cry. Such an effective rallying-cry, it seems to me, is found in the phrase *Obedience to law.* Be the law God-made or man-made, every political evil is the direct result of breaking the law; and such organizations as have been suggested can be and ought to be firmly cemented upon the single demand that every voter, every office-holder, every political organization, every city, every state, and every nation shall obey the laws of God and man.

The laws of God, sooner or later, enforce themselves; but the laws of man must be enforced by men. A genuine enforcement implies, of course, that many laws now upon the statute-books should be repealed as obsolete, meddlesome, foolish or placed there for ulterior, hypocritical or other ignoble ends. Were half the statutes swept away and the remaining ones really put in force, not only would we be better governed, but we would rid ourselves of that widespread disrespect for all law which comes from witnessing the non-enforcement of so many existing, but impracticable statutes. Teach young men to discriminate among laws and you are teaching them both to understand and to respect all law. Base all your political arguments, found all your political indictments upon this single question of obedience to law, and no sophistry, no casuistry, no striking example of the successful rogue can beat down your contentions or confound your facts. By an appeal to fundamental morality, every political problem is reduced to its lowest terms, and its fallacies or its solution are made as clear as the rule of three.

THE WORKADAY WORLD

In one of those mislaid books which is probably on the shelves of a borrowing friend, I remember reading a clever essay on the " bothers of life," wherein the writer depicts most graphically the grinding nuisance involved in getting up, dressing, eating breakfast, answering letters, etc., etc., day after day, perhaps — horrible thought — twenty-eight or thirty thousand times. Merely to read about these " bothers " so tires one that it seems impossible ever to go through the monotonous routine again.

Most depressing is the writer's insistence that none can escape this endless repetition, his emphasis, though he does not employ it, upon the vulgar aphorism that " Life is simply one — thing after another " for every one of us. Our feelings harrowed by reading of the abused workers in mills or mines doing the same monotonous thing over and over, year in and year out, we commiserate them all the more because we contrast their toilsome lives with the supposed ease of the multi-millionaire, or with even our own more modest comforts. But a recent, penetrating book called " The Goldfish " demonstrates that the existence of those multi-millionaires is, in most cases, quite as slavish as that of the dinner-pail worker. The miserable male goldfish swimming around in the limelight focused upon his social bowl, had labored early and late for thirty years to accumulate a fortune, only to be condemned never again to take his ease. On the contrary, at the end of a hard day's work, he finds himself thrust into evening clothes by a censorious valet, in order to eat somewhere a heavy dinner in still heavier company, or to receive these leaden people at his own overloaded table. Even the main object of his strenuous labors, that of giving his daughters social prestige, had deprived those unfortunate girls, owing to the exigencies of Society with a large " S," from meeting any men except other male goldfish possessing more of money and leisure than of brains. Thus far, this poor father-goldfish had seen not one of these chaps whom he would permit a daughter of his to marry; yet by his very, so-called, social success, he had deprived his offspring of practically every opportunity for knowing decent, red-blooded, hard-working youth.

To the treadmill, then,— whether iron or golden — are condemned both the lowest and the highest strata of society. And the great middle-class is in no better case. Every one of us is confined in some species of bowl or squirrel-cage or pint-pot in which he must perforce pursue the same routine, year in and year out, with only an occasional marriage, fire or scandal to vary the monotony, and with death as the unescapable goal.

> " Tomorrow and tomorrow and tomorrow,
> Creeps in this petty pace from day to day,
> To the last syllable of recorded time;
> And all our yesterdays have lighted fools
> The way to dusty death."

All this seems horrible; yet, fortunately for our peace of mind, we early learn that the dull monotony of work is infinitely to be preferred to the deathly tedium of idleness; and sooner or later, moreover, we realize that the earning of one's bread in the sweat of his brow, far from being the primal curse, is the fundamental blessing, the greatest of the many vouchsafed a carping world by an understanding Providence. Furthermore, Darwinian ascent has lifted us at least so far above the veritable goldfish and squirrel that we need accept only a certain proportion of bowl and cage existence, a large share of time and opportunity being ours to spend as we may choose. Although most of us are scandalously inefficient officers in command of very rickety troops, each of us is, nevertheless, for a part of every day at least, " Captain of his Soul."

Starting, then, with the unalterable premise that probably ninety-nine per cent of us must work for practically the whole of our lives, and that substantially all of us must undergo a daily routine which, if we brooded over it, would drive us mad, how are we to escape? Only by establishing, each for himself, a philosophy of life and a manner of living that will do at least two things: give him what President Eliot has so aptly called " joy in work," and fit him to get the most out of those precious free hours during which he is permitted to escape from his bowl or whirligig, or to stretch his mental and spiritual muscles after the dismal treadmill of his workaday task. If one is to find joy in work, he must know how to labor intelligently and with some understanding of what he is working for; if he is to find happiness in leisure, he must be furnished with as many as possible of those things which make for real, lasting mental and moral satisfaction. A sound philosophy of life demands, then, that one be trained not only for efficient work, but also for efficient living; and that he be provisioned, moreover, for the nutritious and ample feeding of his hours of leisure. Sometimes, having only the gentleman-scholar in mind, we stuff the boy's knapsack with such rich food of culture that he becomes mentally dyspeptic and unfit for work. Sometimes, having only the worker in mind, we leave his knapsack so empty that he spiritually starves. Seldom indeed do we succeed in balancing our educational diet with such nicety that the youth finds both work-time and play-time equally stimulating phases of the inexhaustible joy of just being alive. There are in the world thousands of the tribe of Mrs. Gummidge to one of the joyous company of Pollyanna.

Two things have had a far greater psychological effect upon the Anglo-Saxon, and consequently upon the American, attitude towards work than most of us appreciate. The first is the Puritan faith which, in its emphasis upon the curse of Adam and Eve, has degraded labor into a ceaseless punishment. The second is the English social system which for centuries has magnified, as the main distinction of the gentleman, the fact that he does not and must not work for his living. It is significant that in Harvard University the grade of "C" is known as the "gentleman's mark."

The effect of these two fundamentally wrong attitudes towards life has been to overcrowd the learned professions and the clean-collar occupations, to turn the emphasis, in education, upon cultural, rather than upon practical knowledge, and thus to blind men to the fact that there is a true science and art and dignity in every industry and every trade. Work being regarded as a curse, labor with the hands being looked upon as socially degrading, and the Anglo-Saxon inclining to exalt the rule of thumb above the rule of science, it is only within the existing generation that the multifarious processes by which practically every one of us must earn his living have been subjected to any formal, scientific study. Having, thus late in the day, realized the necessity for such a study, we are rushing with the usual American impetuosity to an opposite extreme, and are casting overboard almost everything except what, with cheerful vagueness, we call technical or industrial or vocational education.

Less than twenty years ago, vocational education was such an unaccustomed phrase that it was difficult to disentangle, in the mind of the ordinary citizen, the word "vocation" from the word "vacation." Now, however, vocational education and industrial efficiency are the two wheel horses that draw most of the argumentative load at practically every meeting, be it that of a women's club discussing æsthetic dressing, or that of a chamber of commerce debating preparedness. Every educational crime on the calendar is being committed by knaves or ignoramuses, in the name of vocational training, and every vagary in business or philanthropy masquerades as a *sine qua non* in the blind worship of efficiency.

Having been a backer of both these steeds for at least twenty-five years, I have the greater right to emphasize their inadequacy to meet anything more than a fraction of the needs of the individual or of society. The fixing of public attention upon efficiency and upon vocational training was necessary, has done a vast amount of good, and will show still greater results. But in concentrating our activities upon these two subsidiary things, we are tending towards making the mistake of neglecting matters infinitely more essential to human welfare, happiness and real effectiveness. In limiting education to an instrument for training youth to earn a good living in ways that square with natural aptitudes, we are forgetting that, while the ability to work with intelligence and purpose tremendously increases not only the productive power, but also what one may call the productive pleasure, of the human worker, much more than this is needed to give that "joy in work" which is so essential an element both from the productive and from the human standpoint. Joy in work cannot come from mere technical efficiency; it can result only from that self-knowledge, that breadth of view, that sanity of outlook, that understanding of the true relations among things and between men and things, which ought to be the ultimate outcome of what we vaguely, and too often sneeringly, call education for culture.

To yoke culture and cotton spinning seems rather absurd; yet it is a fact that the main problem, not only in cotton spinning, but in all production and distribution of goods, is not how to make handier workmen, more skilled mechanics, more highly trained technicians, more hustling salesmen, — it is how to develop broader, saner and more forward-looking men and women, how to widen the interests, awaken the minds and stimulate the characters of sentient beings with immortal souls. It is no exaggeration to say that what a workmen thinks and feels and aspires to outside his work hours has far more influence upon his actual efficiency, to say nothing of his personal happiness, than anything which may or can be done to give him technical skill within those working hours or in preparation for them. In most occupations there is a definite limit of actual dexterity, a limit that is often very soon reached. But the value of the worker has no such limitation, provided he be so trained on what, for want of a better term, we call the cultural side, as to give him breadth, understanding and a sense of the relation between what he does and what the world is doing; provided he be so educated as to develop, in other words, his faculties of inventiveness, emulation, loyalty and imagination. The ratio between the worker who is simply a cog in the machine, and the worker who has outlook and vision, is as between one and ten thousand. The need of American industry to-day is not primarily for workmen more highly skilled with their hands; it is for workmen who are aware that they possess, and who are able to utilize, their minds and souls.

This being the case, it follows that while education should diligently proceed to repair its shameful neglect of sound technical training, while it should take every means possible to widen the vocational knowledge and the vocational opportunity of every boy and girl, it should at the same time put greater emphasis than ever upon those things in education which make for clear thinking, for insight, for knowledge of the world, for idealism, upon those things, in short, which make for genuine culture.

All this is very easy to say; and culture, like "Kultur," may be made to cover a multitude of both educational and social sins. Consequently, it is idle for anyone to advocate education for breadth, for culture, for vision, unless he has some notion of what he means by these abstract terms.

He cannot do this unless he first lays down some general philosophy of life, unless he establishes, as the engineer would say, a permanent base for all subsequent reasoning. To my mind there is no shadow of question that the cornerstone of that philosophical foundation must be faith,— not creed or dogma or blind worship; but an unshakeable conviction that somewhere and somehow there is a creative Power with a purpose too high and with ways too profound for our understanding, but a Power that is using us as instruments to an end, an end in the compassing of which every one of us can have,— and indeed, must have — a less or greater share.

Now this Power: call it God, or the Infinite, or Nature with a large "N," or what you please, has put every normal human being under an obligation, or has given him an opportunity (it makes no difference which way it is expressed) by surrounding him with a civilization (imperfect though it be) and with a tamed nature (albeit still pretty wild) representing the accumulated result of unnumbered centuries of human work and achievement. Every individual born into the world, then, provided he is not a hopeless idiot, arrives here with a large patrimony won by inconceivable struggle and capable of almost endless increase. The very slightest acquaintance with history cannot fail to show that the men and women, with conspicuous exceptions beyond our finite understanding, who do most towards increasing this accumulated store of civilization, get most in the shape, either of the material rewards of wealth or of the multifarious immaterial rewards of current or future fame; that the great rank and file of us who try to do our share get at least moderate comfort, neighborly regard and an easy conscience; and that the drones, wasters and "slackers" (again with notable exceptions beyond our explaining) are sooner or later punished, in one way or another, for their disobedience to the established order of the world. Just as in the old days the debtor was sold into slavery until the debt should be paid, so, in our earthly scheme, the only way to reach economic, intellectual and moral freedom seems to be through discharging in one way or another, one's initial debt to civilization. And that debt is in direct proportion, of course, to the original "faculty" (to use an almost outworn term) with which one is born, and to the environment, fortunate or unfortunate, in which one is brought up.

Granting then, as it seems one is obliged to do, that this debt to civilization exists and that satisfaction in living can come only through at least an attempt to pay it, how is it to be wiped out? Obviously it cannot be paid to that Unseen which is the cornerstone of faith; obviously, too, it cannot be discharged directly by working for that vague thing called civilization. It must be paid in tangible ways to beings of flesh and blood. Those beings are myself, my family — which, under Nature's scheme of dual sex, is the fulfillment of myself, — and my neighbors who, in widening circles of relatives, fellow-townsmen, countrymen and the world, constitute that social medium which is as necessary to my existence as is the air to the bird and the water to the fish.

My debt to civilization is to be paid, then, in three ways: by developing to a high point, physically, mentally and spiritually, myself; by making my creative power effective through marrying wisely and rearing my children conscientiously; and by performing at least my fair share of those various community functions without which all that civilization has thus far gained would vanish. Consequently, the chief ends of human education should be the care and training of the body, the strengthening of the mind, will and conscience, adequate preparation for parenthood and homemaking, the arousing of civic spirit, and, as we saw in the first place, the strengthening of faith.

This — the only adequate — view greatly widens, of course, the meaning of vocational training, vastly extends the field of true efficiency. Vocational education that stops at the idea of earning one's living is a poor and sordid thing; efficiency that thinks only of material achievement is a ridiculously mean measure of mankind.

Just to earn a living, no matter how many thousands of dollars it may be measured in, just to be an efficient maker or distributor of commodities, is to degrade one's self to the level of an ingenious machine. A man who does only this sells his soul to the devil of materialism, works without finding any joy in living, and earns the possibility of leisure only to find his leisure a vain and empty thing.

Whatever his particular job or profession, the true vocation of every man is to be not merely an efficient worker, but also a wide-awake citizen, an intelligent and conscientious homemaker, a trustworthy custodian of his own and his children's bodies, a competent captain of his own and his children's souls. His efficiency is measured, not by the money that he accumulates, but by the contribution that he makes to the world of his own time, through his citizenship, and to the world of the future, through the character of the children whom he rears.

Physical education, moral education, will training, education for homemaking, preparation for active and intelligent citizenship and education in the use of one's leisure hours, as well as preparation for earning one's living, are all implicit and should, therefore, be all included in the term: vocational education; and the less chance that the boy and girl have to get this comprehensive training at home, the more must the community, for its own protection and well-being, provide.

At present the chief common agency for doing this is the public school; and great is the turmoil, within and without the schools, over both what they ought to and what they can teach.

As to the "ought," they, or the home, or some other agency, or all of them together, should unquestionably find some way of dealing with boys and girls so that a very much greater proportion of them than now enter manhood and womanhood with strong bodies, self-reliant wills and active consciences. They should enter maturity, moreover, not only with ambition, but also with some sort of preparation for earning a fair living, making a good home, taking an effective part in public affairs, and spending their leisure in something more worth while than frequenting street-corners and barrooms, moving-picture shows or even so-called fashionable functions.

As to the "can" it is simply a question of all pulling together to make the work of the schools, the church, and the community in general really supplement that of the home in every one of these essential ways. If the citizens would provide the money, if parents would understandingly back up the teachers, if the other social forces would actually coöperate all along the line, and if all of us would get it firmly fixed in our heads that the preparation of youth for parenthood, for citizenship, for productive efficiency and for effective, virile living, is a real and serious business, is, indeed, the most important business in the world and one in which every single one of us, including the child himself, is an active and responsible partner,— then the schools could give an education that is an education, then the money spent on them would yield not only visible, but really fabulous, returns. As it is, too many schools are like the famous characterization of a university: "a place that must be full of learning, since the freshmen bring so much wisdom in and the seniors take so little away."

We and our children, however, are in the United States of to-day, not in Utopia: and what can we do with conditions as they exist? These things we can do, these things we absolutely must, at least, begin to do, if we are to make our democracy and our country what it has every possibility of becoming. We ought to bring education to bear on children from the time they are conceived to at least their eighteenth year: first, by so educating the father-and-mother-to-be that they will know how properly to feed and train their young; secondly, by taking the child at kindergarten (or, as we must now say, Montessori) age into a school which will be far more concerned about ministering to his bodily needs, his play instincts, his imagination, his will, his individuality, his social understanding, than about cramming his mind with predigested and more or less unimportant facts; thirdly, by so cleaning up our neighborhoods, our towns and our cities, that they shall be fit places, physically and morally, for boys and girls to be brought up in; and fourthly, by so stimulating the churches that they will actually infuse, as only they have the right to do and, so to speak, the machinery for doing, their people, and especially their young people, with that glowing faith which is absolutely fundamental to any sound philosophy of living.

The edict of Herod was mild as compared with our

modern, needless slaughter of the innocents; the bloody fields of Europe show far fewer dead than peace kills, every year, as the result of a preventable ignorance; what society suffers, each day, because of the untrained minds, the weak wills, the undeveloped consciences and the blunted social instincts of its constituent members, is at once the cause and the measure of human suffering and sin. To prevent all this,— not to perpetuate cyclopedias or to teach trades,— is really the important business of education. To cure the sin and misery of the adult world, to do anything more than palliate their hideous results, is quite out of the question. Sin and misery must be prevented by so bringing up boys and girls that they shall not be, as most of them now are, physically, domestically, socially and morally, almost as ignorant as the Kaffir and the Hottentot.

We are rapidly changing from a country-bred to a city-bred people; but you cannot rear healthy, normal children in towns unless you give them abundant play-space and help them, moreover, to organize their play. Hence the movement for playgrounds, physical training and organized games.

We are fast being transformed from a "handy" people to one that supplies all its needs at the bargain counter or by parcel post; but you cannot train the senses, quicken the faculties and develop the gumption of boys and girls unless you provide something to take the place of the farm and household work of the simpler pioneer days. Hence one of the main reasons for manual training, prevocational training and vocational education.

We are speedily being reorganized from a society that gave free play to the individual into one where the man is lost in the mass, the worker is swallowed in the machine, the child is overpowered by the very numbers with whom he must work and play; but you cannot preserve and strengthen the will, the imagination, the character, of the child unless you deal with him as an individual to be developed in the way that is best for him. Hence the crying need for social education, for an education, that is, which gives free rein to individuality while gradually preparing the child to live, work and play as an efficient factor in the complex social group.

We are rapidly changing from a homogeneous, slow-growing people to one having all sorts of differing traditions and standards, with all of us going a fast and faster pace; but you cannot have moral young men and women, you cannot secure a sound civilization, unless from the first the child has definite ethical training and is prepared, furthermore, for what is likely to be his chief real responsibility in life: that of parenthood and the making of a home. Hence the need for moral education and for definite teaching in homemaking.

We are fast being transmogrified from a folk self-governed by the town-meeting into one boss-governed under the complex and impersonal system of a modern city; but you cannot have a free people unless its youth are brought up in the knowledge and restraint of political self-control. Hence the crying necessity for training in citizenship, for some kind of education that will do for the boy and girl of to-day what the New England town-meeting did for the first ten generations of Americans.

We are very rapidly indeed changing from a comparatively poor, to an ultra rich people, what used to be luxuries having now become necessities; but prosperity like this greatly weakens the moral fibre, for with morals as with muscles, hard exercise is needed to keep them sound and strong. Hence the necessity for everything in education that strengthens, toughens and makes resilient the will. Moreover, wealth means increasing leisure; but leisure without a mind stored to use it, is a veritable curse. Hence the need for training the mind, in youth, to seek, understand and enjoy those things which are the essential food of leisure.

So, if we be properly fitted to enjoy it, this workaday world of ours is not so humdrum after all. The daily "bothers" none can escape in themselves, but the serene mind makes them largely automatic and therefore negligible. Hard work cannot be run away from, but the trained worker finds ceaseless and increasing zest in conquering tough jobs. Sorrows and disappointments are met at every turning; but the sound body buries them in sleep, the poised intelligence sees into their deeper meaning, the basic faith makes them constituent and essential factors in its life-philosophy. Youth loses infinite time and wastes incalculable effort in making needless mistakes; but it is only through such experience as this that he can exercise his will, develop his imagination and build up his character. Age gains wisdom, only to see death standing at his elbow; but, if he has done his share, he has the reward of knowing that the world is richer and wiser through his having lived.

But all this satisfaction, this " joy of living," is denied to the vast majority of men and women, because society has failed to give them much of any capacity or knowledge beyond that of the dumb beasts. Implicit in them is the pure delight of perfect physical health and strength; but society lets them, through ignorance and lack of physical training, drag through their lives half sick. They have the power to procreate; but society denies them a training which would make home-keeping and child-rearing a joy and satisfaction instead of, as it too often is, a hideous burden and a hopeless failure. They have hands with capacity, minds with innate intelligence, souls that aspire to the beautiful and fine; but society leaves their hands incompetent, their intelligences dulled by routine, their souls drowned in the sordid vileness of the streets and slums. And even where there are physical well-being, opportunity and leisure, our educational methods leave those more fortunate children of men, as a rule, quite blind to the real pleasures of life and quite ignorant of the true significance of living. The pressing business ahead of us is to change all this.

THE HUMAN HOME

MOST men and women, and certainly all children, are under the delusion that education is "going to school." To them the chief purpose of schooling is to cram the child and the youth with facts which may be secreted again through the process of an examination, the sole aim of such an examination being to push him forward into the next grade at schöol or into college.

In the true sense, however, education is nothing of the sort. Real education is simply the sum-total of the physical, intellectual and moral forces which, acting and reacting upon you and me and our neighbors, thereby create what we call our characters.

Growth is the law of all living things,— a steady growth until the highest point of efficiency is reached. Then follow, just as inevitably and just as naturally, gradual decay and death. But there must be always movement. If that movement is not forward, it must be backward. Nothing in nature can stand still. In mankind the growth which shapes all later progress takes place between birth and, roughly speaking, twenty-one. In this period the main currents of life are determined, the forming influences exert their greatest force. In this time, therefore, the principal work of education must be done. To be effective and sound, education, whether it be carried on in the school, the home or the fields and streets, must follow the laws of all organic growth. It must expand, not repress, the child; it must lead, not force him; it must develop him towards complete ripeness, not towards early decay. Education, in short, must be a steady process of opening the individual from within, not of trying to shape him from without.

Moreover, all physical growth, in man, is simply a development from the simplest beginnings, all mental growth is but an enlargement of the infant's first perception, all moral growth is a strengthening of the first exercise of the childish will. The athlete, in his physical perfection, is nothing more than the puling infant plus the milk and meat, the water and air and exercise, of a quarter of a century. The scholar, dealing with the most abstruse problems, has the same brain that, by associating certain vague sensations, produced the baby's first real thought. The hero, whose moral force carries him through a seemingly impossible crisis, started with a will power no stronger or better controlled than that common to infancy. Each of these men, in a thousand devious ways, has been educated out of the helplessness of babyhood up to the physical, mental and moral power of efficient manhood.

Education, then, has triple work to do: to build up the body, to feed and train the mind, to develop, strengthen and direct the will. With all these three, teaching, whether carried on in the home, in the school or in the community, must unceasingly concern itself. Ever before the parent and the teacher must be the questions: Am I doing all that is possible to conserve and develop the child's health? Am I doing what is best, not on general principles, but in this particular, individual case, to enlarge the child's mind? Am I losing no opportunity to build up to its highest possible point this child's whole character?

If a child goes to school every day from his seventh to his fifteenth year, he gets, under the best conditions, only about eight thousand hours of schooling; while his waking hours, from birth to his fifteenth year, are approximately eighty thousand. One tenth of his time in the schoolroom! But during the remaining nine tenths, he is nevertheless at school, his teachers being the household, the street companions, and that big hurly-burly of experience which we call his environment. And it cannot be too many times repeated that, for that nine tenths, as well as for the one tenth spent in school, the home is directly and almost entirely responsible. It is the duty of the father and mother to choose as good a school as it is possible for them, under the circumstances in which they live, to secure, and it is their duty, also, to coöperate with the teachers in making the school instruction count for something; but it is still more urgently their duty to make sure that in the nine tenths of the child's time passed outside the schoolroom he gets as real and effective an education as in that comparatively short time during which he is under direct school influence.

It is idle, therefore, to consider education apart from morals. An unmoral education is, in the very nature of things, immoral and, however highly finished, cannot be good. But it is equally idle to believe that morality in education is secured by the formal teaching of ethical and religious truths. These truths must be the basis, the backbone, the ultimate aim of all teaching; but they must reach the child through the hidden way of sympathetic understanding, for by that path alone can they actually enter his life and form his character. To find that path and build that way should be the aim of every school, of every community,—above all, of every home.

This mechanical age of ours, elated with its rapidly growing power over nature, is elaborating the mechanism of instruction at the expense of real education. It is lavish of apparatus, penurious of teachers, eager that the child shall have a wide range of information, unconcerned that his character be formed. A wise secularizing of the schools which freed them from dogma has become a dangerous mechanizing which is robbing them of morality. The essential ethical principle of education is lost sight of in a wilderness of pedagogical machines.

The remedy is simple and close at hand. It is not to make the schools church schools, it is not to read more chapters of the Bible, it is not to teach formal ethics and to repeat maxims; it is to educate the teachers in such a manner and to such a degree that they shall understand what education really means; it is to give each teacher so small a number of pupils that she can establish between herself and each of them a path of understanding and of sympathy, and can send all her instruction straight along that path to the inner chambers where character is building. The essence of the remedy, however, is to emphasize and reëmphasize the fact that the home is the centre and mainspring of all education, and that the father and the mother, who are the responsible heads of that home, must learn and must practice their profession as the chief and finally accountable educators of the coming citizens.

In view of this fundamental and unalterable responsibility of the home for the real education of each succeeding generation, it is most fortunate that the modern developments of science, and the applications of science to the needs of daily life, are strongly tending to make fathers and mothers, both as parents and as members of the community, realize more and more every year what the real, permanent, effective education of their boys and girls actually involves. A somewhat new attitude of moral optimism has released us, too, from the old belief in "original sin," and has convinced practically all those who think that substantially every child born has the capacity for becoming an efficient citizen, provided the conditions of hygiene, of education and of morals under which he is brought up are favorable to physical, mental and spiritual growth. If he is reared in a slum, his physical and moral life will be poisoned by the slum; but if he is brought up under conditions where the laws of health can be observed, the laws of intellectual development followed, and the moral laws obeyed, a good man or woman, with a sound body and a strong efficient mind, will almost surely result.

To begin, then, at the foundation: the physical life; science has taught us that to have sound bodies we must eat proper and well-cooked food, must keep ourselves and our surroundings clean, must breathe fresh air, must take an abundance of rational exercise, must wear hygienic clothing, and must surround ourselves with an atmosphere of cheerfulness, good temper and high ideals. The homemaker, therefore, must know how to choose food and how to cook it, must appreciate the virtues of cleanliness and fresh air, must understand the hygiene as well as the æsthetics of clothing, must know what proper exercise really involves and, of equal importance, must understand how to create a true home atmosphere. We have the basis of knowledge necessary for such training; science has placed at our disposal all the facts about food, air, clothing and sanitation that are necessary. Most of us still need, however, to get over the erroneous notion that anybody can keep a house; and we must, on the contrary, realize that housekeeping and homemaking is not only a real profession, but the greatest of all.

The physical side of homemaking, however, is only the foundation of the homemaker's task. The body must, of course, be made sound, so that it may last for eighty, ninety or one hundred years; but those long years will be more than wasted if that body is not made also efficient; and efficiency is a quality that cannot be manufactured in any school unless the broad foundations of it have been laid in the home.

What are the essential bases of efficiency? Expertness of the senses; a well-trained mind; and self-control. Our senses are, as a rule, very little developed and are, therefore, exceedingly inefficient. How few of us, unless we are artists, really see with our eyes; how few of us, unless we are musicians or lawyers or diplomats, really hear with our ears; what a pitifully small proportion of us can actually do anything with our hands except grasp like monkeys; and above all, how very few of us have our senses so trained that they help one another by focussing sight, hearing, touch and even smell all at once upon everything that comes along! Almost all of us might be many times as clever as we are in taking in facts and in drawing conclusions had we been trained in childhood to use our senses as they ought to be exercised and used.

It is mainly in those earliest years and in the home that this essential training of the five senses can and should take place. While the powers are growing and developing, while they are eager to learn, is the time to exercise them by making the small child really see with its eyes, really hear with its ears, really discriminate with its touch, and actually coördinate all its senses so that they shall form a true and powerful partnership. It is wonderful how eager the little child is to use its budding powers; and it is criminal how many little children, even in so-called good homes, are being punished for doing not only what they ought to do, but what it is our business as adults to see that they should all the time be doing. It is a small matter whether or not we teach children the alphabet or two times two; but it is of life-long consequence to that child, whether or not we help him to acquire a real, thorough, coördinated use of all his physical powers.

Efficient senses are, however, worse than useless unless they are under wise command; and the greatest responsibility of the homemaker is for the teaching of self-control. It is superfluous to say, of course, that the chief way of teaching self-control to children is through example; and that the "grown-up" who has not learned self-control for himself, has little hope of seeing its growth in the younger generation. Not only by example, however, but by direct teaching, the child must be trained to self-control, to be the master of his own special, individual will. The ruler of both body and mind is the will, and the child himself must be trained by daily exercise to self-mastery.

This teaching of self-control can best be done by a steady appeal to the certainty and supremacy of law. Hardly ever is a child too young to appreciate the fundamental truth: that obedience to law means happiness and that disobedience to law means sorrow. We elders may have to hasten the working of the law by providing artificial punishments; but the principle is early grasped by the child, and, if wisely looked out for, he gets ingrained into him the idea that all nature, all life and he himself are under the rule of laws which cannot be disobeyed without suffering, and obedience to which gives order, satisfaction and true happiness to the very end of life.

This training of the will is the most important part of education, is indeed education itself; and its chief purpose is that the animal side of us may be kept in subjection; that greed, selfishness and sensuality, which are natural to us, may not get the upper hand of friendliness, unselfishness and self-respect, which are also natural to us. But a secondary and almost equally important outcome of the discipline of the will is in the training of judgment, in accustoming us to make sound decisions, in getting us into the habit of doing nothing upon impulse but only after careful thought and due weighing of results. Training in self-control, therefore, is the best sort of intellectual training; and because this is so, the home, where the will is trained, is also the place where, mainly, the mind should get its discipline. The school exists primarily to impart information and to give social experience; in the home must be prepared a mind fit to take in and utilize that information and so trained in judgment as to profit by the special forms of discipline given by the school.

A good home atmosphere and a sound home training must and do result, therefore, in strong, well-disciplined bodies, in trained and active minds, in self-control, self-reliance and self-respect; and out of these arises that quality of which the world stands, and always will stand, most in need: individuality. The rank and file of men and women simply exist. They take life as they find it, add nothing to it either of special good or special evil, and civilization is neither richer nor poorer because of their having lived. All advance in civilization is made, not by such negative characters, but only by men and women who have individuality, who have, that is, character, strength of will and definiteness of purpose. The chief end of every teacher, whether a pedagogue in school or a parent in the home, should be, therefore, to foster and to strengthen individuality, to encourage in every boy and girl those traits which are special to that child and which are likely, under the process of evolution, to lead that individual to the doing of some real and lasting work for the world. The homemaker must not only make the home environment favorable by securing the best physical condition, she must not only make it stimulating by thorough education of the senses and thorough training of the will; but she must make everyone in that home feel the greatness of the truth that since everyone is an incalculable debtor to civilization, only by doing some genuine and lasting, and if possible some original, service to that little piece of the world in which he lives can he begin to pay back that debt.

Every physical illness, every mental weakness, every moral short-coming of every individual is a drag upon the progress of the entire world. Could we measure these things in terms of money, we would doubtless find that the world is losing through unnecessary illness, laziness, incompetence, intemperance, and all the rest of the bad qualities of men millions upon millions of dollars every year, to say nothing of the happiness that these physically, mentally and morally sick folk, through ignorance or wilfulness, are all the time throwing away.

And most of this loss is due to the lack of home training, is due to physical ills which the proper food and hygiene of a real home would have averted or cured, to mental flabbiness that right home training of the will would have overcome, to moral weakness or ignorance that a true, wise home would have strengthened or cleared up.

The home, therefore, is at once the centre and the source of all that is most important and permanent in education. As family life strengthens or weakens, a nation grows or decays; in the building up of the family unit lies the chief interest and the main resource of modern education. The immediate object of that education is, of course, the specific individual; but the all-important instrument of real education is, and always must be, not the individual, but that group of individuals which constitutes the family.

THE HUMAN FAMILY

THE present is the greatest period of industrial ferment and of social change that the world has ever seen. Large questions of civilization are being considered as never before, and vast propositions for social reform are ordinary themes for discussion. Behind all these spreading plans for world peace, for universal education, for a socialistic state, and for all the rest of the things which are to introduce the millennium is, however, the fundamental question of the family. Are we or are we not, in these days, preserving the family life which is the necessary basis of all real civilization? If we are, all these needed reforms will come in good time. If we are not, then these grand projects for making the world better are nothing more than idle and impossible dreams.

It was John Fiske who first pointed out that the reason why we to-day are better than savages, why we are living in houses and in cities instead of in caves, is because the young of man, unlike that of all other animals, is practically helpless for the first three or four years of life. This helplessness makes it necessary for the parents to provide shelter and food, requires them, therefore, to have, even among savages, a home life, and most important of all, compels them to educate their offspring. This educating of the children, moreover, is what has educated the parents and has gradually brought mankind out of the state of the brute into that of the comparative refinement, wisdom and moral power of to-day.

This helplessness of the children, furthermore, has made it not only necessary for a family to stay together, it has gradually evolved the modern idea of monogamy as the simplest and most nearly perfect type of family life. The development of monogamy has been a conspicuous example of that process of scientific adjustment to conditions which lies at the foundation of the whole process of evolution.

Why, aside from our inherited prejudice against polygamy and polyandry, is the monogamic home best? The helplessness and feebleness of infancy requires a definite and settled place of shelter such as is best given in a monogamic home; the senses of the infant are so delicate that the surroundings must be narrow and unvarying, such as one finds in the ordinary household; and, of greatest importance, the growth of the emotions and the will,— which are the most important factors in human development,— demand an atmosphere of affection and of solicitude such as can be furnished only where there is the trinity of father, mother and child.

In the home, whether it be a palace or a one-room tenement, are determined and practically settled for life:

The physical condition of the child.

His knowledge of and acquaintance with life.

The range of his emotional and æsthetic powers.

His will-power and, consequently, his power of self-control.

To be more specific: if an infant and small child is wrongly fed or underfed, it fails to get the proper physical start in life, and, no matter how much it may have to eat later, it will usually be anemic, rickety and easily subject to disease. If a child is permitted to walk too soon and to carry heavy burdens too early, its body will always be stunted and misshapen. And the sole persons responsible for giving the child these absolutely essential foundations of physical welfare are the father and mother in the home.

Whether a child gets right ideas concerning truth, honesty, unselfishness, temperance, and all the rest of the virtues depends on whether or not he is brought up in an atmosphere where the truth is spoken, honesty and unselfishness are practised, sobriety is exercised and the other virtues regarded. It depends, that is, on whether he is brought up in a slum and on vice-infested streets or whether he is brought up in what the Puritans in a narrow sense, and what we in a broad sense, call a Christian, God-fearing home.

A tremendously important part in life is played by the emotions and by the love and appreciation of the beautiful. And whether or not the child's emotions shall be high or low, whether or not he shall know what beauty means, depends on the kind of environment which surrounds his earliest years.

Finally, the character of the child and the man is the result of the development of his will power. And who has any interest in helping that child get control of his will except his father and his mother? Most of the really powerful influences outside the home are interested in breaking that will-power down rather than in building it up.

It follows, therefore, that a home, to be a true home in which the child gets that preparation for life to which he is entitled, must have in charge of it persons who know how to surround the growing child with right conditions as to food, clothing, sleep, cleanliness, ventilation, sunshine, exercise, etc.; how to bring knowledge and experience to his growing consciousness in orderly sequence, in such ways as to make a real and lasting impression upon his mind, and at such a rate of speed that the immature brain may be kept always properly stimulated and nourished without being at any time over-excited or over-fed; and how to cultivate the emotions, while at the same time strengthening and educating the will.

Usually, however, when this general program is agreed to, it is taken for granted that the homemaker who is to do all this is the house-mother. As the magnitude of the task is beyond the strength of most women, no matter how willing or wise, the major part of it is shifted to the servants, if there are any, to the school, to the Sunday-school, and — in not infrequent instances — to the neighbors and the community at large. But home-education is not a one-man or one-woman task. It is a partnership responsibility, in which every one of the household, educators and " educatees," is concerned; in which the children who are to be brought up should have a share as definite and in its way as important as that of those who are doing the bringing up; and in which the whole community must take a hand.

In other words, family life should be an organized life, with unity of aim and definiteness of function on the part of all involved. And it should always be kept in mind that, since the family exists because of the needs of the child, family life should centre around the child or children. Their interests should be paramount, for as those interests are looked after or are neglected so the child will make a success or failure of his life. And if a sufficient proportion of children, through bad education, make failures of their lives the community will, in the next generation, go to rack and ruin.

Therefore, the most important business in any community is that of properly running a home; and the most important profession to be prepared for is the profession of homemaking. The chief interest of the state is that the small children now in the world or to be in the world in the next ten or fifteen years shall be strong physically and sound mentally and upright morally, so that they will add new wealth to the world instead of being either a burden upon the wealth already existing, or an actual danger to progress and to civilization itself.

The fundamental of any business, whether it be making shoes or bringing up a family, is order. Order is indeed Heaven's first law; and it is the first law, therefore, of that most potent agent of Heaven, the human family. The failure of so many households which really try, as the phrase is, to "do well by" the children, is because of their total lack of system, of plan, of that order which is fundamental.

In business the main things upon which order depends

are organization and, using the word in its large sense, bookkeeping. In a successful business there must be someone responsible for every detail, he must definitely know what his responsibilities are, and the methods of keeping track of every person and of every detail must be so complete that those at the head may always know just where they are.

In a family, no less, the father, the mother, the other adults, if there are any, the servants, if any, and the children themselves, must have definite responsibility for definite things, and must feel that the whole success of the family life depends upon those things being done at the right time, in the right way and with the right results. There has been much jesting over the question in the last census as to who is the head of the household; and that head is usually pictured as a formidable female towering over a henpecked man. But every household, not only in the legal sense, but in its aspect as a place to bring up children, must have a head, and as a rule that head should be the mother. She should lay out the plan of the household, devise its organization and see that the duties of each person under that plan or organization are assigned and are performed.

Moreover, having the responsibility for the organization, it devolves upon her to supervise the bookkeeping side: not only to manage the household expenditures in the narrow sense, but also to have a system of cost-accounting by which she may know both the probable limits of expenditure, and also the limits of outlay within the main divisions of the household economy.

The first and most important division of that expenditure is for the securing of bodily health and strength,— expenditure, that is, for food, shelter, clothes, fresh air, sunshine and exercise.

The second important division of expenditure is for education in the larger sense, for the wise and effective training of the body, the mind, the emotions and the will.

The third and hardly less important expenditure is for recreation, for the re-creation of body, mind and soul.

The thing to be emphasized in connection with the first of these divisions of expenditure, that for bodily welfare, is that all these material outlays,— the largest and fundamentally the most important,— should not be made haphazard, but with the knowledge which to-day any intelligent man or woman, though far short of having had a college education, can acquire, with a sense of relative values, and with understanding on the part of children as well as of adults why they are made as they are.

The second division of expenditure, that for the wise and effective training of the body, the mind, the emotions and the will, is not primarily a question of money — most of the money of the home will go for the first and third divisions,— it is a question of things much harder to secure than money: intelligence, patience, self-control, wise affection and a sense of eternal values. As has already been suggested, it is in the family, not in the school or the Sunday-School, certainly not in the streets and back alleys, that this real training of the mind, the emotions and the will must take place. In the home and within the compass of three persons, or six persons, or perhaps a dozen persons, is an epitome of all the world. It is a sort of rehearsal, on a scale not too large for the ignorant and tender mind of the child, of the real drama in which, as a man, he must enact at least a minor part. And upon the thoroughness of that rehearsal and the skill and wisdom of the older, experienced actors in training the new actor, depends the success of the growing youth upon that later stage.

Moreover, to carry the metaphor further, since acting is largely mimicry, so the early training of the child is largely imitation. And what it imitates most closely, what becomes second nature to it in all its subsequent playing of the part of life, are those actions and opinions and points of view with which the child has come in contact within the family itself. The training given by the household is not so much, therefore, what the family does, as what it is. Those qualities of mind, of heart, of will which we would have a child possess, he does not learn, he acquires or, rather, absorbs from the atmosphere of the place in which he is brought up.

The expenditures under this second heading, then, are expenditures of self in maintaining self-control, in presenting high examples of living, in cultivating fine and lofty emotions, in creating for the child an atmosphere in which all the high sides of his nature shall be fully fed and all the low sides shall be starved and killed. Precepts will be of little avail, if practice is not parallel with them; admonitions to be good and pure and filled with high ambitions will be laughable, if the preacher of those things is bad, impure and mean. And it is useless to try to cover these things up. There is no hypocrisy through which even the average child cannot quickly penetrate.

Because these expenditures of physical and moral energy for the training of the children are so intangible, it is almost impossible to deal with them, and it would be impossible to explain them at all to a foundling or to one who had not had any sort of genuine home care. But home influence is not a matter of chance, it is not a thing to be left to grow up by haphazard. It is just as definite a duty of the father and of the mother as the furnishing of food and clothing, and, in its way, it must be subject to the same organization and the same bookkeeping as those material things placed in the first division.

Consider, for example, bodily development. Having looked after the food, clothing, fresh air, etc., there still remains the very large question of physical exercise, and, from baby-jumper up to the training of the collegian, regular exercise suited to the age and physical strength of the individual is one of the essential things of an efficient life. Exercise, however, to be really beneficial, must always have in it some of the play spirit. Therefore the family life must make provision for exercise that, on the one hand, shall meet the varying needs of the several members of the family and that, on the other hand, shall have in it the "doing together" element which makes exercise a play, and therefore an effective agent for development. Here is the chance of which most American parents do not half avail themselves: the chance of keeping themselves young while at the same time doing the best thing for their children, by playing games with them and joining in their sports, just as far as it is possible for elders to do without trenching upon the very definite need of young people to associate in sports and plays with those of their own age.

Considering next the training of the mind, the will and the emotions, these, fortunately, need not be considered separately for — and this is especially true of home training — all these ought to be educated together, and the educating of one of necessity trains at the same time the others. Here again, however, things cannot be left to chance. Not only must there be established in the home a standing good example and a steady ethical atmosphere which cultivate and train through imitation, but the father and mother must deliberately consider those things within the ability of that household to secure which will do most to develop those faculties thoroughly and well. They must study, moreover, each child as a separate problem, for what would be best for strengthening the will of this child would be very inefficient in the case of the other; what would have a most salutary influence upon the emotional life of the elder child would perhaps be disastrous to that of the younger. Of all these things there must be kept, so to speak, an individual ledger account, and definite effort must be made to provide what is needed for the moral and mental solvency of each member of the family.

And all tied up with this problem is that of recreation,

of the "re-creation" of the body and the mind. Americans have been very slow indeed in regard to this side of family training, and have much to learn from the English, the Germans and the French, as to recreations that are cheap, that take in the family as a whole, and that leave those who take the recreation rested and refreshed, instead of more jaded than when they began. Most of the ways of amusing themselves that Americans indulge in are enormously expensive, fearfully fatiguing and are entered upon not for recreation but for display. The quiet family excursions that the Germans used to take before the war, the pleasant little picnics of the English, are things almost unknown in this country; and therefore, unless we have money enough to keep automobiles and yachts and to give extravagant entertainments, we think we cannot have a good time. Or else the men go off into the woods, where they can really get next to nature and can relax, leaving their wives and daughters in a summer hotel, where they fry in an attic chamber, eat canned food and spend their days gossiping with other forsaken females on the piazza.

It would seem that wives and daughters are largely responsible for the poverty of recreation in this country. They are, so many thousands of them, anxious to make a foolish show, anxious to outshine some other woman, anxious to do what they cannot, rather than what they can. To restore things to their proper balance, the family must be taken as the basis of recreation, and must undertake those simple things which can be afforded and in which all can share.

In emphasizing — as it cannot be too strongly emphasized — the fundamental importance of the family life, we must not forget that, like every other good thing, it is liable to abuse. There is an intemperance of family life just as there is intemperance in eating, in self-improvement and in recreation. It is not uncommon to find families where all the members are true partners, where each literally lives for the happiness and welfare of all the others. But if they live — as is frequently the case — wholly within and wholly for the family, if parents think only of the children and children only of the father and mother, then their lives get narrow and narrower until all of them degenerate, under the law of evolution, into a mere mutual admiration society, acting and reacting upon itself with absolutely no effect whatever upon the progress of the world.

Family life must all the time be enriched and renewed by contact with and by working for the community around it. For that community is the larger family in which the education of the family in the ordinary sense has its exercise and motor effect. Nature is interested, apparently, in communities, states and nations, rather than in individuals; and only as individuals are prepared, by their training, to be of service to the community, do they really count.

The basis of valuation of the individual is that of service; and service always involves more than one person or one group. A man cannot serve himself alone without becoming a monster of egotism. He cannot restrict his service to his family, without that family becoming a group of concentrated selfishness. The only way in which the individual and the family can, so to speak, fulfill themselves, is for them to serve the community as a whole and according to their ability.

What does such service imply? It involves, on the part of the individual as an individual, and on his part as a member of the family, the same coöperation in the work of the community as he should exhibit in the work of the family. For the community is nothing other than a larger family in which, on a larger scale, we have the same problems of housekeeping, of education, of moral development and training that are met with in the home. The basis of good citizenship is sound, intelligent family training; and all training in "civics," to be understandable, must be bottomed on knowledge of and experience in a real and effective family life.

THE HUMAN COMMUNITY

"The education of the child," says Dr. Laurie,[1] "is the bringing of him up in such a way as to secure that when he is a man he will fulfill his true life — not merely his life as an industrial worker, not merely his life as a citizen, but his own personal life thru his work and thru his citizenship."

This wise and comprehensive definition, with which most intelligent Americans agree, but which few seem disposed to put in practice, requires that, in some way, there be given to every normal child an opportunity to become, within his capacity, an efficient worker, an intelligent citizen and a true man. Can the school, now or ever, provide this comprehensive opportunity? No. Is the community able, if it will, to furnish it? Yes. That being the case, the final responsibility for the real efficiency of the public schools, lies not with the teachers but with the citizens.

Dr. Laurie's admirable definition suggests, moreover, the best hypothesis upon which to base education. This hypothesis is that the child's nature is threefold and yet indivisible, that he has a physical, a mental and a moral nature, each deeply involved with the others, and all combining to form the essence and end of a human being:

[1] Institutes of Education, Lect. II.

character. Education, of whatever nature, has to deal, at one and the same time, with an animal whose thoughts and impulses, no matter how complex, are conditioned upon his health; with a thinking being whose physical and ethical states are governed by his percepts and concepts; with a willing (or moral) being whose appetites and thoughts are swayed by an unknown, inner force called conscience. Every step in education must rest upon the premise that the child, as well as the man, is simultaneously an animal, a thinker and a soul.

Popularly, however, education has lost a large part of its real significance, and even those who ought to know better have fallen into the habit of associating it with but one of the three phases of human development, that of the mind. Consequently, since intellectual training is peculiarly the province of a school, we have persuaded ourselves that education means simply schooling and, conversely, that the youth who has been schooled is educated. Many communities have indeed adopted, with more or less enthusiasm, the catch-phrase: "Send the whole boy to school;" but most of them as yet fail to appreciate that the school to which the larger part of the boy still goes has unlicensed teachers, unsupervised studies and, too often, the devil for headmaster.

In primitive Puritan days, the whole boy did go to a comprehensive school controlled in every department by the entire community. His mental training, by modern standards, was pitifully narrow; but his teachers were literally God-fearing men, and the minister, the lawyer and the squire had personal knowledge of every boy's advancement. His physical training was rude and laborious; but it was mainly out of doors, and was personally looked after by the father or the master, both having a direct interest in making that part of his education thorough and effective. His moral training was hard and unlovely; but, such as it was, no youth was permitted to escape it. And over all phases of the boy's daily life, the parson and those indefatigable lieutenants of his, the deacons and the tithingmen, kept strict watch, being held to high supervisory efficiency by that vigilant theocracy which, as their own creation, the grim New Englanders liked better than the laxer rule of kings.

Whatever its shortcomings, the early New England town was an ideally many-sided school wherein to educate, in fact as well as in name, the threefold nature of a growing boy. The range of activities was limited and the stage — if one may use so scandalous a term — was small; but for that narrow theatre the training of the actors was strikingly complete. Physically, the active life, with its varied farm tasks and household " chores," its exposure to the weather, its cold sleeping-rooms, coarse fare and early hours, made strong, wiry men. Manually, the wide variety of homely industries, most of them requiring skill, dexterity, keen observation, correlation of head and hands, and multiform activities, developed a Yankee ingenuity which assured industrial success. Mentally, the district school, kept usually by college students who, because of primitive conditions, lived among the people and knew the pupils and their families through and through, served at least to foster individuality. Politically, the town meeting, training boys from early youth in principles of liberty, democracy and social responsibility, and establishing in them the habit of free debate, was a school of citizenship unmatched in history; while, ethically, the ceaseless pressure of meeting-house and public opinion, upholding the weak and strengthening the strong, kept the average of morals singularly high.

To study the substantially complete educational efficiency of an early New England town is a chastening experience. Such an investigation shows the absurdity of placing, as we are too fond of doing, the modern palatial school-building beside the " little red schoolhouse " and bidding the awed spectator observe how much more we do for the child than our great-grandfathers did. In many ways, of course, we do; in richness of school curriculum we are far ahead; but were we to meet to-day's conditions as comprehensively — considering modern needs and resources — as those poverty-stricken forefathers fulfilled the demands of their crude time, we would have to show many things other than piles of brick and stone, many educational forces additional to those now active. Did some ancestral ghost, gliding fearfully through marble corridors adorned with works of art, and peering wonderingly into chemical laboratories resplendent with plate glass, summon courage to whisper: "Where do you educate your children's morals, where their hands, where their bodies, where their ingenuity, where their power to work, where their sense of duty to the state, where their ability to take efficient share in self-government?" what could you and I reply? Could we point to the churches, if there were any chance of that ghost remaining for the Sunday worship? Would we carry him to our city halls or ask him to read the yellow newspapers, to learn how we implant good citizenship? Would we take him into some tenement district to show how we develop human bodies and immortal souls?

Not that those elementary times are to be regretted or are to be brought back by living the so-called simple life. Better, on the whole, an hour of rich, modern complexity than a century of that narrow Puritan Cathay. The growth of our multiform resources, intellectual breadth, industrial power and fabulous wealth has been a glorious evolution and would be an unmixed blessing had education, in the true meaning of that term, advanced with corresponding speed. Emphatically, however, it has not kept pace with our rapidly differentiating social needs; and if we do not appreciate this lagging of genuine education, if the fathers and mothers, if all the members of a modern community, do not realize that they are responsible on a large scale, as the Puritans felt themselves responsible on a far smaller scale, for the all-round development of all boys and girls, then modern progress will culminate, and at the same time will come to an end, in rank materialism.

One should not exalt unduly the wisdom and prescience of the Puritan Yankee, whose educational difficulties, as compared with ours, were trivial. But we cannot too highly extol his sense of individual responsibility and the splendid results which that conscientiousness produced. Neither can we too strenuously maintain that real democracy must be bottomed upon the conviction of at least a majority in every community that each citizen is morally liable for the physical, industrial and spiritual welfare of his entire city or town. Not simply in extent of resources, but also in breadth of educational view, no American community but contains many persons far in advance of their Puritan forebears; but, from one cause and another, the proportion of citizens having a sense of civic responsibility is to-day much less; while the problems confronting them are incalculably more complex. The burning question of democracy is how to interest a greater number in every city, every town and every village in these vital problems, and how to inspire them to aid in solving them.

As to rural communities, their educational problems are not markedly greater than in the early nineteenth century, but the forces for meeting those problems are vastly different. Then the small town gave general allegiance to an individual church having both temporal and spiritual power; to-day half a dozen sects are struggling, often in quite un-Christian spirit, for mere domination. Then a homogeneous population swayed by active, wholesome public sentiment, governed the village as a genuine democracy; to-day, with the strongest men and women gone to the cities and their places filled by a heterogeneous and often decadent people, license, not liberty, frequently holds the reins of power. Then the varied industries of farm and house and village-shop served as an education in themselves; to-day their place is taken by ill-cared-for farm machinery, crazy pine furniture and slop-shop clothes. Then village pride and satisfaction centred around the school, feeble and insufficient though that school might be; to-day, in hundreds of rural communities, there is but a grudging, perfunctory compliance with the law, the wage of the teacher being, in many instances, actually lower than fifty years ago, her status correspondingly depressed, and her influence in even greater measure gone.

Serious, however, as the situation in many rural places has become, the problem for them is far less pressing than for cities and suburban towns; because here, at the very outset, the imagination is staggered and the energy paralyzed by the element of size. This element has become so obtrusive and insistent that, in many cases, it alone is grappled with, resulting in great school-machines satisfied to handle in military fashion large numbers of pupils, to give them some sort of mental drill and to drive them so far through a formal curriculum as to keep the number of technically illiterate, in spite of almost overwhelming immigration, astonishingly low. But to believe that in meeting the perfunctory tests of registrars of voters the community fulfills its educational duty is to place ourselves on the level of the little girl who, having with great difficulty mastered the alphabet, asked with an air of assured omniscience: " What more is there for me to learn? "

Every one of us, despite his probable disavowal,

is party to an elaborate socialism which, being negative, is largely ineffectual. The necessity for self-preservation has driven us into a kind of *ex post facto* socialism which, at public cost, establishes hospitals for the sick and insane, almshouses for the pauperized and houses of detention, jails and prisons for the morally diseased. Such punitive and palliative socialism is the result, primarily, not of economic enlightenment, but of collective fear. A wise socialism would provide the ounce of prevention rather than the pound of cure by furnishing, at common cost, a genuine, fit and thorough education for all three sides of the nature of every child in the community. It needs no special wisdom to understand that, if we are to have socialism at all, preventive measures are far cheaper than remedial ones, and that the saving in human souls, through such measures, is incalculably greater. To ward off idleness, disease, crime, pauperism and their attendant evils from naturally well-disposed children costs immensely less than to try to cure them in hardened adults, and it means, moreover, the moral preservation of many now wasted lives. Therefore, unless one adopts an attitude wholly *laissez faire* by saying that the state should do nothing at all for self-protection, unless one is ready to give up prisons, hospitals, police, almshouses and all kindred things, then he must acknowledge that, on economic, if on no other grounds, the state has not only a right, it has a solemn duty to provide means for developing every boy and girl physically, mentally and morally, to the full measure of each child's capacity.

Of course much is being done in all these directions towards right education; but such work has thus far been sporadic, desultory and vaguely experimental. What is being attempted toward comprehensive education has not the whole community, but some individual, club or association behind it; and that little is subject, moreover, to the whims and spasms of economy of kaleidoscopic school committees. Before real advance can be made, there must be approximate consensus of expert opinion, an authoritative policy, fixed without being rigid, and, above all, an appreciation on the part of the public that education really pays only when it is not cheap; that not until we reach a high level of expenditure are we likely to secure a general schooling worth paying for at all. At present the smell of the bargain counter is over the public schools, cheapening the teachers, substituting shoddy for genuine mind-stuff, depriving children of the right of self-development, and defrauding the community, economically and morally, to an extent immeasurable.

Such a program of genuine education as this demands adequate revenues and the spending of them by men and women who will use them honestly, wisely and effectively. In other words, we are confronted with the formidable task of making democracy itself efficient before we can give an education adequate to the needs of democracy. To attempt what education ought to undertake while the control of great sums of money and huge bodies of children is left in such hands as those into which, stupidly and lazily, we so often surrender our city or suburban governments, would mean financial disaster and an educational cataclysm. Therefore the fundamental responsibility of every community toward education is to clean its municipal house.

But you and I and our neighbors are the state and it is our duty, therefore, to make the government genuinely democratic, to preserve and develop all the children of the community on the physical side, by cleaning, materially and morally, the whole city, town or village, destroying slums, providing playgrounds, baths and gymnasiums, keeping the supply of milk and other indispensable foods clean, pure and cheap, and employing rational means to educate mothers in hygienic living. All this is socialistic, but it is wise socialism; while to establish hospitals, almshouses, homes for the insane and crippled, to say nothing of prisons filled with victims of foul environment and want of training, without at the same time attempting to stop the supply of inmates for those institutions, denotes a very stupid and extravagant socialism.

The second series of problems for you and me and our neighbors to take up are those relating to that basis of civic life and morals — the family, our families. Therein most of the child's training will take place whether we want it to or not, and therein, almost without exception, the ultimate usefulness or worthlessness of the boy or girl will actually be determined.

The next business before us citizens is to prepare the child for that industrial usefulness, to himself and to the community, which is fundamental to good citizenship.

He is virtually but half educated so long as he has not acquired such necessary industrial qualifications as manual control and dexterity, coöperation of brain and hand, quickness of adaptation, fertility of resource, concentration, "gumption," and has not been given, on top of these, ample opportunity to secure the groundwork of some special trade or industry. Without such essentials, he is likely to join that appalling army of "floaters" who, without a trade or any chance of learning one, wander from one casual occupation to another, depressing wages, inducing enormous industrial waste and swelling at last the costly ranks of vagrancy.

Having thus provided for his physical welfare, for the right family atmosphere, and for the training of his body and hands, it would be logical to declare that we should next take up the task of furthering the child's mental and moral growth. But, practically, there is no such task remaining. Give a normal child hygienic and uplifting surroundings, with plenty of opportunity for physical and manual development, make every effort to keep sound the family influences which shape his life, imbue him with those qualities which lie at the root of industrial effectiveness, surround him with the evidences and results of good government, and — provided only that he be furnished with the necessary tools of human communication, such as reading, writing and numbers — the mental growth and moral stability of that child are made almost absolutely sure.

II. IN INDUSTRY

THE BOY IN BUSINESS

Not so very long ago the merchant, the manufacturer, the teacher, the young man and the public in general were under the spell of the boys' magazine wherein the first prize: the prize of partnership in the business and marriage with the "old man's" daughter, was awarded to the boy who kept his hands clean, brushed his shoes, picked up stray pins on the office floor and carefully saved the twine from his employer's parcels. To do these things was indispensable; but, besides that, the aspirant for partnership (and the daughter) must also, according to the story-books, write a perfect hand, never make a mistake in addition, never forget a message, never have a deceased grandmother on the afternoon of the ball-game, never think of aught except mastering every detail of the business, never, in short, be anything but the kind of prig that real, red-blooded boys are not.

The so-called Manchester school of political economy was built around a supposed economic man wholly unlike any human being ever born. Consequently, there were promulgated for nearly a century a lot of solemn fallacies which have given, and are still giving, endless trouble to civilized society. In much the same way, the supposed demands of business upon boys have crystallized around these story-book heroes and have led the business man, the boy and the boy's teacher into all sorts of difficulties, misunderstandings and wild-goose chases after educational impossibilities.

It may be that the story-book boy and the story-book employer — and even the daughter — did exist at some period anterior to the middle of the nineteenth century; but since that time all three have been as extinct as the dodo; yet much of the thinking and much of the talk about the demands of business are based, even now, upon these ancient and mendacious tales.

We must get from under the obsession of these romantic fallacies and face the facts. The clean hands, blacked shoes fallacy has ruined thousands of boys who, if they had pitched in and got their hands dirty, would have turned out first-rate mechanics and mill men, instead of sixth-rate clerks. The pin-picking and twine-saving fairy-tales have started many a boy on the downward path of petty, two-cent economies, instead of on the upward path of large-minded, far-seeing business policies. While, as for the other things demanded by the story-books, they are about as obsolete as quill pens and sealing-wax.

Who really cares about long-hand writing, when all real business to-day is done by shorthand and the typewriter? What is the use of drilling a boy who has cost the community $4000 into becoming a fairly accurate adding machine, when one can buy an absolutely accurate metal one for a hundred dollars? Why lay so much stress upon errand running, when the telephone takes and returns all messages? Why talk about learning all the ramifications of an industry, when the main hope of business success is in becoming a first-rate specialist? Why even specify that the boy shall know how to wield a broom, when the incorporated cleaning company will sweep the offices and sweep them well for far less money than even the wages of a greenhorn?

Should the present agitation over vocational education come to nothing— which is inconceivable,— it will have been worth while if it forces teachers, boys and, eventually, employers to ask themselves straight questions and to face actual conditions. What does modern business really require of the average boy? How fully can the boy meet, or can he be trained to meet, those requirements? And finally, what can the school do and how far can it go in bringing the boy into line with the reasonable demands of a rational, up-to-date mercantile or manufacturing concern?

Just now everybody is in a turmoil and pother over all three of these problems; for all of us: business men, boys and schools, are in a transition state. Business itself is in the travail of readjustment — as witness the attempted regulation of it by the Congress and the states, and as witness, also, the vogue of anything that labels itself scientific management. The young man, still reading the old story-books about business, is finding out that those tales and the real conditions are not even fourth cousins one to another. While the schools, tired of putting boys through the treadmill work demanded by formal college entrance examinations, and looking for some better incentive to hold before the pupil, are turning (generally with more eagerness than knowledge) towards preparation for business as something at once tangible to them and interesting to the youth.

But it is a tremendous point gained that all three of them: business man, boy and pedagogue, are working at the same problem, each from his own angle of vision, but all seriously; the business man being desperately in earnest as he finds that profits are in inverse ratio to lack of really trained men; the boy being more and more driven, by modern competition, to weigh the problems of his after-school vocation; and the schools, as the educational tax gets heavier and heavier, feeling ever more keenly the need of showing tangible returns for the millions given every year to their support.

No business man can have the face to say, however, that those millions are thrown away so long as he, the average manufacturer, is every day wasting so much good material (both human and inanimate) through his haphazard, antiquated and unscientific ways. But since he is manfully buckling down to the problems of real conservation in manufacturing, transporting and selling goods, so must the teacher, also, get down to actualities. For in all industries the chief element to be conserved is the human element; and the teacher is paid by the state to educate, guide and give a right start to his quota of those boys and girls who are to be the producers, distributors and consumers of the coming time.

For years and years everybody has been saying that the real work of the schools is to produce good citizens; but no one, broadly speaking, can be a good citizen unless he is an able producer and an intelligent consumer. Those are the cornerstones of good citizenship. Education that is not founded upon them produces dreamers, parasites and social anarchists. Education that is founded upon them is at least in line to produce self-reliance, self-respect and social responsibility, the three main bases of sound citizenship.

Therefore, it is not merely the teachers in the commercial school, or in the commercial department of the high school, who must take the problems of modern business seriously, it is every teacher. And however high the ideals of all teachers should be, however strongly they should insist upon breadth and culture and " uplift " for their pupils, every one of those noble things of education should be soundly bottomed upon the no less noble demands of self-respecting, intelligent, purposeful winning of the daily bread. What higher and finer goal for all school life than the founding of a family and the rearing and training of the next generation? But how absolutely bound up with that true ideal of a civilized state is the ability to earn a living, in ways congenial to the earner and in such an amount that ease of mind, comfort of body and education for the mind and soul shall follow for the worker himself and for those depending on him!

Using the word " business " to cover all the fields of human activity along material lines: the fields of production, distribution and consumption, every boy and girl in every school is going to find his chief interests and his chief medium for development in the business world. Therefore, every teacher should understand, at least in a broad way, what business is, what it demands and how those demands are to be met,— so far as they can be met,— by the school.

Obviously, however, the most zealous of teachers could not acquaint himself intimately with more than one general line of business activity; and it is a serious question whether or not, if he had so trained himself, he would not then be doing the teaching profession a service by leaving it. The teacher must never forsake the teaching point of view: the view, namely, that his duty is not to train the boy for business, but to use business as a powerful instrument for training the boy. To do this, however, the teacher must understand not only boys in general, but also business in general. And, however great may be the differences between manufacturing and merchandizing, between banking and baking, there are certain fundamentals characteristic of substantially every branch of that production, distribution and consumption of commodities which we gather under the one comprehensive term: modern business.

The most striking characteristic of modern business is the rapidity with which it is moving from a competitive to a coöperative basis. This is resulting, on one hand, in the "trusts" and other combinations, which furnish so much good copy for the newspaper and the congressman; on another hand, in the so-called public service corporations, wherein quasi-public needs are supplied by quasi-private bodies; on another hand, in that genuine coöperative production and distribution with which we are less familiar than are the Europeans; and finally, in that public ownership, pure and simple, which many modern politicians are hastening to promise to the people in exchange for the people's votes.

But, in whatever form it appears, coöperation results in two things: bigness and complexity. When two men form a partnership, the profits may be out of all proportion to the business paraphernalia. But when oil producers get together, and then (at the behest of Congress) unmix themselves again; when the "elevateds" that run below the streets, the "subways" that run above the ground, the tunnels and the surface lines, knit themselves into a single great transportation cobweb; when the workingmen of a whole county decide to buy their flour at a single purchase; and when forty cities and towns combine to supply themselves with water — then there results not only a bigness that has taught us to talk in billions as easily as our fathers talked in hundreds of dollars, but also a complexity which staggers us poor outsiders and, there is reason to believe, staggers the insiders as well.

The third feature of modern business, growing naturally out of the characteristics of bigness and complexity, is that profits to-day are made by the geometrical progression of innumerable small gains, instead of through the adding together of a few large gains. Selling one or two hundred things at a good profit in a country store in New York State brought in to Mr. Woolworth's employer a few thousand dollars a year. Selling millions of things for not exceeding ten cents each enabled Mr. Woolworth himself to capitalize at $75,000,000 and to erect the highest building in the world. The mining fortunes of yesterday were made by working the richest veins and pockets, leaving the rest as waste. The mining fortunes of to-morrow will be made from the dump-heaps of abandoned plants. The day of the telescope in business, the day of seeking new worlds and skimming the cream of their natural resources, has gone by; and the day of the microscope in business, of getting infinitesimal profits infinitely multiplied, has come. Thus far we have been a world of wasters; henceforth we are to be a world of savers, and are thus to outwit Malthus and to make the world's resources not less, but greater, by every added baby born.

The fourth characteristic of modern business, consequently, is (in merchandizing) frequent "turn-overs" and (in manufacturing) the utilization of what used to be called waste. The stream of trade flows so fast through a modern department store that the one cent profit here and the two cents profit there aggregate in the course of the year a huge amount of money. According to their own statement, the beef barons actually lose on sirloin steaks and choice cuts of pork; where their profits are made is in converting every scrap of the animal's carcase into something that can be sold.

To keep a river of business flowing through a

great store, and to make it profitable to save every hair of every beast in the Chicago stockyards, however, there must be highly developed organization, highly complicated machinery and just as little as possible of that most expensive of motive powers, the human hand. Human hands are still wanted, and in proportionately greater numbers than ever before in history, but merely as servants to machines that multiply hundreds and thousands of times that initial force. It is nonsense, however, to talk of this as slavery to machinery. On the contrary, it is mastery of the forces of nature —an ever increasing mastery, which is, so to speak, kicking the brute laborer, the pick-and-shovel man, up into the ranks of the machine-user, and is kicking the machine-user up into the ranks of the organizer, those ranks where brains are every day setting hundreds and thousands at new work, and every day bringing what used to be luxuries down to the horizon of the commonest man. The cost of living is high, not because of the scandalous luxury of the rich, but because of the commendable luxury of the poor. It is true that the desire for the good things of life is growing somewhat faster than the devices and economies of modern industry can bring those good things within reach; but this is simply a question of gradual adjustment. And the fact that more men are every day wanting and demanding more things is one of the surest guarantees of a continuous and genuine prosperity.

An inseparable accompaniment of machinery, however, is speed. Therefore, the next notable characteristic of modern business is whirlwind pace. Thirty years ago, Boston, New York and London were horse-car towns, with clerks nodding over pigskin ledgers, errand boys playing marbles in the roadway, with no telephones, no rapid transit in the modern sense, with scarcely any devices for making speed or saving time. To-day, even London, the archetype of conservatism, is a whirlpool of motor-buses, speeding men and clamoring advertisements.

Consequently, not merely what the business man, but what modern business itself, demands of the high school graduate is rational and orderly speed. In the high school, in the schools below, in that larger school, the community, and, above all, in the boy's home, he must have been trained (if he would succeed in business and, therefore, in good citizenship) to " go the pace," not of dissipation, but of modern industry.

Since, however, no one can get speed, without a breakdown, out of a weak or badly-built engine, so one cannot get efficiency from a half-sick or ill-developed youth. Consequently, now as never before, the business world must have boys who are sound in body and in nerves and who know the value of good health, clean living, exercise, right eating and fresh air. The average boy of eighteen has cost the community at least $4,000 to " raise," — most high school boys have cost a good deal more. Moreover, to train that $4,000 boy to the point where he is a real asset in the business costs that business a large additional amount. Therefore, the community cannot afford — the business into which the boy goes cannot afford — to have him break down because of a weak body, poor nerves or dissipation, just when he is beginning to bring in fair returns upon his capital cost. The first thing, then, that modern business demands in its apprentices is sound bodies, steady nerves and a good working knowledge of hygiene. These things are worth much more than a knowledge of double-entry bookkeeping; and the school, in coöperation with the parents and the community, must provide this kind of teaching.

The next essential for speed is quickness of mind, nimbleness of body and good coördination among all the senses. One doesn't acquire these, however, by stewing all day at a desk or in an armchair, over a lot of books. One gets them by using all his muscles and all his senses in a wide variety of exercises, mental, physical and manual, directed in educative ways and by rational progression towards well-defined ends, — not occult ends, seen only by the inner consciousness of the teacher, but tangible ends, visible to the boy himself.

The third essential of speed is team-play. Every schoolroom should be an organism as well knit, as thoroughly balanced, as purposeful as a 'varsity football team; for that is the kind of coördination towards which every mercantile and manufacturing enterprise is rapidly, and with full understanding of its value, tending. The teacher who still uses competition instead of coöperation as the main spur towards speed, is woefully behind the times and loses that most valuable aid in education: working together for a common result.

Effective team-play, however, is founded upon

promptness, ready obedience, willingness to subordinate one's self to the general good, enthusiasm and that comprehensive quality called loyalty. All these are at the very root of every successful enterprise; and what modern business asks most eagerly is that the boys who come into it shall obey orders intelligently and promptly; shall see how much, instead of how little, they can do to further the interests of the concern; and, in whatever they do, shall show the essential virtues of team-play: enthusiasm, self-subordination and unflagging loyalty.

But a man cannot be enthusiastic and effective if he lives in a mere groove. Therefore, while the youth who is to succeed in the complexities of modern industry must be a specialist, he must be a broad one. A man may move fast in a treadmill, but he gets nowhere. On the other hand, a motorist, though tied to a roadway, makes his twenty-five miles an hour because he sticks to that well-surfaced track instead of trying to wander through bushes, potato-fields and gravel banks. He does not leave the road, but he sees and knows the whole surrounding territory. Consequently, a fourth essential of speed is thoroughness in one line, with an outlook into many lines, with an intelligent interest in many things, and with a broad attitude towards all human interests.

And a fifth essential of speed is the cutting of red tape. Circumlocution, that curse of the law, is being rapidly driven out of business, because a merchant or manufacturer cannot afford to waste time and lose headway in doubling and twisting. If there is a short way of doing a thing — be it in business or in school, — do it; and save time, money and nervous energy.

Therefore, in demanding of the high school graduate rational and orderly speed, modern business asks the teachers of those young men and women:

(1) that they do everything possible to send into business life sound animals who appreciate the value of good health and who know how to conserve it;

(2) that they give those pupils such studies and exercises and in such a way as to result in activity of mind, thorough coördination between mind and body, well trained senses and an eagerness to work and to learn;

(3) that all the school work be so carried on as to foster a spirit of team-play, a sense of the value and power of working together for the common weal;

(4) that to this end the teacher subordinate the memorizing of facts to the inculcating of promptness, obedience and loyalty;

(5) that the studies which make for breadth of view and variety of interest be emphasized, and those which make for mere information, technic and drill be minimized;

(6) that, to accomplish this, subjects like arithmetic, bookkeeping, grammar, rhetoric, etc., be cut down to their lowest terms and fewest principles, throwing out all processes and exercises which are obsolete, little used or cumbersome, putting in all the short-cuts and labor-saving devices which are of general application; and that those subjects, such as history, economics,

political and economic geography, etc., which make for breadth of view; those exercises, such as rightly-conceived manual training, ordered games, free-hand drawing, etc., which make for quickness and control of the body; and those general school relationships which promote team-play, loyalty, the spirit of working together for a tangible and desirable end, be fostered, amplified and in every way encouraged.

Finally, and above all, the high school should be the medium for leading the boy and girl from the irresponsibility of childhood into the responsibility of men and women. With that end in view, the school days and weeks should be on a business basis, with long hours (diversified, of course, with a proper alternation of mental and physical activity), strict accountability on the part of the pupils, and an organization based, as nearly as possible, upon the best business and factory models. So long as youth of seventeen and eighteen do not take their high school work seriously, they will not take business seriously. And it is this lack of seriousness, this failure to realize that success in business can come only from strict attention to business, which lies at the root of most, if not all, of the complaints made by business men against the products of American schools. Those employers find many, if not most, of the boys and girls who come for employment unfitted for and, if I may use the word, unfittable into, the complex demands of modern life. Remembering the story-books, they think it is because these aspirants cannot write and cipher and spell. But they are fast finding out that the causes of the trouble, in most instances, are weak bodies, or untrained senses, or sluggish minds, or lack of purpose, or general immaturity, or ignorance of how to work with others, or an all-round irresponsibility, or a combination of from two to seven of all these human defects. Secondary schools cannot, of course, make silk purses out of sows' ears; but they can make it their chief business to deliver to the business world boys and girls whose bodies, senses and minds have had so much organized training as Heaven has permitted them to receive; who have passed out of the state of "kids" into that of men and women; who have a conception of and experience in coöperation and team-play; who know what loyalty means; and who have taken school work so seriously that they are prepared to look upon the earning of one's daily bread as something other than a listless game.

Modern business demands these things. Experience has shown that a rightly ordered secondary school system can produce them. That all schools do not is the fault partly of the teachers, partly of the employers, partly of the community in general, mainly of the parents. The fathers and mothers, and the rest of the community, must be educated to give moral and financial support to this effective type of education. But the only persons who can educate them are the schoolmasters; and they must do it in a roundabout way by gradually introducing this rational, real education into the higher and lower schools. The results will be so immediate, and in many cases so startling, as to make even the over-worked business man take notice. And when he begins to realize that the school is really trying to meet his needs, when he begins to see that the millions poured into the public schools are producing efficient young men and young women, he will cease growling over his school taxes, and will turn some of the fortunes that he now gives or bequeathes to colleges into the lean treasuries of the higher and lower schools.

THE HUMAN FACTOR IN BUSINESS

WHAT is big business? One man in newspaper articles cleverly designed to stimulate the lust for gambling, says, with many wonderful words, that it is a hideous curse; another, nonchalantly referring to a million dollars as "a small sum," maintains that it is an unadulterated blessing; while those of us who are coming in contact with it every day, find it to be just a normal manifestation of the good and bad — inextricably mingled — in common human nature.

But the unthinking public and certain lurid newspapers which cater to it, will not come out of their prevailing state of hysteria regarding "big business" until they look at it, not as some mysterious legerdemain carried on by supermen, but as the simple effect of every man's desire to get the most money with the least work.

From the standpoint of efficiency, however, as well as from that of good-will, the principals in this big game ought to play fair and to observe the rules and regulations of team-play. Be it little or big, every business is a partnership in which the three partners are the employers who steer the game, the employees who do the work and the public which pays in its good money at the gate; and the reason why we are usually in such turmoils of investigation and crimination and recrimination is because some of the partners are convinced, with good show of reason, that they are not getting a square deal.

Under the old free-competitive system among small businesses, the public, as a consumer, did get, under normal conditions, a square deal and the cost of living was low. But that same public, as a producer under competition, had a hard struggle to make both ends meet; and, as an employee, was forced to accept an unreasonably low wage. Those were the days of the debt-ridden farmer and the real wage slave.

The obvious way out of the dilemma of poor wages and minus profits was through combinations of one sort or another: pools, gentlemen's agreements, trusts, etc.; but in order to give these combinations a good start it was necessary to shut out free competition from abroad. Hence the protective tariff, with its much advertised solicitude for American labor and with, incidentally, its temptations to extravagant management. Behind this safe barrier, big business grew with such whirlwind speed that to-day we think and talk in millions.

But, while business combination has produced such fortunes — real and paper — as were before undreamed of; while it has made us a world power politically; while it has undoubtedly greatly raised the general level of prosperity; it has not brought with it that increased efficiency which its beneficiaries so loudly promised; and it has done little towards making this country that leader in the markets of the world which our natural advantages should long since have brought about.

Business combination does insure, without question, marked economies through the use of huge capital, the elimination of middlemen and the prevention of needless duplications. Not only these advantages, however, but also those due to the increasing application of science to agriculture, commerce, transportation and manufactures, have been more than offset by the extravagant promoting, syndicating and stock-watering burdens which have been foisted upon almost all such combinations by those who brought them about. These were long concealed from the general public, however, through the abundance of those natural resources which formed the basis of most of these combinations, through the rapid growth of home markets, through the fact that wages could be kept down by the inflowings from the enormous reservoirs of cheap foreign labor, and through the sudden blossoming of extravagance which made the American public indifferent to the rapid rise in the cost of living, until that rise had reached the startling figures which confront us to-day.

That increased cost is due, of course, to many other things besides the trusts; but someone must pay the huge and wholly unnecessary expense of promotions, manipulations and general watering; and that somebody, age-long experience has shown, is the ultimate consumer.

But that patient elephant has turned; and the burden of costs cannot much longer be placed upon the public's ample and well-seasoned back. Therefore business — big and little, for the little men have to follow the big —

realizes at last that it is "up against" the problem of a drastic cutting of costs.

Under such a necessity, the first refuge is, of course, to reduce wages; but there business finds itself confronted with, on the one hand, a fairly well-organized body of labor which, far from submitting to a reduction, is demanding an increase with which to meet the mounting cost of living. It finds itself confronted, on the other hand, with a Frankenstein which it has itself evoked: organizations such as the I. W. W., with menacing ranks recruited from the cheap labor which big business has been so industriously bringing in without making proper provision for its training for American citizenship. So that way out is barred.

The easy alternatives, either of putting the burden of extra cost due to inefficiency (or worse) upon the public or of taking it out of the employee, being thus cut off, the managers of big business have been forced to look within their own domains and to see if costs cannot be reduced through what is vaguely called scientific management. And, with the help of eager specialists, what a host of panaceas have we successively discovered!

First: scientific accounting which, it is true, revealed many leaks, but which, in itself, is expensive. Next: cost accounting, which did much to shake our former self-satisfaction, but which touches only the fringe of the problems of reduction. Next: development of piece and bonus systems, stop-watch studies, and a whole academy of Taylor doctors, Emerson surgeons and other eminent specialists sitting at the bedsides of our sick businesses for months, making infinitesimal diagnoses and prescribing, sometimes a cure, and sometimes remedies worse than the disease.

Nevertheless, the whole efficiency propaganda has been infinitely wholesome, for it has waked business men up and has proved, what some have long suspected, that the so called Captains of Industry are not, after all, to be regarded as great business executives, but merely as colossal manipulators of established enterprises.

They are not, however, to be blamed. After giving the matter a fair trial, we might as well acknowledge that it is not humanly possible for any single man to administer efficiently one of the huge business or public-service aggregations of to-day. The small competitive business proved inefficient because it could not command funds big enough to run it economically. The large combination is proving even more inefficient because it cannot find men big enough to run it economically, or even honestly. For not Argus himself could keep an eye on every leak when there is a constant inpouring and outpouring of tens of millions of comparatively "easy money." And big business has so many things to look out for that it fails to see what little business does generally perceive: that every enterprise, large or small, has three equal and always to be remembered partners, (1) the employer, who should do honest financing, (2) the employee, who should do honest work and (3) the purchasing public, which objects to paying high prices for shoddy or for watered goods.

This means that real business efficiency is only to a

minor degree a question of raw materials or machines or time-clocks or newspaper advertising; it is a question of sound, well-balanced human relationships, of men and women working together loyally, heartily and honestly for the good of the business and, through it, of themselves. And every such business, or the small federated units into which every big business ought to be divided, must be so compact that those human relations may be kept close and vital.

In other words, having tried free competition and found it wasteful, having tried unrestrained combination and found it even more extravagant, we are driven by the logic of circumstances to try what we long ago found was the only sound road towards political and social efficiency, namely, coöperation: within the business itself and between that business and the public which it serves.

So long as the employer studies only his machines and office methods, leaving out of consideration the human forces which enter into his business (those forces being the managers, the foremen, the workmen, the sellers and buyers and the general public good-will) he will be saving at the spigot and wasting at the bung. So long as the employee seeks only to force the highest wage for the least return in work, forgetting that he is the partner with most at stake and that the cost of every wasted hour or bad job comes out of his and his fellow workmen's pockets, he is doing more than all the "grinding monopolists" put together to depress the real wage-scale. So long as the public, through harassing laws, sensational charges, a foolish encouragement of fake advertising and shoddy buying, and the election of fools or knaves to office, puts all sorts of needless burdens upon business, it is doing all that it can to keep the cost of living on the upward climb.

Efficient business management, then, means honesty, reasonableness, fairmindedness and "gumption" in handling and in dealing with men. The manager who assumes large responsibilities in business must know how to choose assistant managers, foremen and other lieutenants so that they will do team work as well-balanced as that of the finest foot-ball eleven; must know how to handle workmen so as to get from them, not task work, but loyal service of the highest possible effectiveness; must know how to deal with the public so as to get its confidence and to make it appreciate that the aim of that particular business is so to eliminate wastes and so to promote efficiency as to save the public every needless cent of cost.

The greatest source of inefficiency in most large or small businesses to-day is to be found in the management; and the best service that high schools, colleges and technical schools can render to the common weal is to train young men and women who shall be competent to handle commercial and industrial enterprises in a scientific and statesmanlike way.

The business men having large responsibilities to-day may be roughly divided into four classes: (1) the grandsons of their grandfathers, who have usually inherited all the "old man's" weak points and few of his good ones, and who wholly lack his experience in the school of hard knocks;

(2) the men who have worked up from the bottom and who, with an intimate knowledge of every detail of the business, are usually lacking in social experience and breadth of view;

(3) the men who, in the hurly-burly of business politics, have been pitchforked into high office and who are kept busy spreading out the few things they do know in such fashion as to cover up the many that they do not; and

(4) the men who regard business as a real profession and who have made a study of every fact and feature bearing upon the efficient conduct of their particular task.

Needless to say, the type of man for which there is to-day everywhere a crying need is the last; and in the case of a big business involving large responsibilities, this is the way to create him. Begin far down in the lower schools to develop the boy's initiative, gumption and knowledge of human nature by encouraging him to work out things for himself, to do things, build things and carry out schemes with the rest of the "gang" in the same spirit in which he captains the baseball team. Impress him early with the fact that he will be compelled to earn his living and that to be efficient in doing it is one of the finest goals in life.

When he gets to the high school, don't waste his time cramming him for college examinations. Find a college that is sensible enough to take the school's word for his proficiency. But in that high school try to get the coöperation of the manufacturers, the merchants and the farmers so that the boy may spend a considerable part of his time in real, paid-for work, learning how to apply his books to business and finding out what kind of help business needs from the books and other school paraphernalia. All this means sound, genuine industrial training from top to bottom of the schools, as well as a new spirit and attitude towards, and in, education. In that high school, moreover, give the boy even more opportunity than he had in the lower schools, to rub up against other boys, to get experience of bossing and being bossed, of planning and organizing, of buying and selling and of getting "sold."

In college, help the youth to choose a well-rounded course that shall, in the first place, bring him in contact with real men, — not with "greasy grinds" grown into cub instructors, — and that shall, in the second place, give him, through history, economics, sociology, applied science and studies of that type, familiarity with and knowledge of men and of man's development, of the principles of organization, order and true efficiency. Pitch him early, too, into politics, and teach him that public service is not merely his duty but his opportunity.

In his summer vacations, and possibly in a year between high school and college, in college or right after graduation, let him see just as much of his own country and of other countries as can possibly be managed. If he knocks up against the world in the right way, by roughing it, tramping, and living with the people, he can do it without much expense, and the problem of making a little money go a long way will do him untold good.

Finally, let him start in business at the very bottom, doing real, hard, continuous work in every department, rubbing up against the workmen long enough to get their point of view, and rubbing up against the public, through the selling end, until he appreciates their coöperative possibilities.

Above all, and from the very beginning, impress in every possible way upon that boy and youth the fact that if he is to succeed as the executive of a great business, he must know men, be able to work with men and to make them work with him. Impress him also with the fact that if he is to get the highest efficiency out of his enterprise, it will be through the intelligent conservation and the wise and just exploitation, through coöperation, of all the human factors concerned.

A man so trained will have studied business as a real profession; and when he gets to the top, he will know what efficiency means, and will have that understanding of men and that hold upon men which will enable him to extend and to enlarge his enterprise upon the only sound and lasting lines: those of thorough coöperation between the management that creates, the workman that constructs and the public that "pays the freight."

ART IN HUMAN LIFE

ONE who argues for the development of art in the United States must begin by denying with all possible vigor that there is any actual distinction between the arts called manual (or useful), and the arts called fine. Between the genuine craftsman and the genuine artist there is no real line of cleavage, and consequently there can be no distinction between the things which one or the other of them produces. The painter of great pictures is but the culmination, or the flower, of a group of designers and decorators who, being artist-craftsmen, have imperceptibly gone over the imaginary line between designing and painting, and in so doing have evolved from out their group one or more genuine painters who, when they shall have been dead long enough, will be called " old masters."

The sculptor, in the same way, is but the flowering of the potter, the wood-carver and the stone-cutter, any one of whom, if he honors and loves his craft, may at any moment step over that same invisible line into the noble company of great plastic artists. Architecture, no matter how magnificent, is but the logical goal of honest carpentry, sound masonry and artistic cabinet making. Even music must have behind it the craftsmanship (exquisitely perfected, as in the case of a

Stradivarius violin) of the instrument maker, and is in itself the effect of the high craftsmanship involved in the perfect manipulation either of a musical instrument or of the human voice. The drama, of course, loses half its value unless it have behind it the stagecraft which helps to create the dramatic illusion. Moreover, it is no forcing of analogies to regard the perfect gesture, the studied posture — so perfect that it seems unstudied — and again the manipulation of the voice, in acting, as a fleeting but no less real form of craftsmanship.

Literature alone would seem to have no ancestry in any manual art; but there is, nevertheless, direct parallelism between the cabinet maker who designs, proportions and exquisitely finishes a piece of furniture, and the writer who, having a great thought to embody, so shapes his sentences, smoothes his paragraphs and proportions his entire presentation as to make that great thought a living force, enduring from generation to generation. Shakespeare, for example, greatest of writers, is also greatest of craftsmen, his very faults being so manipulated by his transcendent genius as to give added emphasis to what he desired to express. " Craft," in perhaps both senses, was behind the remarkable " Cross of Gold " speech made by Mr. Bryan, a burst of studied oratory which markedly changed the course of American history for at least twenty-five years.

It is of the utmost significance in this connection that the period of greatest " all-roundness " in the fine arts is also the period of greatest flowering in craftsmanship: the era loosely called the Renaissance, to which belong so much of the great painting, sculpture, architecture, literature, and even music of human history. A majority of the transcendent names in that marvelous period were primarily craftsmen; and it is difficult to know whether to admire their masterpieces most for their embodiment of what we call fine art or of what we call pure craftsmanship. The greatest cathedrals, looked at as a whole, are superlative specimens of art; viewed point by point, they are equally astonishing examples of craftsmanship; and even one who knows nothing of painting understands that the technique of the old masters is quite as extraordinary as their powers of emotional expression. No argument is needed, of course, to prove that in many instances besides that of Shakespeare the technique of the great Renaissance writers is equal, and in some cases superior, to the content of their writings. And were such men as Benvenuto Cellini and Peter Visscher merely craftsmen, or were they superlatively artists, too?

While the Renaissance is doubtless the most conspicuous proof of the thesis, there are many other examples in history ready to sustain the argument that great leaders in the fine arts do not appear in any number unless there is a widespread facility in, and a popular appreciation of, the manual arts. Consequently, if we are ever to be — what we now are not — a nation producing painters, sculptors, architects, dramatists, musicians and writers of undoubted first rank, we must begin by creating a general understanding among everyday people of what true craftsmanship means, and by rearing up, also, numerous accomplished and devoted craftsmen, capable both of seeing visions and of making those visions real. We must have, in other words, not a few scattered individuals, but large groups of men and women, a part of whom know how to manipulate, with supreme artistry, wood and stone and metal, and others of whom know how to mobilize their bodies, hands and voices — and their minds as well — with that almost superhuman skill possessed by the consummate actor, musician, orator, dramatist or poet.

Probably a vast majority of Americans would argue that the need for creating craftsmen — or, rather, artists — of this superlative type is open to much argument. In a country like ours, they will contend, the aiming to develop supreme masters in the fine arts is a wasteful use of national energy. They will maintain that, situated as we are, we should limit our endeavors practically to the field of mechanical skill, a field in which we are already near the front. In many directions we are making machines fully equal to those of any other nation, and in possibly a majority of those directions we are making machines the finish and perfection of which no other nation can approach. "Isn't it glory enough," they will say, "for the United States to make the best motors and watches and sewing-machines and typewriters, and similar practical objects, without trying to create those rare, artistic things which, after all, have very little immediate, intrinsic value?" "What good," they will continue, "are pieces of superlative craftsmanship that only connoisseurs understand; and, as to pictures and statues, what use are they except for critics to wrangle over?"

"Moreover," the hard-headed American will say, "Are not these well-nigh perfect machines products of art in themselves? And isn't it better for us to concentrate our energies on creating these pieces of perfection worth so much, cash down, rather than to strive after the uncertain, and always tardy, laurels awarded the fine arts?"

This last contention of theirs is easily answered, of course, by pointing out that where and when a machine or a bridge or a sky-scraper is indeed a work of art, it is primarily because of its design; and that the designer is not a mechanic, but is an expert craftsman and, in most cases, a true artist. Consequently, even in this comparatively narrow field of development, the United States cannot maintain its supremacy unless it is all the time creating great designers; and such cannot be created except as part of a well-conceived scheme for developing, through training in perfect craftsmanship, what may properly be called a general atmosphere of art.

Therefore, even should the United States deliberately determine — which of course it cannot do — to limit itself to the narrow field of expert machine, bridge and structure building, it would still be obliged to train up designers who must be artists, and that can be done only through developing a widespread system of sound craft training. But, of course, a country with our possibilities would not for a moment be satisfied to limit itself in this way. Everything seems to be conspiring to push us into world leadership, and it would be both cowardly and foolish not to fit ourselves for the highest leadership of all, for acknowledged supremacy, that is, in all the arts called fine. We cannot think of confining ourselves to the mere raising of foodstuffs on a colossal scale, to the mere production of vast quantities of raw material such as cotton, pig-iron, etc., or to the mere manufacture by tens of millions of things that are virtually raw material, such as structural steel, coarse cotton goods, and so on. Neither can we be satisfied to be the great machine builders of the world, or even to become the centre of the world's finance. We cannot stop short of producing, in time, the greatest architects, painters, sculptors, musicians, writers, poets, of all history; for only through making such intellectual and spiritual contributions to civilization can any nation hope to endure.

Notwithstanding conspicuous exceptions, it is an established fact that these supreme flowers of civilization are not sporadic growths. They appear in such numbers and of such quality as to give the stamp of genius to a whole nation only when and where the intellectual, æsthetic and spiritual soil has been long and carefully prepared. Consequently, if we are to become a truly great nation, we must put into concrete shape our present vague aspirations, we must definitely seek to be a great exemplar of the fine arts and of literature, and we must lead, therefore, our system of general education into channels which will so æsthetically water and so spiritually fertilize the great mass of the people that within two or three or four generations there will spring out from this widely and wisely enriched soil those great painters, sculptors, musicians, actors, poets and writers through whom alone undying fame can come.

We have *in posse* all the constituent elements of such a rich, artistic soil, so that, as in the case of a western desert, which produces nothing until the stored-up waters of the mountains are brought to it, and then shows a fecundity truly amazing, we have but to bring to our somewhat arid materialism the waters of a sound artistic spirit and a wise artistic education. We have not only widespread well-being, a great variety of climate and of natural scenery; we have not only freedom of thought and limitless opportunity for individual initiative; but we have also a rich mingling of races transplanted here from all quarters of the world and, because of that transplanting, growing with new life and vigor.

It may seem astonishing that with nearly a century and a half of such special advantages, we have not yet produced in any large measure those geniuses (except inventors) who are the real evidences of a nation's greatness. But any doubt of our artistic future, because of such barrenness hitherto, is wholly unwarranted. These hundred years and more had to be devoted to exploring and taming a savage territory, to putting it at the service of the world, and to fitting it to be the dwelling place of a huge, cosmopolitan people. The time has now arrived, however, when that work is so far complete that the best energies of the nation should be turned towards producing, not the ephemeral things of material welfare, but the enduring things of genuine civilization.

This being the case, and it having been shown that the fine arts must be a direct outgrowth from the manual arts, it follows as a matter of course that from this standpoint of true national greatness, if from no other, American education should put ever stronger emphasis upon a sound training in, and a thorough practice of, sound craftsmanship.

Thus far the extraordinary material wealth of this country has come largely from the production and exportation of what, broadly speaking, is little better than raw material. Our rich soils have produced abundant foodstuffs, with which we have kept our own population at a high standard of efficiency and have fed other nations at profits bringing us great wealth. Moreover, our vast and varied acres, our forests, mines and water powers, have enabled us not only to develop rapidly our own manufacturing, but also to supply the world with such indispensable raw and semi-manufactured materials as cotton, coal, pig-iron, pig-lead, structural steel and lumber. But this second use of our natural resources has been inconceivably wasteful, for it has in many directions robbed the country of stored resources which can never be made good, and has secured in return for those precious possessions little more than the bare cost of getting them out of the ground and of carrying them outside the country. We have been not much wiser than those classic optimists who were going to support themselves in affluence by taking in each other's washing. Had we been far-seeing enough not only to conserve, — instead of prodigally to waste — our natural resources, but also to convert them, by thoroughly skilled labor, into articles of high intrinsic value and of enduring beauty, we would not now be facing probable exhaustion of many of these natural bounties. Moreover, by using but a fraction of this raw material which we have so wickedly squandered, we would have brought into our country a thousand times as much return in actual money value, and ten thousand times as much in commercial and national prestige. The problem of conservation involves not merely the renouncing of our stupid destruction of forests, robbing of mines and exhaustion of soils, it involves also a study of the wisest use, from every point of view, to which a virile and intelligent population like ours should put the raw material with which, as a nation, we are so lavishly endowed.

Take Massachusetts, for example. It is conceivable that, by drastic measures, this state might have been kept purely agricultural. The result would have been that, producing hardly enough to keep its own inhabitants alive and having nothing to export to other states or nations, the Commonwealth would have accumulated no capital and its citizens would have simply existed, like savages, from hand to mouth. Or if, seeing the need of something beyond mere daily bread for themselves, its people had deliberately sold such few natural resources as they had: their trees, their building stones, etc., they would long ago have parted with these things and would have reached a state of squalid bankruptcy. The right policy, however, was that which New England has pursued: the policy of giving up the cruder forms of agriculture, which require vast spaces and a dependable climate, of placing emphasis more and more on intensive farming and the raising of what may be called luxuries, wherein the element of brains is of much more importance than that of soil and climate, and of putting their main energies into the converting of raw material, raised elsewhere, into manufactures requiring those things which they preëminently possess, namely, a ceaseless stream of sturdy laborers, good water powers, Yankee "gumption," brains, a high level of general education, wide and accessible markets and abundant capital.

Whether as a fundamental error, or whether as a necessary step in evolution, Massachusetts has thus far developed, as its principal manufactures, those things in which the cost of raw material and the cost of brains stand more or less equal in the finished result. For example, the manufacture of cotton and woolen goods, of shoes and of other like staples, involves bringing to New England, often from long distances, raw material in itself expensive, the transportation of which adds greatly to first cost, and the conversion of which into finished material requires only a minimum of brains on the part of the workers, the real intellect having been put, of course, into the inventing and developing of ingenious machines. Had Massachusetts, instead of this, put her energies more fully into such intricate manufactures as that of watches, automobiles, fine tools, optical instruments, sheer muslins, etc., where the cost of the raw material as compared with the price of the finished product is almost infinitesimal, and where the final value is given almost wholly by the skill and brains of the workmen, the State would to-day, probably, be far richer than it is, and it certainly would not be in a panic at seeing so many of its industries taking flight to other regions in order to get close to the sources of their raw material.

Whether or not New England has erred in the past, there can be no doubt as to its course in the future. The day of wide margins of profit has forever gone, and the manufacturer can in these times succeed only by cutting out every avoidable expense — such as that of transportation of bulky goods from a distance — and by utilizing to the fullest extent every former waste and by-product. New England, remote from Western markets and from raw materials, has, however, advantages of which she should make the utmost: nearness to European ports, giving wide foreign markets; extraordinary harbors, facilitating commerce and the building of ships; well distributed water powers, which, through modern electrical transmission, can be advantageously harnessed; a population trained to manufacturing for generations; and an educational prestige which should enable her to keep always ahead in the work of preparing for intensive, intelligent, artistic manufacturing, her native and her acquired peoples.

All these advantages, however, point without shadow of question to ever greater emphasis, in her manufacturing, upon the production of fine and artistic goods in which, on the one hand, the handicap of distance from raw materials is minimized, in which, on the other hand, the advantages of foreign markets, of manufacturing skill and of education, count for their full value. Consequently, whatever may be argued for the United States as a whole, there can be little doubt that the material, to say nothing of the moral and intellectual, future of New England depends upon beginning at once to take every step needed to make this section the Paris, the Vienna, the Belgium, the Switzerland, the South Germany, of America, — the place, that is, where one turns instinctively for the finest and most exquisite things that human hands can make.

Granted, for the sake of argument, that in this matter of broad, sound, effective craft training only a very limited number of the community can ever be appealed to on the philosophical basis that America should create a popular soil, rich in its possibilities for producing, two or three generations hence, great masters in all the fine arts. Nevertheless, practically the whole people of New England would respond enthusiastically to a more immediate and concrete plea for developing markets through extensive and intelligent training.

To convince that people, it will be necessary, first, to make them see that such skill and craftsmanship as will make New England the "fine goods" centre of the world, must necessarily be founded upon a manual, craft and æsthetic training given to practically all their boys and girls; and, secondly, to make them believe that the schools themselves are both ready and able to provide such comprehensive training. To show New England these two things is primarily the task of men and women engaged in teaching the crafts; and it is superfluous to say that they cannot create an artistic soil, they cannot persuade the general public even of their ability and willingness so to do, as long as any of them is satisfied to limit manual training to a more or less perfunctory pottering with carpentry, woodturning and the rudiments of work in iron.

Most of what manual training has already done is useful and has proved its value as a minor force in the general curriculum; but what is now involved is something which goes far deeper, spreads much farther, and has as its aim nothing less than the gradual lifting of a population contentedly buried in a fog of commonplace materialism up into the daylight of enduring beauty, illuminating art and true human and spiritual values. To accomplish such a task as this, manual training, — whether or not its unhappy name be changed — must be broadened to include not simply the few branches to which it has thus far been limited, but also the training of the eye for painting, the training of the hand for sculpture, the training of the voice for speaking and singing, the training of the body for rhythmic, dramatic and oratorical expression, and the training of the whole being for music, literature and the other highest forms of æsthetic understanding and expression.

Of course this large program cannot be applied to every pupil, and of course it cannot be carried out within the limits of the usual school day. Consequently craftsmen and craftswomen should agitate with special zeal for three things which those who have been given the somewhat dubious name of " social educators " are also working for, namely: (1) a diversified, flexible training, adaptable as far as possible to the special needs of each individual pupil; (2) organized group work in which, through the principle of interest and coöperation, a large share of their education can be carried on by the pupils themselves, and in their homes as well as in their school; and (3) a development of school plants along the general lines of what is popularly known as the Gary system, under which the school buildings and grounds shall provide for every side of a child's activity, under which the school program shall be so arranged as to utilize the entire plant for at least fourteen hours every day in every week, and under which that " whole child," regarding whom we have so long meaninglessly chattered, shall really get the benefit of wise, all-round education during substantially all his waking hours.

Let the individuality of the child be understood and his right development looked out for; let the forces of childhood interest and adolescent interest be utilized as friends of the teaching plan, instead of fought against as enemies; and let the school plant and the school day be made truly efficient instruments for educating every side of the growing child; then there will be every incentive and every opportunity to give to the whole youthful population a real, effective manual training, a training covering, in accordance with the child's individual bent and capabilities, his hands, his body, his senses, his emotions, his constructive, critical and æsthetic faculties, and especially his mind and will. Within two or three generations such broad and effective training as this not only would produce, unquestionably, that widespread facility in craftsmanship which is needed to make us the industrial leaders of the world, but also would amazingly enrich that artistic soil out of which alone can come, and out of which always will come, the sublime masters in painting, sculpture, architecture, music and all forms of literature, — masters, that is, of those things in a nation which, when all lesser, transitory deeds and fames have vanished, still endure.

INDUSTRIAL ART IN HUMAN LEADERSHIP

In the seventeenth century the United States was born great; in the 300 years intervening she has acquired material and political greatness; and now the opportunity for intellectual and moral greatness is being thrust upon her by the world war. She was born great because history gave to some of the best selected stock of the world the task of founding, in a region insulated from the turmoils of Europe and having every natural opportunity, a new nation; she has become great through the fortunate working out of those unique conditions; and now the cataclysm of stupendous war has thrust upon her a new greatness: that of taking, in the forthcoming reconstruction of the world, acknowledged leadership.

So far as concerns material things, there is no question of this new responsibility being hers. The United States is the one powerful nation not in any measure exhausted; geography made it practically certain that the war could neither violate her territory nor seriously affect the tenor of her daily life; her political and social habit is so in accord with the spirit of the times that no violent readjustments are needed in either her government or her systems of education; and her wealth in products and in money will almost surely cause New

York, rather than London, to be, sooner or later, the focus of the world's trade.

The attaining of such supremacy as this, an achievement that, even as late as the beginning of the century, would have seemed chimerical, carries with it, however, moral responsibilities not only enormous in themselves, but big with the future of the world. If the opportunities placed by an extraordinary combination of circumstances in this country's hands are received with boasting and self-satisfaction, they will certainly come to naught; if, on the other hand, they are accepted gravely, humbly and with a national determination to rise to the unexampled heights presented, they will make the United States actually and forever great.

Whether they vanish or whether they remain depends upon ourselves as a people. If, knowing this country to be incalculably rich, we seek material domination, we shall be powerful only until some other country exceeds ours in possessions. If, realizing the exhaustion of those nations that have borne the brunt of the fighting, we try, through trade laws and commercial exactions, to absorb more than our share of the world's commerce, we shall create a legacy of hate which, sooner or later, will lead to our destruction. If, drunk with the wine of imperial dominion, we seek, directly or indirectly, territorial aggrandizement, we shall build up but another mushroom empire, bearing within it as did Persia, as did Rome, as did the realized world-dominion of Napoleon, and as does the unrealized world-domination of the Kaiser, inherent decay. The only national supremacy that does not carry within itself the seeds of self-destruction is that which comes through moral leadership, through the desire of a people to serve not alone itself, but all civilization, through its ambition to advance not only its own fortunes, but those of all mankind.

If the United States determines to make democracy in America a real government by and for the people, she can, in time, convert the civilized world to, and make it safe for, democracy. If she demonstrates what effective common schooling can really do to lift men out of ignorance, folly and evil doing, she can, by example, force genuine popular education upon all the great nations and upon most of the little nations of the hemispheres. If she uses industry, and those handmaids of industry: training, invention and research, as a means of enriching all the peoples of the world; if she proves that wealth is not an end in itself, but is merely an essential means of raising men out of ignorance and degradation into mental and spiritual freedom; then she will get and will retain enduring authority in the affairs of the world, then she will indeed prove herself worthy of that special inheritance which permitted her to be born great, to become great and to have this final greatness of moral leadership thrust into her willing and efficient hands.

Paradoxical though it may sound, this country has actually suffered from the prodigality of Nature. Raw materials have been so abundant, riches have come with such ease, it has been so much less trouble to exploit the unworked fruits of the earth than to convert them into finished things, that we have remained, far longer than was necessary, crude industrially, crude artistically, crude intellectually. The first raw period of our national life, a period that was already fast coming to an end, has been closed abruptly and forever by the war. If, on the industrial side, we are now to assume and to retain leadership, our manufactures must be made truly competitive, our industrial art must be brought up to the European level, our business minds must be taught to think and to plan in international terms. Only so much of our raw materials must be sent abroad as we cannot advantageously convert into finished goods ourselves; those goods must meet much higher standards both of use and of art than we have, in most cases, yet set for ourselves; and from this time forth we must appreciate that industry and commerce are not haphazard things to be developed by luck and rule of thumb, but are complex professions upon the building up of which all the resources of intellect, of science, of art and, no less, of ethics, must be brought unceasingly to bear.

It is a truism that any article manufactured by the hand of man must have, if it is to be considered at all, some use for someone. But to most persons it has not yet become clear that in addition to, or as a part of, the use value there must be beauty value. Few, if any, things in the world serve, however, a real use unless they subserve, also, the universal craving of mankind for beauty. The satisfaction which comes through fineness of line, perfection of color, harmony of all the component parts of an object, whether that object be from nature or from man, is a fact so patent as to need no demonstration. Though the artist's ideas of beauty and those of the savage may differ very widely indeed, they have this in common: that the use of a thing and the beauty of a thing are closely intermingled, in the minds of both of them, in substantially every phase of their widely divergent experience of life.

The general level of æsthetics in the United States, while far above that of the savage, is nevertheless still that of the pioneer. Most of us have had little time and less inclination to develop that side of our nature, to know that there is such a thing as beauty and, much less, to analyze and understand those feelings which make us prefer, as the case may be, rag-time to Debussy, wax flowers to the Winged Victory. The important fact, however, is that we do prefer something, that we have, untutored though it be, the æsthetic longing and at least the foundations of æsthetic taste. But an even more important fact, at the present juncture, is that the peoples of Europe, of the Near and the Far East and, to a certain extent, of South America, have built up, on the side of beauty, standards in many cases far above ours, standards which, if we are successfully to enter the world markets, we must hasten also to attain.

As we come forward, after the Peace, as chief purveyors to the world's needs, it will be found, of course, that those demands are, at first and mainly, for just those crude products which, up to this point, we have been most busy and most interested in exporting: foodstuffs, ores, lumber, cotton, coal, oil, etc. Exhausted by conflict, the purely material necessities of the nations must first be satisfied, their cities must be restored, their industries reëstablished, their normal stream of daily, material living as quickly as possible resumed. For that immediate work of reconstruction, our huge supplies of crude products will be of transcendent importance. If, however, we are to dominate or even to hold the world markets beyond this first reconstruction period, we must depend upon things far different, far higher, far more complex, than are associated with digging ores, felling trees or raising wheat. Moreover, in the great dearth of money following this incredibly destructive war, we cannot afford to carry on commerce in the wasteful ways of the past. We must make our not inexhaustible natural riches realize their utmost possibilities, giving them, through processes of artistic manufacture, a value twice, ten times, possibly a hundred times that which, as crude products, they originally possessed. To hold foreign trade that is worth the holding, to develop domestic trade along sound avenues, and to make both foreign and domestic trade bring in adequate revenues, the manufacturer, the salesman, the merchant and, still more, the workman, must be educated, both as producer and as consumer, to appreciate true beauty, to understand its elements, to utilize them in the things they make and to demand them in the things they buy.

That general comprehension of the æsthetics of industry which is fundamental to our economic future can come, of course, only through gradually educating the people as a whole to understand beauty and its manifestations, to appreciate art and its applications. But special preparation for this new, artistic commerce of ours is the particular province of those schools and colleges wherein the arts are taught, and wherein men and women are specifically trained in the applications of art to substantially every form of industry. Moreover, while performing the special and immediate task of training industrial artists, those schools must never lose sight of the fact that they should be also the chief centres from which is to emanate that general appreciation of applied art essential, as has been suggested, to the country's welfare.

As a first, and an immediately important step, towards converting the people of the United States from an inartistic into an artistic nation, industrial art can make great headway and can, at the same time, demonstrate its value merely from the money standpoint by taking a leading part in reaching and holding as much of the markets of the world as may be our fair share. To that end those interested in promoting industrial art must carefully study the markets most readily open to this country, must delve deep into the complex study of exports, especially as those exports have been revolutionized by the war, must determine where and in what directions the United States can make the most enduring impress upon foreign territories and, with this study as a basis, must adapt the teaching in industrial art to the immediate needs of special industries from this specific point of view. In this connection the schools of industrial art will find a strong ally in the fast growing interest in part-time education. If those schools can get hold of youth actually working in industries where art can be of the most immediate service, can give them, out of their working week, four, eight or twelve hours of training in the principles and applications of industrial art, they can accomplish more for the immediate development of American standards than in any other way.

Business itself has, of course, an important task in adapting its methods to meet not only the needs, but also the idiosyncrasies, of the many new peoples that will be looking to us for their supplies; but this mere mechanics of the export problem will not get us far unless the goods which business is preparing itself to supply meet those artistic standards which, to a large part of the American people, are still a sealed book.

The fibres in an ugly cotton print may be as strong as, or even stronger than, those in an exquisite muslin; the wool content in a hideous piece of goods may be as high as in one of beautiful design; but the market for the ugly will be with the degraded and the savage, while that for the beautiful will be with those whose custom is worth while. The "watch that made the dollar famous" serves an excellent purpose, but the timepiece that has given America a reputation in watchmaking is not only dependable as a mechanism; it is beautiful as an object of art. The American motor-car could not have made the market for itself that in a few years it has, had it depended solely upon either its mechanical make-up or its cheapness; it has made its way mainly through the beauty, simplicity and grace of its design. And the extraordinary part of it is that this artistic quality which adds sometimes several hundred per cent to the selling value of an article is, in itself, as a rule and from the purely material point of view, a cheap thing. The actual raw material used, the time consumed in manufacturing, the mere labor cost of a beautiful product may be no more than for one hideously ugly; but the selling value of the lovely article is always higher, and is often many times greater, than that of the object which brazenly proclaims its want of taste.

This question of selling value, important as it is, has far less bearing upon the problems of our commercial future, however, than have other, more intangible considerations. The expression of beauty in things made reacts incalculably for good upon the maker; the appreciation of beauty in things purchased influences the general public to a degree which most of us have hardly begun to understand. Real beauty has a psychological and a moral influence of the highest consequence. Through the senses of sight, of hearing, and even of taste and smell, character itself is in no small measure formed. The intellect is refined by beauty, coarsened by ugliness; the moral nature is strengthened and upheld by what is æsthetically sound and true, is hardened and degraded by what is æsthetically gross and bad. The character of a city people is markedly affected by that city's beauty or its ugliness; the life of a family is influenced in surprising measure by its surroundings, orderly or disorderly, lovely or hideous, æsthetically stimulating or æsthetically debauching; and the life-value of the individual is in large measure gained or lost through the æsthetic and emotional forces which surround his developing career.

Therefore, immediately following upon or coincident with the special work of helping the country to hold the right type of foreign markets, those having authority in industrial art should set out deliberately, buoyantly and with holy conviction of the greatness of their mission, to raise the level of æsthetic understanding on the part of the great mass of the people of the United States. To that end they need to determine first of all what one may call the American standards (for there is an honorable nationality in æsthetics) for industrial art, standards based not upon fashions or fancies or the whims of petty schools, but based upon those sound canons of art concerning which there is substantial agreement. Having arrived at those standards, there should then be inaugurated what, for want of a better word, may be called propaganda for the understanding and acceptance of those canons in the wide and varied fields of architecture, of so-called landscape architecture, of street and house decoration, of dress, of furniture, of all types, in short, of personal, household and civic decoration.

No more fortunate time than the present could be found for such propaganda. As a people we will be greatly chastened by the war, and will be wholly in the mood to listen to the preaching of that simplicity which, in industrial art as in almost everything else, is the foundation of æsthetic satisfaction. The great majority of us do not really like the hideous buildings, brick or brownstone in the city and wood in the country, that disgrace the profession of the architect; substantially all of us are affronted by the billboards, unkempt vacant lots, dirty alleys, vile slums, and the rest of the horrors compounded of greed, laziness and want of taste that stamp our cities and towns with a common seal of ugliness; we are ripe for rebellion against the atrocities with which that anonymous scapegoat, "the fashion," strives to take all dignity and grace out of the human face and figure; and there is not a comic paper which does not reflect our widespread discontent with the gewgaws that masquerade as household decoration. And half of the restlessness and nervousness of the typical American is due to the fussiness, the flashiness, the overmuchness, the general hurly-burliness, of the alleged decorative side of his daily life, that side which it is in the power of those who preside in the realm of industrial art to reform. If we are to be saved from ourselves, we must be educated into a taste that will sweep away all this phantasmagoria of the superfluous, banish dirt and litter and all that corrupting crew of ugliness, and make our streets, our houses, our parks, our hats, our gowns and even our shirts and ties, preachers of the blessed gospel of simplicity, of fitness and of restful beauty.

The very fact that all this sounds to a degree fantastical is one of the strongest proofs that we are as yet in the pioneer stage of national civilization. We are still rather ashamed of beauty, still feel that there is something effeminate about the man who advocates the all-importance of æsthetic understanding. A good deal of our civic and domestic ugliness has its foundation in the fear that public opinion will condemn as namby-pamby and old-womanish any undue attention even to neatness and good order. It is out of this state of mind that, as a nation, we must lift ourselves if we are to be a world-power; it is to a diligent and respectful study of beauty and of its embodiments in the so-called fine and the so-called applied arts that we must give ourselves if we are to command international respect; and, since we are fundamentally an industrial people (using that term to include the greatest of our industries, agriculture), our first attention must be given to that aspect of art which we denominate industrial. If we bring about during the next generation or two a high development in the design of our machines and their products, in the ornamentation of our cities and our homes, in the artistic quality of our fabrics, whether of cotton, silk or wool, not only shall we make certain of our markets abroad, not only shall we immensely widen our markets at home, but we shall raise our standards of living, of thought, of all that we include in the term civilization to the point at which will begin to emerge great artists in the realms of building, of sculpture, of painting, of music, of literature,—those artists through whose work, and through whose work alone, is to be fixed, in the relentless verdict of final history, the everlasting status both of the ancient, and of the modern, nations of the world.

THE SCHOOL AND THE MANUFACTURER

THE war was hideous,—so hideous that those of us who were obliged, during it, to spend the greater part of our time in Washington, feel as if we had been living through a dreadful nightmare. Yet many of the lessons that, in this hard and sorrowful school of conflict, the country learned, not only are salutary, but are of the highest moment to the future of the United States. One of the most important of those lessons is that, as a nation and as individuals, we have been wasters and that this waste, from now on, must cease.

To no one more vividly than to the manufacturer has this fact of scandalous waste been shown. He is dependent upon steady and assured power; the coal situation of 1918 made him see, at immense cost, how clumsily we have handled and, unfortunately, still are handling this main sustenance of industry. It showed him, too, how stupidly we have failed to develop that almost limitless supply of power which we might get from our unharnessed rivers. The manufacturer is helpless, of course, without a dependable stream of raw materials; the upsetting of the world's markets proved to him how careless and happy-go-lucky he has heretofore been in supplying himself with such materials. Without transportation to bring his raw stuff to him and to take his finished stuff away, his labor as a manufacturer is worse than wasted; the congestion, and in many instances the utter breakdown, of the railways made clear the folly of the past handling of the railroad situation, including, on the part of the Government, pernicious meddling and, on the part of the railroads, not only graft, but the needless killing, in so many cases, of good auxiliary means of transportation. To produce goods and to have no markets in which to dispose of them, is the beginning of bankruptcy; yet, as the war proved, we have never given any real, constructive thought to this essential aspect of the industrial problem. Above all, though industry knows itself to be helpless without an adequate supply of suitable labor, it required this worldwide war to bring the manufacturer to consider questions, such as those of labor overturn, of industrial training, of labor efficiency, of organization, that, up to this time, he had smiled at as being dreams of the much-despised " professor." Taking all these and many other minor things together, the average manufacturer is realizing for the first time in his life that manufacturing is not merely the buying and fabricating of raw materials, that merchandizing is not a simple question of buyers and salesmen, that the bringing and sending of goods is not just the telephoning of an order to the railroad, that the question of markets is not solved when he has beaten some particular rival, and that the labor question involves many things beyond the hiring and firing of such casual labor as may happen to come to the mill door.

This being the chastened condition of the manufacturer's mind, it would seem, as it is, an admirable time in which to place before him the fact that all these and many other problems lead back for solution to the question of right education. If the manufacturer himself, if his customers, if those who supply him with materials, transport his goods and handle his labor problems had all been generally trained in economics and specifically trained in the jobs they have to do, they would understand that all these questions of coal and railways and markets and labor are tied up with one another and that, if one is to make a real success in industry, he must make a study of these fundamental things as well as of the comparatively minor problems of how to make his goods and how to find salesmen to place those goods, directly or through effective advertising, upon the market.

The educator has indeed ground for rejoicing that at last he is to come into his own and that throughout the whole industrial world there is to be such an appreciation as never before of the value of sound education. But while thus exulting, he will find his ecstasies somewhat tempered with the grim realization that, having uncorked this bottle of appreciation, on the part of the manufacturer, of the value of education, he has at the same time released, as in the old story of Sindbad, a djinn that will sooner or later spread out and fill the whole educational heavens, a djinn who is going to ask the school and the college and the university: why do you do this? why do you teach thus and so? why do you cling to such and such methods? what is your justification for teaching in the twentieth century subjects that were taught in the seventeenth? and, especially, what is your excuse for teaching them in the same old way?

The manufacturer, in his new mood of self-study and of the study of industry, will no longer accept old ways of schooling, will no longer remain indifferent to what the schools are doing with his children and with those other children who are soon to be either his employees, his suppliers of materials, of power and of transportation, or else his customers. When the leaders in industry get really aroused to the fact that success or failure in any particular industry, or in the commerce and manufacturing of a region, or in the development of the country as a whole, is largely a question of right education, they will demand that the schools be made over to meet the existing economic and social situation, that those responsible for the schools shall make themselves thoroughly familiar with that economic and social field, and that there shall be provided from the common funds revenues adequate to carry forward education in a manner consonant with the genuine needs of modern, civilized society.

I do not in the least mean that the manufacturers are going to demand that the schools shall train boys and girls solely or specifically for manufacturing. On the contrary, when those industrial leaders really understand the relation of schooling to industry, they will call for an educational plan much broader than we have, a system that will give the boys and girls of the coming generation initiative, mental flexibility, ambition, that will fill them with ideas concerning the interdependence of industry, labor, transportation, legislation, citizenship and daily life, concerning the prevention of material and human wastes, concerning their duties as members of a civilized society, that none of the earlier generations has had, in its rank and file, any sort of opportunity to secure.

The first thing that a manufacturer would do with education, if he had the power, would be to make it real, immediate and interesting to the growing child and youth. The schoolmaster has a great deal to say about the doctrine of interest and about apperception; but in most schools there is neither any atmosphere of interest nor any genuine connection between the school tasks and the child's apperceptive experience. It is only for a very short time that the school can hold the child at all; and from the point of view of a business man it is a wicked waste that this short time should not be made as fruitful as is possible. And common sense teaches that the only way in which to render it fruitful is to make the school period interesting, to see that its subject-matter is comprehensible, and to place before the child, as far as possible, a visible and understandable aim for the work that he is told to do. Make it interesting, simple and with a definite objective, and there is almost no limit to the amount of work that one can get out of even the commonplace child; and that work will be secured with far less mental and physical fatigue, on the part of both pupil and teacher, than under the methods that now hold in most public and private schools.

The next thing that the manufacturer would bring about in education, if he could, is to make it business-like. The most important period in a human life, so far as future character, happiness and success are concerned, is that of the school years, including at least those of the secondary school. Yet that most vital time is usually treated as if it were of little consequence, as if it were not until the period following school that the really serious business of human life begins. Whereas, anyone who has had anything to do with childhood and youth knows that unless the physical, mental and moral character is firmly established before the eighteenth year, there is almost no hope of doing anything thereafter. Consequently, education should be treated as a business: the business of establishing health, mentality and character, and should be subject, therefore, to the rules and methods of business, adapted, of course, to the age of the person concerned and to the special nature of the business that is being carried on. The essential thing is that the child, the parent, the teacher and the citizen in general,—all should realize and should act in accordance with this realization, that in the period between five years of age and sixteen, eighteen or twenty-one years of age, as the case may be, all of them ought to attend industriously, earnestly and with full understanding of what they are undertaking, to the business of making each particular child into the best citizen, physically, mentally and morally, that he is capable of becoming.

A third thing that the manufacturer would bring about if he could, is an understanding on the part of the pupil in school of what his future responsibilities are almost certain to be. It should be made plain to the boy that he has an important part to play in the coming generation, that it is his business in the childhood and adolescent years to prepare himself for his part, and that his duties range themselves under three main heads: the duty of earning as good a living as he possibly can, so that he may make due return for all that the community, during his unproductive years, has done for him; the duty of establishing himself as a real part of society by marrying and bringing up a family; and the duty of taking his full share in those common responsibilities for the welfare of the community as a whole which are comprehended under the general term, citizenship.

It is for these three things that, in the main, the education of the child is carried forward; it is because we believe these ends worthy and desirable that most American communities appropriate a large part of their revenues to public education; yet, when it comes to using the money so appropriated, cities and towns lose sight almost entirely of what that money is intended for and spend it upon a kind of so-called education that in many cases has only a very remote bearing indeed upon either vocational competence, sound family life or intelligent citizenship.

It will be objected at once that these aims are too large and too vague, that there are certain tools of speech, writing, number, etc., which the child must not fail to acquire, and that there is not time enough to do so much as these wider objectives imply. To this there is ready answer that, if the schools really availed themselves of the doctrines of interest and apperception, if they actually treated the education of the child as a business to be pursued during hours corresponding to those of the industrial world, and if, during those hours, they devoted themselves not merely to training in book-learning, but to the real development of the child as a future citizen and homemaker, all the above things could be accomplished with much less pain to the pupil than at present and with the far more important result that such teaching would really influence, as most of the present textbook work does not, his subsequent social, vocational and moral life.

A fourth thing that manufacturers are beginning to ask of the schools is why they keep themselves so much apart from the other educative forces of the community; why they do not coöperate with the parents, the industries, the civic life in general, using them as aids, as laboratories, as co-teachers, in the upbringing of the boys and girls. The schools maintain, of course, that coöperation should come from the other side, and that the school, as an agent of the community, cannot take such initiative. As a manufacturer who is somewhat familiar also with school conditions, I am convinced that the initiative must come from the school side, and that it is a legitimate duty of the schools to educate the parents, the industries and the community in general as to what they can do and ought to do to help in this most important of all social duties: the preparation of boys and girls for an effective adult life.

There are several ways in which the school and industry, whether that be manufacturing, commerce or agriculture, can get together for mutual and immeasurably important help. The school can use the factory, the farm, the office or the store as a laboratory in which, under proper supervision and safeguards, the boys and girls may get that acquaintance with real things which it is impossible to give in the schools. Impossible, because the air of reality is lacking in the school, and because no community can afford to fit up in its school buildings those complete industrial and commercial plants, or to surround the school buildings with that extent and variety of agriculture which, in most communities, are to be found, within a reasonable distance of the school buildings, in the factories, stores and farms which are themselves the economic heart of the community.

Another way in which the school and industry can coöperate is by using the former as an adjunct to the factory, the store and the farm, opening its facilities, both day and night, to those boys and girls, men and women, who have had to go to work at an early age, or who for one reason or another have been denied proper schooling, or who, their ambition roused as they get into the thick of earning a living, desire systematic training for higher economic service.

A third way in which the school and industry can

coöperate is by definitely dividing the work of educating the boy or girl during certain adolescent years, the pupil spending half his time in school and half his time in remunerative industry, the so-called practical work in the shop, store or farm being illuminated by the theory taught in the school, and the theoretical studies of the school being given life and meaning by the practical work of industry.

The machinery by which these several types of coöperation are to be brought about is that of the evening school, the part-time continuation school and the coöperative day school. In the first will be cared for, mainly, those older men and women who are employed throughout the day and who can receive instruction, therefore, only in the evening hours; in the second will be served, chiefly, those youth between the ages of fourteen and eighteen whose schooling is so defective as seriously to interfere with their economic and social progress; while the third will cover the cases of those thousands of ambitious youth who, unable to afford the loss of time involved in securing a higher education, can, by working and earning half the time, so far support themselves as to be able to devote the remaining half to systematic study.

A fourth way in which the industries can be of service to the schools is in connection with the all day vocational school, wherein the boy is deliberately preparing himself for a specific vocation. The teaching in such a school is the more effective the more it utilizes the factories, the stores and the farms of its vicinity as laboratories in which the pupils are permitted to get the main part of their practical experience.

The manufacturer has no anxiety as to the readjustment of our public and private schools to meet those exigencies which the war has so keenly brought home to us, provided education in the United States continues, as it has so well begun, to develop sound vocational education in its schools and colleges. That development not only compels the schools to measure up their courses in actual terms of the real achievement of their boys and girls, it compels them to study and to get into line with the real forces that dominate the social and economic life of to-day. Moreover, vocational education, from its very nature, must bring about increasing coöperation between school and industry, through the day industrial school, the evening school, the part-time school and the coöperative school. That being the case, the manufacturer is as certain as one can be of anything in this uncertain world, that the old traditional methods of teaching cannot long endure, that the so-called academic studies will remain only after they have proved their right to live by reshaping themselves to meet the true needs of modern life, and that the schools as a whole will get more and more awake to the fact that they are supported by the public, not to fit boys into an ironclad system, but to fit a very varied and flexible system into the actual needs of individual boys.

This general awakening is being helped to an unexpected degree by the working out of the so-called Smith-Hughes law for the promotion of vocational education.

Under that law, every state in the Union has created a State board for Vocational Education, and, in increasing amounts, the federal government stands ready to subsidize the teaching and supervision of secondary training in agriculture, the teaching of boys and girls over fourteen in the trades and industries and in home economics, and the preparing of teachers along these three general avenues. To the manufacturer it is of great interest that at least one-third of the money appropriated by the states and matched by the federal government for the training in trades and industries must be used for part-time instruction. This provision emphasizes the interest of the government in strengthening education at one of its weakest points. That point is the lack of educational supervision of the boy and girl between fourteen, when, in most cases, he can leave and does leave school, and sixteen, seventeen or eighteen, when he arrives at the age for beginning really productive work. During those intermediate years, unimportant from the point of view of industry but perhaps more important than any others from the point of view of psychology, morals and education in general, part-time schooling permits of the school keeping hold upon the youth, advising and training him with a view to his effective future, and supplementing his remunerative employment with studies that will improve his outlook upon life, give meaning to his daily work and strengthen character at the very moment when it most needs wise support. The part-time continuation school, thus fostered by the Vocational Education law, has educational possibilities beyond our present conception; but it cannot be made really effective until the states pass, as they should, compulsory laws requiring school attendance between fourteen and sixteen, for all youth. This attendance should be for the entire session if they are not at work, and for at least eight hours a week, out of their working time, if they are regularly employed. Those manufacturers who oppose, or who are even indifferent to, such legislation as this are not only working against the welfare of all boys and girls, they are perpetuating that blindness and folly from which have arisen most of the wastes and losses under which industry is suffering.

Another form of education which the Vocational Education law permits and encourages, is the formation of evening classes for men and women at least eighteen years old, in subjects supplementary to their day employment. This gives new and added opportunities for those ambitious workmen who desire to fit themselves, as modern industry makes it so difficult for them to do within the industry itself, for those higher positions which are the first rungs on the ladder of industrial competence. As to the day industrial school and the coöperative part-time school, it is for the schools, as already said, to educate the manufacturers, the merchants and the farmers as to the important part that they should play in making public education really serve the boys and girls, by opening their plants and their facilities to those youth who, eager to get a thorough schooling, want to get it while at daily work. Young men and women so trained will be, without question, the best source from which to secure those real leaders in industry for which the manufacturer, the merchant and the farmer are forever clamoring.

There will continue, as there now is, a shortage of labor in this country, and especially will there be a shortage of men and women competent for leadership, for the exercise of initiative, for the carrying of industry out of those ruts from which it must be lifted if we are to hold our own in the great markets of the world. The only way in which that shortage of leadership can be made good is for school and industry to work shoulder to shoulder in educating boys and girls to assume responsibility. This they can do if they will; and they have the sanction, both moral and financial, of the federal and state governments for doing it. And in thus coöperating, freely and wisely, for the development of leaders in industry, they will not only be helping production, they will not only be giving to the schools such vigor, due to purpose and interest, as they have never before had, but they will at the same time be building up a generation that will not tolerate such indifference, such waste, such slacking in the matter of active devotion to the duties of the citizen as we saw before the great war —that war which, with blood and iron, taught us in bitterness what we were too indifferent to learn in the easy, prosperous and purblind days of peace.

III. IN TEACHING

EDUCATION: THE COMMON HUMAN TASK

MOST of us are surprised to realize that whether we wish to be or not, each one of us is every day an educator. There is no escaping the responsibility. Even if we have no children to train, we must all the time be educating ourselves; and, in addition to that tough task, most of us are under the ceaseless necessity of attempting to educate the employers for whom we work, the employees who work for us, and the public whom, in the slang phrase, we are in one way or another " working."

Consequently, education is in a wholly different category from the other great professions. It is proverbial, for example, that the man who tries to be his own lawyer has a fool for his client; and, while not one of us but spends a large portion of his time preaching to others, we really have no immediate concern, except when we are christened, married or buried, with the clerical profession. While we have to be more or less active participants in the experiments of the medical profession, the less we know of medicine the better; and as for the other professions based on scientific knowledge, such as engineering, they are quite outside our ordinary range of understanding.

The profession of education, however, is a wholly different matter, for we are it and it is **we**. It is as much a part of our existence as is the food we eat; and whenever **we** assume any responsibility whatever, we find ourselves confronted with educational problems of the most far-reaching character. Therefore, while it is meddlesome for the layman to concern himself with the details of other great professions, it is not meddlesome, it is necessary, for him to take an active part in that profession which is fundamental to all others: education. It is essential, however, that he should not be active except in a rational, helpful, understanding and effective way.

While it is natural for us to believe that the particular period in which we live is the most important in all history, it is scarcely an exaggeration to say that the last ten years have been the most significant in the entire progress of American education. For in that period we have placed ourselves, more than at any previous time, face to face with real questions. As a result, we are learning to what a degree every one of us — whether father, mother, employer, employee or ordinary citizen — is responsible, along with the teachers, for the solution of its difficult problems. We are looking at education from a new point of view, one which, in another generation or two, is going to transform enormously the whole conduct of teaching.

What is this new point of view? It is that education **is** not alone the concern of the church, or the college, or the learned professions, or the school board, or the schoolmaster; but is the concern particularly of the plain, ordinary citizen. And as such, education must conform, within reasonable limits, to his real and fundamental needs as a citizen, as a parent, as a worker and as a human being.

The first need of the civilized human being is for sound health, both for himself and for his family. His second need is for high standards of right and wrong and for a satisfactory working morality. His third need — since no man can be a good citizen unless he is first an effective and self-respecting earner — is for a trained efficiency. His fourth need is for skill and information along the common lines of human interests. His fifth need is for an appreciation of social responsibility, of what we call good citizenship. And his sixth need is for an understanding of beauty, whether in nature, in art, in living or in character.

Education, therefore, should be a rounded process through which the child, the youth and the man ought to get and to keep good health, sound morals, efficiency, skill, useful information, a sense of social responsibility and a love of the beautiful; for the man or woman who is deficient along any one of these lines is not securing the most and the best out of this wonderful and interesting experience called life which, so far as we know, comes to us but once.

Obviously no one teacher can cover all these sides of education; obviously, moreover, no school can educate in all these directions unless it has the fullest and most active coöperation from every live force in the community. Good health can not be learned out of textbooks; it can be secured only by the working together of doctors, nurses, parents and other citizens, all combining to promote sanitation, to head off epidemics, to teach hygienic living, to warn and safeguard against every abuse of this great gift of life. A high standard of morals can not be maintained unless, not only the schools, but the churches, the whole body of citizens and especially the parents, work shoulder to shoulder to keep the boys and girls straight and to protect them from every needless contamination and temptation. Efficiency and skill can not be developed in children unless we know what the world's standards of skill and efficiency are; and here is needed, therefore, the active coöperation of men and women who are doing the world's work: employers, employees, merchants, manufacturers and artisans.

Information and knowledge can not be got into the pupil until, out of the infinity of possible facts, are intelligently selected those which are of real and enduring use to that particular boy or girl, as an individual. Social responsibility can not be instilled unless the child and youth are brought into direct contact with those whose business it is to run the city or town. Love of beauty can not be aroused unless the pupil sees pictures, hears music and gets genuine inspiration from high-souled men and women.

This is the underlying reason for our attempts — sometimes wise, sometimes unwise, but always worth while making — at an enrichment and expansion of the school program; this is the origin of the many organizations and groups that are bringing earnest persons together in a serious endeavor to help the public schools; this is the real foundation for the widespread interest in vocational education, vocational guidance, social education, moral education, and all the other new forces — or old forces revived — in modern teaching. Every one of these things has its foundation in our new understanding of what education really means and in our determination to do what we can to make the next generation roundly, soundly and efficiently trained.

Since education, like civilization, is always in process of expansion, it is impossible to lay down any one definitive school program along these newer and broader lines. But the following, as the result of placing ourselves face to face with facts, are seen to be some of the most conspicuous needs, here and now, in practically all our systems of public education.

We need better health conditions, not merely in matters of ventilation, heating, etc., but in lighting, seating, freedom of movement, exercise, the teaching of hygiene, the control of minor epidemics (such as colds), the following of pupils into their homes, in order to give training there in personal and domestic hygiene, in right feeding, clothing, sleeping, playing, etc.

We need more moral teaching, — not instruction in dogma, but a ceaseless, daily exercise in the great ethical truths which underlie all sects; and especially do we need a sweeping away, both in city and in country, of all sorts of needless evils and temptations, now undermining and corrupting youth.

We need much more training for real service in the world, — not merely vocational training in the narrow sense of fitting to earn a livelihood, but such a rational and thorough training of the senses, of the head, of the hand and of the will, that every average youth shall acquire the habit of doing as a matter of course whatever comes to his hand, of doing it thoroughly, intelligently and efficiently, and of taking pleasure in the mere act of doing it.

We need a better understanding of what is and what is not worth while to learn, so that so much of the child's time may not be wasted in memorizing useless facts, in performing foolish "stunts" and in merely marking time.

We need coöperation between the employers and the school so that as the boy and girl approach the time when they must leave school, the two agencies shall work together in leading the youth gradually and wisely out of school education into work education, through some system of continuation or part-time instruction.

We need intelligent training for our boys and girls in the meaning and in the practice of home-life, for, whatever else they may be, the vast majority of them will be fathers and mothers, and unless they are intelligent parents and efficient homemakers, their children will be frightfully handicapped and the community unwarrantably burdened. To get this training we need the closest friendship and understanding between the home and the school.

We need more "follow up" work with boys and girls,

so that the school shall not lose sight of them until they are started, and well started, on the right road towards earning a living not only sufficient for early marriage and the bringing up of a family, but also permitting of skill, initiative, interest and growth.

We need more and earlier training in the sense of social responsibility, so that, from the beginning of his school life, the child shall realize what he owes to civilization in general and to his own community in particular, and shall be filled with the ambition to pay back that debt by rendering effective service to his town and state.

Finally, we need to arouse appreciation of the beautiful not merely as it appears objectively in art and subjectively in character, but as it assumes the homelier forms of neatness, order and tidiness, as it takes shape in the " clean up and paint up " slogans of the day.

How are we to get these things which, we must all agree, are essential if the child is to come into his rightful heritage as a useful and happy citizen? We shall not get them through any miracle, but only through hard study to find out what education really means and through hard personal work to bring about true school reform. And we shall not get them at all unless every one of us does his part, be it large or small, in making all the conditions as far as possible right in our own community. We are all, perforce, educators, and unless each of us finds out what his part in education is and does that part as well as he reasonably can we shall get practically nowhere.

Much of our school machinery is outworn; like enlightened manufacturers we must have the courage to "scrap" it and get new. The correlations between the school and the home, the school and industry, the school and citizenship, the school and real life are in most cases far from satisfactory; everything possible must be done to bring about those correlations so absolutely essential to effective education and efficient living. A large part of the process of education is carried on wholly outside the school: in the homes, on the streets, in the factories; we citizens must do all we can to make those homes intelligent, those streets morally, as well as physically, clean, those factories wise to their own best interests in the enlightened handling of the human forces which they use.

Most of the evil and misfortune in the world, which we are at such incredible expense in trying to palliate through prisons, hospitals, asylums and other so-called remedies, need not exist at all, were we to use education, as it should be used, to prevent incompetence, immorality, crime, pauperism, disease and premature death. But education will not be the great force that it should be, to keep children well, to preserve them morally sound, to endow them with the ardor of good citizenship, to lift their eyes out of the gutters and fix them on the stars, until the schools are wholly divorced from politics, until thoroughly trained teachers are given substantially untrammelled opportunity really to educate, until classes are made small enough for the teacher to know and to train each child as an individual, until there is just as much attention given to what the pupil does out of school as in, until the home and the school work hand in hand to keep the child sound and strong, and until every one of us realizes that he or she is personally responsible for what this generation and this community do for the training of their boys and girls.

EDUCATION FOR EARNING

ABRAHAM LINCOLN said that God must love the common people, else he would not have made so many of them. Whether or not that be so, without the so-called common people industry, democracy and civilization itself, would disappear.

Only the uncommon man gets into the pages of history; but it is the common man who makes history. It is the one youth in a hundred who acquires leadership; it is the ninety-nine other youths who are shaping the channels in which that leadership must run. It is the scattered thousands who make the shining crust of culture upon the loaf of life; it is the solid millions who make up the body and substance of that loaf.

Therefore, education is not mainly concerned with the industrial leaders, the men of the professions, the exceptional individuals who, by force of favorable circumstances or of their own personality, are bound to make their way. It is concerned, rather, with the business man's clerk, the professional man's office boy, the manufacturer's green hand who, numerous as the sands, hold the very life of the community in their grimy hands. They are the future citizens, they are the future voters, they are the future workers, and as they do their duty, as they vote and as they work, so the United States will rise or fall.

This typical urchin, of whom there are millions upon millions and of whose collective or individual existence the business man and the statesman are scarcely aware, is, nevertheless, the final arbiter of all their fates. Yet with his education for the duty of settling the country's future, few of us condescend to be concerned. Neither do we seriously trouble ourselves that he is pulled out of school, or leaps out of that place of unpleasant tasks, on the stroke of fourteen years or, if his parents are not averse to perjury, a year or two before fourteen.

The boy is removed from school in order, ostensibly, to supplement the family income, and he is generally glad to come out because it gives him greater freedom and at least a percentage of his earnings to spend on cigarettes and "movies." Moreover, neither he nor his parents see (and no more can most of us perceive) much relation between the school work that he is giving up and the life work that he is going to do.

Certainly, for whatever he undertakes, — except it be the duties of a clerk, — his schooling has given him no direct preparation. This would be of minor consequence had that school given him any indirect preparation, had it given him, that is, those qualities and aptitudes, those powers of mind and hand, those fundamentals of character which would enable him to take up any piece of work with that grip and that self-reliance which are bound to lead any boy and youth having them, regardless of his book knowledge, to genuine success.

For good reasons, such as duty to a widowed mother, or for bad reasons, such as a desire to keep up with the gang, the boy is anxious to earn as much as possible; therefore he seeks what will pay him most at first, regardless of the future and of the opportunity to make a real career. So he secures, generally, a job which leads nowhere and in which he is more than likely to go to economic and spiritual waste. Moreover, if the boy does happen to get into an occupation offering chances for advancement, in most instances he has no opportunity really to learn that trade excepting as he may pick it up in the intervals of routine work. Therefore, in the valuable years between fourteen and seventeen, when the boy ought to be laying the foundations for his future career, he, as a rule, is learning practically nothing excepting idleness, shirking and vice; and when the time comes that he might be regularly employed in some effective industry, he is, to use a vulgar phrase, industrially rotten before he is industrially ripe.

The average boy drifts into a blind lane in this way, not only because he has no one to show him the folly and loss of it, but for the more weighty reason that he is not able to pick and choose. He comes into the industrial market at fourteen, — or even at sixteen or eighteen, — with a pair of hands totally untrained, with a mind most imperfectly developed, with no technical skill and with an unformed, or deformed, character.

While the average business man seems utterly indifferent to any particular wasted urchin, he is far from being indifferent to the waste of urchins as a whole.

On the contrary, he is highly exercised about it and has very decided views as to the kind of training that those urchins ought to have, though he is even vaguer than the schoolmasters as to how that kind of training is to be given. And the business man and manufacturer has those decided views because he is confronted every minute with the problem of waste. He has to fill his bins with ten times as much coal as, theoretically, he needs, because about nine tenths of that coal does absolutely no work. He has to stock up with many more machines than, theoretically, he requires, because of the losses through friction, breakage and general inefficiency; he has to buy much more raw material than, theoretically, he should use, because of the many chances for loss in passing from the raw to the finished state. Science and skill can do much to overcome these losses; but the largest source of waste is one that cannot be accurately reckoned, is one that no science within the mill can do much to stop, is one that if he were able really to calculate it, would be perfectly staggering;—and that is the waste of human energy and life. The main sources of this human waste are, of course, physical weakness, involving absence through sickness and loss through early death of men who have been years in training; carelessness, through which one man may stop a great plant for days; indifference and shirking, which necessitate the employment of a large force of foremen to keep the men up to even a moderate degree of efficiency; and above all, ignorance. Not so much ignorance of the work that the man is supposed to do, as ignorance on his own part of how to utilize his physical and mental strength. We are so accustomed to human inefficiency that we fail to appreciate how little we actually get out of a man in comparison with what he is really capable, were he rightly trained, of accomplishing.

The enlightened business man who is doing everything to perfect his machinery and to stop his material leaks and losses is practically helpless in the presence of this human waste. It is almost impossible to reform men who come to him, as a rule, only after they are grown and after their habits, — or want of good habits, — have become ingrained. He turns, therefore, to the schools and asks more and more loudly that they give him boys and young men who have, first and foremost, mental, moral and physical good-health; who have, secondly, efficiency — that is such coördination between head and hands, such self-poise, such self-reliance, such self-respect that the man does what he has to do with the least real exertion, with the least waste of time and material, and with precision, finish and sureness of result. And, thirdly, he asks that the school give him, in his workmen, vim, go, hustle, loyalty, or any other word which expresses the attitude of the man who likes to work and who knows, — as only the well-trained man can appreciate — that the greatest happiness in life comes from work effectively and thoroughly done.

The complaint of the average man that the schools of to-day are not giving a good training in the common branches is quite without foundation. So far as concerns the gymnastics of the mind and those tools of education which we call the three R's, the boy of to-day is far ahead of his grandfather and is considerably in advance of his father. The real difficulty, and one of the reasons why boys and girls seem to-day inadequately trained, is because modern life demands infinitely more than it used to even twenty years ago. The trouble is not with what the school does to the boy; it is with what the world demands of the boy after he leaves school. It is like the congestion of freight, a few years ago, in the Middle West. The shippers made vigorous protest to the traffic managers, who met and gravely replied that the trouble was due, not to a shortage of cars, but to an excess of products.

The responsibility for this inadequacy of the schools does not lie with the teachers, who are doing fairly well with the means at their command; it certainly does not lie with the children, who are helpless in the matter. The responsibility lies with the citizens who have seen the enormous development of industries, who have seen the increased demands upon everybody, young and old, who know that life is rushing at automobile speed, and yet who do not furnish moral and financial support to those schools and to those communities which are seriously trying to fit boys and girls for these new conditions.

The original conception of education, of course, was that of a process for maintaining class distinctions. Men were to receive the special education of the priest or knight in order that as holy men and gentlemen, they might be kept apart from the vulgar herd. It mattered little what those privileged classes studied, so long as it gave them erudition of which those beneath them could not even dream. Out of the caste idea of education grew the so-called culture theory which, carried to an extreme, is embodied in the Oxford professor of higher mathematics who thanked God that he had never taught his students anything of which they could make the slightest use.

When, by the spreading of democratic aspirations, the caste theory became impossible and the culture theory more or less untenable, there arose the informational theory of education, the idea so industriously promulgated in the late eighteenth and early nineteenth centuries that if a man be only instructed in right ideas he will be wise and good. Out of this notion grew the schools of the Gradgrinds in which helpless infants and unhappy youth alike were gorged with facts.

Next, as a sort of child of the culture and informational theories appeared the doctrine of disciplinary education, the hallucination that the mind needs to be kept in condition by doing hard, dry and disagreeable tasks, very much as one's teeth are to be kept firm and white by gnawing bones and crusts.

The present chaotic and fast-crumbling notions (they cannot be dignified as principles) have grown out of these three ideas concerning education: the idea of it as a means of perpetuating caste, the idea of it as a purveyor of information, the idea of it as a gymnastic for the mind. The coming school, however, the only kind of school which can meet modern conditions and needs, while not rejecting or neglecting culture, information or formal discipline, will be based upon the principle of giving the child the use of himself, of developing in him to the fullest his innate powers, of making him an efficient social, industrial, political and moral force.

Culture is a desirable and essential goal of all education; but to strive primarily for culture is to produce a plant all leaves and flowers, without any roots to give it nourishment. Facts are a fundamental basis of all education, but to pursue facts as facts is to be like Solomon John in the Peterkin Papers, who conscientiously read the encyclopedia until he got to Xerxes, and then, his book-mark slipping out, had to begin again at A. Formal discipline is a necessary part of all youthful training, but to keep a child at a task simply because it is disagreeable is like making him pull chest weights without ever giving him opportunity to use his muscles in real work or play. We want these things in our scheme of education, but we want them simply as agencies in the producing of power. Power should be the aim of the whole educational process. Power to think straight, power to work effectively, power to control one's self and to influence others, power to add something to the sum of human wealth and happiness, — that is what makes a man, and it is this sort of power which the schools must develop, to a greater degree than most of them now do, if they are to furnish genuine men and women to the world. The watchword in all business and manufacturing to-day is efficiency. The brains of inventors, the wisdom of managers, the powers of industrial captains are focused upon securing the greatest product with the least expenditure. Similarly in the business world. The trusts were formed, not to cheat and oppress the people, but to avoid wastes in buying and selling, to save needless duplication. The great department stores were established, not because Mr. Wanamaker wanted to sell automobiles and pins under the same roof, but because by putting everything under a single management, the efficiency of the establishment could be greatly increased.

Carlyle, in his savage way, once declared that there are — I forget how many — millions of persons in England, "mostly fools." This was the verdict, of course, of a chronic dyspeptic; but there is an appalling number of fools in the world, — not fools in the ordinary meaning of that unpleasant word; but fools in that they never count for anything in the progress of humanity, never are of any real use to themselves or to anyone else. These unhappy persons are not naturally fools; neither are they fools from choice; they are simply called fools because they are inefficient. For its own sake as well as for theirs, the world should take these hundreds of thousands out of the fool class and put them into the effective class by deliberately and wisely educating them for personal and industrial efficiency.

Industrial efficiency is fundamental to the real prosperity of the country as a whole, and to that of every mill-hand, mechanic, farmer, craftsman, merchant, professional man and other citizen in the United States. It is vital to our domestic progress, to our foreign trade, to our national welfare, that slipshod workmen, ignorant mechanics, shirking clerks, incompetent public servants, and "faking" professional men should no longer be tolerated or excused.

It is essential to the maintenance of a democracy that the mediæval distinctions between the "clerk" who does not soil his hands and the "laborer" who does, should be broken down; and that youth should be brought up to respect manual labor and industrial processes by having had some experience in both.

It is educationally necessary that boys and girls be taught to use their hands as well as their heads, and that — whether they are to make use of them or not — they be made acquainted with, and more or less proficient in, those industrial ideas and processes which lie at the very roots of modern life.

If this American experiment in democratic government — an experiment never before undertaken on so huge a scale — is to succeed, we must breed a more active and responsible citizenship. In doing that, however, we must recognize that the essential foundation of good citizenship is the ability to earn a living ample to support a family, and to earn it with that sense of satisfaction which comes only from a knowledge of being competent to what one undertakes. The urgent demand of to-day, therefore, is for a vocational education which shall give this sense of competence to that more than nine tenths of the people who must earn their living, directly or indirectly, through some form of mechanical, agricultural or domestic work.

Consequently the educational authorities, using that term in a pretty broad sense, need to make provision for the following groups: (1) for youth in general who, whatever their future station or occupation, need to have some first-hand knowledge of the principles and processes which lie at the basis of all production; (2) for those youth who are to be the industrial captains, as engineers, directors or administrators of large productive enterprises; (3) for those youth who are to be foremen, superintendents and other minor officers of those same enterprises; and (4) for that great host of boys and girls who, by limitation of mind or of capacity are certain always to remain in the rank and file of industry, but upon whose competence, skill and economic faithfulness the whole success of modern industry depends.

The educator need concern himself very little, however, with the training of group two, being sure that in the nature of things the education of the industrial captains will always be looked after by those officers themselves. What we do need to consider is the training of the other three groups, and in this inquiry we need give consideration only to groups three or four, the petty officers and the rank and file of industry, since in providing proper education for them, we shall be certain to furnish a type of training which will meet also the needs of youth in general.

As a necessary basis, not only for this industrial training, but also for intelligent citizenship, there should be woven into all schooling, from the earliest years, that training of the senses, that practice of the hands, that feeling of social responsibility and of the importance of producing something useful to the community, that ability to work with others, which lie at the foundation, not only of efficient industry, but also of effective living. This means that for much of the rote-work and text-book grinding characteristic of the school of to-day, there must be substituted a large and varied body of the right sort of team-work and team-play, of hand and sense training, of sound education in civic duty, personal responsibility and social responsibility, of good manners and right morals, of what, for want of a better term, we call pre-vocational training — training in those things which are fundamental to efficiency in every trade and profession.

All this cannot be done, however, in the school day and school year as we now understand them or in the face of the extremely difficult conditions under which most teachers are compelled to work. The child's education, — certainly from the beginning of his tenth to the close of his sixteenth year — is the main business of the child's life, and should be dealt with, therefore, not in an occasional and haphazard manner, but in a thoroughly regular and businesslike way.

The school, at least during the seven years specified, should control practically all of the boy's or girl's daylight time. Theoretically, the parents should take care of the manners and the morals, the social life and the vocational preparation of the children for whose existence they are responsible; but as a matter of actual fact, they do not and they cannot. Modern life is too complex, and the conditions of society are too diverse, for us to leave this most important of all businesses, theoretically to the care of the home, but practically to the tender mercies of the street. On the other hand, however, it is absolutely essential to such an enlarged school activity, that the parents, both as individuals and as citizens, should take a much more intimate and more responsible part in the work of the school than most of them now do.

If the school is to assume this larger task, it should be a matter, not of five hours a day, five days in the week and thirty-five weeks in the year. School should be made the unremitting and really moulding influence upon every boy and girl through every day of the week and substantially every week in the year, during at least the important years from nine to seventeen.

This greatly extended school day and year would be worse than useless, however, were it merely a multiplication of the present formal, memoriter and not seldom profitless school exercises. On the contrary, these days and years should be ones in which children, in groups of not over twenty, should be under the steady supervision of teachers competent to educate and enthusiastic in educating every part of the child: his body, his mind, his senses, his capacities, his will, his character, his soul. A large part of this extended school time should be given to games, physical exercise and group work, in which the muscles and senses of the children may be fully trained and developed; another large part should be given to moral training, not through sectarian teaching, but through self-active work and play tending to strengthen and to fortify the immature will; and in at least the last four of the seven years there should be an increasing emphasis upon fitting the child vocationally, upon preparing him, that is, to take his due part, as an active and competent worker, in the business of the community in which he lives.

This lengthening of the school day would abolish that experience, demoralizing for most children, which we call "home lessons"; it would destroy that Moloch — the idling on street corners and in vacant lots, — which is devouring so many of our boys and girls; it would, by organizing and supervising games and plays, make them what they should be: builders up of body and of character; and it would, as a rule, give us children, at fifteen or sixteen, who are ready to take up seriously, enthusiastically and effectively, the work of fitting themselves, either through university training, or through the school of actual experience, for what is the main business in life of substantially every man and woman. That main business is the establishing, before twenty-five years of age, of a genuine family life, under which the efficient father shall be steadily employed, under which the competent mother shall run her house economically and wisely, under which the children, as they arrive, shall be amply nurtured and properly educated, and under which all the family shall appreciate and shall exercise their full duty as responsible citizens in their town and state.

Such a school life will be long in coming, for it will be tremendously expensive; and we are not yet civilized enough to realize that large expenditures in childhood save enormously greater ones in after life. We are not yet wise enough to see that, however expensive the right sort of schooling may be, it can never be so costly as are the hospitals, jails, asylums and other dreadful buildings in which we try to hide our social mistakes and to repair the damage which society inflicts upon so many of its helpless members by failing properly to protect and educate them in their early and adolescent years.

This elaborated education will be long in arriving, moreover, because it will be hard to overcome, on the one hand, our conservatism, which cannot imagine any schooling different from what we have and, on the other hand, our misplaced tenderness, which makes us think we are giving our children freedom when we are really condemning most of them to aimless idleness. But we can take a long step towards this real, thorough education of the whole boy and girl, by doing all that we can at once to further vocational training: that is, to further the wise and thorough preparation of every child and youth for an efficient, and therefore a happy, life as a worker and as a citizen.

What are the essentials of such an efficient and happy life?

First: good health. This means physical education from the very beginning, ordered play, a trained use of all the muscles and senses, hard, regular work with a definite object, fresh air, bodily freedom and ceaseless activity.

Secondly: honesty, self control and self respect. This means ceaseless moral training, through good example, through wise, individual talks and through working and playing together in natural groups where there shall be every opportunity to exercise and strengthen the undeveloped will.

Thirdly: a sense of responsibility. This means early and continuous training of a sort that shall make the child realize that he has no use or right in the world unless he eventually becomes a competent earner, a wise spender, a responsible head of a family and a citizen who does not shirk.

Fourthly: culture. This means a good knowledge of books and men, of the earth and of its people, of music, pictures, nature and all the rest of the beautiful things which give life breadth and interest.

And, fifthly: religion, which to some means definite teaching within a creed, to others, indefinite teaching outside a creed; but which should mean to all a looking beyond one's self and the material things of life, up to those ideals that are the stars to which our wagons, — be they little go-carts or great touring-cars, — must, if we are to get anywhere, be firmly hitched.

To come back, however, to earth. The school, for the child under ten years of age, need not be very different from what it now is, provided it begin early enough with the right sort of kindergarten, provided parents and teachers work understandingly together, provided the children be divided into groups so small that the teacher may know and really develop the personality of every single boy and girl, and provided that body-training and will-training have a much larger share of the day than mind-training and memory-training.

Beginning with the tenth year, however, education for life should begin. There should continue to be, of course, reading, writing and arithmetic, but these should be used as means, not ends; as tools, not accomplishments. There should be history and geography and civics, but taught in such a way as to bear directly upon the life and experience of each individual child in his own particular community. But in addition to all these old things thus made over, there should be much time given to playing purposeful games and making useful products, to collecting things and finding out about them, to working and playing together in little groups and in big groups, all of this emphasizing to the child the fact that he is and always will be a citizen who has to work with other citizens, a youth whose business and whose privilege it is to prepare himself for the noble responsibilities of a competent, free, self-respecting man or woman, the father or the mother of a well-cared-for family.

The person needing immediately to be dealt with is that, at present, most neglected of individuals, the boy or girl who can leave, and in the vast majority of cases does leave school at fourteen. That child now emerges from the process of so-called education as little fitted, generally, to cope with the world and the world's demands as is a babe-in-arms.

For these fourteen-year-old children there need to be established at once, wherever it is possible, at least four types of school: (1) the industrial high school in which the whole day shall be given to preparation for efficiency;

(2) the apprentice or journeyman school, in which a youth may get, though under far better conditions, a training similar to that given in the days of apprenticeship; (3) evening industrial schools, combining the opportunities of the industrial high school and of the apprentice school, but with more flexible conditions as to hours, length of time for graduation, conditions of discipline, etc.; and (4) part-time schools, in which the public and the manufacturer shall coöperate in training those youth who cannot afford the time necessary to follow a course in an industrial high or in an apprentice school.

The industrial high school should have running through it a strong backbone of humanistic or so-called culture studies; but those studies should be in no way subservient to the existing, absurd college entrance requirements; and the English, the economics, the history, the ethics, etc., should be simple, direct and aimed at the real problems of everyday life. Moreover, this industrial high school should every day bring theories to the test of practice by using them in the solving of immediate, real problems. To that end, this school should have extensive and thoroughly equipped shops of all kinds wherein would be epitomized, so far as practicable, all industrial processes, and wherein the problems met with would be real and the results arrived at would be genuine.

Such a school as this is beyond the reach of a large majority of American youth. There must be provided, therefore, three other types: (1) the part-time school,

(2) the apprentice school, and (3) the evening school. The apprentice school should follow very closely the lines of the industrial high school, but should have a more distinctively trade atmosphere. Being intended mainly for youth who have determined upon their life occupation, the course should be intensive and should follow as nearly as possible real shop conditions as to hours, management, etc. For this reason the work can be crowded into a shorter period, can be carried into some of the evening hours, and should occupy, of course, what are now vacation weeks.

Evening schools should not be carried on for boys just leaving school, or for boys employed throughout the working day. They should be planned mainly for adults and should be an emergency means, so to speak, for making good the defects in training of those who, because of age or responsibility, cannot give up their regular daily tasks, and yet who need better fitting for those tasks or wider training for positions of larger responsibility.

Evening schools, therefore, because they must meet a wide range of needs — from the requirements of the immigrant who, skilled in his special occupation, is ignorant of English, to those of the man who needs but a little added training to enable him to step out of the ranks of the led into the ranks of the leaders, — should make provision for a broad range of subjects and should be as flexible as possible in matters of regulations and attendance. And because they are mainly supplementary means of teaching, they should make as much use as possible of existing educational agencies. In other words, they should be, to the fullest extent, grafted upon schools already established, from the primary public schools whose rooms and forces may be utilized to teach English to adult immigrants, up to the laboratories and lecture rooms of colleges and schools of technology, which should be open to everyone who can make good use of their facilities.

The best way, however, of providing that industrial education for which so many individuals and communities are clamoring is through the part-time school. Just what form that combination of schooling and working shall take depends largely upon local conditions and the nature of the business or industry; but this system, under which the youth beyond fourteen spends part of his working day in some paying occupation and part of it in school studies bearing directly upon that special business or industry, meets better than any other the main difficulties of the vocational education problem.

The part-time plan overcomes one of the most serious obstacles in the way of vocational education, that of cost. Where the manufacturer or merchant provides the industrial plant and the specialized instruction for the so-called practical side of the teaching, he takes care of the most serious difficulty; and he can afford to do so since the ultimate benefit accrues to him.

Part-time education overcomes the objection made by parents — and, unfortunately, too often justified — that they cannot afford to keep children under instruction after fourteen.

It overcomes the unwillingness of many children, especially boys, to remain in school after the legal limit of school-age.

It vitalizes the school-work by giving it a definite and worth-while job to do, bringing new meaning into education for both teacher and taught.

On the other hand, it illuminates the job by showing the dependence of every industrial or commercial process upon sound training in certain fundamental school things.

And, finally, part-time schooling establishes new, intimate and solid relations between the schools and the community, emphasizing to each of them their interdependence, and giving each of them new meaning in the eyes of the other.

STANDARDIZATION

SOME makes of motor car have been so thoroughly standardized that they almost put themselves together and, so the humorists tell us, will travel fifteen miles with no other motive power than their reputation. That kind of standardization is essential to the making of popular-priced machines, but is fatal to the making of efficient men. A conspicuous proof of this fact is found in the breaking down, under the stern test of war, of the most thoroughly standardized nation that the world has ever seen.

The fundamental difference between the machine and the man is that the latter thinks; and, when thinking is standardized, the result is not a citizen, but a sheep. Education should make men not alike, but different; for it is only the " different " man, the man with individuality, who really counts. Education is practically useless unless it stimulates ambition and develops character, unless it cranks, so to speak, the intellectual and moral engine so vigorously that the individual, thus set going, will make for himself a satisfactory career. A standardized education does not stimulate thought; it stifles thought, for it stuffs the child's head with cut-and-dried opinions and ready-made facts instead of stirring up that mind to arrive at its own opinions and to find out facts for itself.

The sole advantage of a uniform system of education is that it is cheap and easy. Democracy requires that millions of children in the United States shall every year be schooled; and we taxpayers, who ought to want to do it as well as we can, really endeavor to do it as cheaply as we can. Seeking cheapness, we have learned that the secret of schooling children inexpensively is that long ago discovered by the makers of cheap machines: standardization.

Therefore, we put our school children through a substantially unvaried routine, with arbitrary methods of teaching and uniform textbooks. Few children really fit into the system; the methods do not result as, theoretically, they should; and the textbooks seem to benefit nobody except the stupid teacher who uses and the far from stupid man who makes them. Moreover the system crushes out individuality, squeezes growing minds and lops off developing character, leaving many children for the rest of their lives mentally and morally maimed. Nevertheless, they have been schooled, and — greatest of all triumphs of machine efficiency — the process has been carried out at the lowest possible cost per capita.

Almost anybody can be a teacher when he has only to follow a carefully arranged schedule, under which no attention need be paid to the special characteristics of the individual child. Therefore, elementary school teachers can be secured for wages lower even than those of pick-and-shovel men; and, since the wages also are standardized, there need be no invidious distinction between the dummy who hears recitations and marks them according to rule and the genuine teacher who, appreciating that to educate is to develop a human soul through training a human brain to think, tries to teach accordingly.

The greatest advantage of standardization, however, from the point of view of cheapness, is that, through its aid, fifty or even sixty children can be schooled by a single teacher. By dividing this preposterous number into squads, she can hear one batch of children recite from the prescribed book the preappointed lesson in arithmetic, while a second batch is preparing its cut-and-dried lesson in geography, and a third is doing "busy work," that polite school phrase for killing time.

All this, however, is not education at all. It is school-drill of a very meager and unenlightened sort. Of course, it is not wholly without value. Repressive discipline, learning things by rote and marching about with fifty or sixty other children, all have their useful place in education; but it should be a very minor place. In most schools, however, this insignificant part of education is about all that the pupils get.

It is true that they learn to read, write and cipher after a fashion, and that some of the facts which the teacher tries to drive into their heads stick. But the members of one of these overgrown classes are seldom required really to think; they are almost never taught how to use their minds, their hands, their senses or their wills; and, far from stimulating initiative, the usual public school does all it possibly can to kill initiative, for it practically forbids the pupil to study things, or plan things or work things out for himself.

As to the development of character, which should be the chief aim of education, what can a teacher who must keep forty or fifty children quiet find out about the needs and aspirations, the thoughts and visions, of any one of them? She cannot even learn what the boy or girl is best fitted to do in life, for that takes time, patience and quiet conversations with the pupil, his parents and possible employers. If there is no time to do this, which concerns merely the bread and butter side of life, how much less time is there to get at those mental and moral characteristics which make John absolutely unlike Henry and a knowledge of which is essential to his real education and right development.

So long as schooling is standardized, a comparatively inexperienced and consequently a cheap teacher can handle and hustle on to the next higher grade forty or even sixty children; but not one of those children will have received even an elementary education. To educate requires training, competence and insight; and teachers having these qualifications are difficult to get at ruling salaries. Even such teachers cannot really educate their pupils unless their classes are limited to not over twenty children. Only when he is in a small class can the pupil be dealt with as an individual and given those things to study, to plan and to execute which will best develop his body, train his senses, stimulate his mind and build up his morals. Only when his schooling is fitted to him — and not he to the schooling — will it really help him to become an efficient worker, a clean head of a family and an intelligent and conscientious citizen.

CHILD IDLENESS

THE phrase " child labor " goes to everybody's heart, and anyone seeking to prevent employment under fifteen or sixteen is always backed by strong public sentiment. Long hours in bad surroundings, monotonous and heavy tasks for youth are universally condemned. Yet, bad as are such forms of child labor, there is something infinitely worse: child idleness. The wreckage from exploiting children in unscrupulous factories and sweatshops is terrible; but it is relatively small compared with that resulting every day from simple idleness.

Every child, we all agree, should be kept active, should have definite duties and should work, physically and mentally, if his body, mind and will are to be developed properly. Yet in most communities everything seems to conspire to keep the average child, to fourteen and even to eighteen years of age, practically idle.

Of course, he goes to school; but under the usual machine methods — methods made necessary by too large classes and too small appropriations — the child gets scarcely five minutes of personal attention, and is forced, during the rest of the school day, to sit in a stuffy room and to go through the motions of doing lessons which fail to engage his mind. Even the dull (to say nothing of the bright) school child has not enough to keep him really busy, and the little that he actually does has neither interest nor meaning.

Moreover, this inadequate school work occupies far less than one fifth of his waking time. The rest of his education is carried on, as a rule, without supervision, in back yards and streets. Modern home life seldom permits of regular daily tasks; the indulgent American parent would hesitate to impose them; the child craves youthful companionship; we want him to play outdoors; and the result is that nine children out of ten pick up that part of their education which determines character, from older companions, from loafers and from their own ignorant and unbridled whims.

Fortunately the vast majority of youth survive this educational neglect and become good citizens; but this idleness during the most impressionable years of life breeds, by thousands, the tough or hoodlum; and the tough is almost certain to develop into either the incompetent, the loafer or the actual criminal. One of the chief feeders of prisons, hospitals, asylums and all the other expensive backwaters for hiding social derelicts is, without question, our ignorant or mistaken tolerance of this needless curse: child idleness.

Theoretically, the father and mother are responsible for the child outside the schoolroom and should see that he has right physical and moral training. Actually, however, most parents are too busy, earning or spending money, to give him any real oversight. Moreover, the herding of youth is not only natural but right; for the chief function of education is to prepare a man to deal with, and to understand, his fellowmen. There is infinite difference, however, between the organized, supervised group, and the unorganized, mischief-making "gang," between children working and playing together under wise direction, and children idling together in dark alleyways.

With mistaken kindness we have relieved the young of the burden of regular labor; but in so doing we have imposed the far heavier burden of aimless idleness. A majority of boys and girls, fortunately, have sufficient initiative to organize work or play — and there is no real distinction between the two — for themselves. But an appallingly large minority, unable to rescue themselves from idleness, fall an easy prey to evil influences, within or without themselves. From them is made up the huge army of loafers, unemployables and criminals which burdens and threatens the body politic.

Without relaxing our efforts concerning the thousands suffering from the iniquities of child labor, we ought to consider the hundreds of thousands whose lives are being stunted and perhaps ruined, by child idleness.

Neither parents, nor Sunday schools, nor any other of the good agencies can of themselves transform discontented idlers into happy workers; but with the coöperation of the school they can. It has the necessary machinery and authority, and should take the lead in the fight against child idleness. The school cannot make itself effective, however, so long as it has control for only a few hours a day, five days in the week and thirty-five weeks in the year, so long as it dumps fifty pupils upon one teacher, and so long as it subjects the child to an irksome routine of purely mental and, as a rule, perfectly futile tasks.

Education being the most important business of the child's life, the school should take him after breakfast and keep him until late afternoon, every day except Sunday, and substantially every week in the year. With the parent and the community helping, with teachers enough to give each pupil individual attention, it should educate the child physically, by training body and senses through hard work and thoroughgoing play. It should educate him mentally, not merely through books, but through his observation, reasoning and personal initiative. It should educate him morally by setting him tasks designed to strengthen and train his will, by making him from the beginning a responsible citizen of the school community. Above all, it should impress upon him in every way the blessedness of work.

Such schools can be developed only gradually and will cost much money; but their cost can never equal the cost of the jails, hospitals, asylums, etc., in which we try to undo the evils of bad education, or that of the losses suffered by industry and citizenship through the laziness, sickness, disloyalty and general inefficiency of men and women who, not naturally bad, are the victims of this widespread evil of child idleness.

COLLEGE TRUSTEES AND COLLEGE FACULTIES

It is a common cry that teachers, whether in colleges or in schools, are underpaid; and the complaint (especially in view of what common labor gets) seems amply justified. The imperative need of American college faculties, however, is not higher salaries; it is larger professional authority and more genuine freedom. Those attained, the wage question will take care of itself. It is true that teaching offers no such money prizes as does law or medicine; nevertheless, the average professor or school-master is in many ways better situated than the average lawyer or physician. Despite this patent fact, the number of youth who deliberately prepare themselves to be teachers, by years of serious study, is comparatively small. Young men of power and ambition scorn what should be reckoned the noblest of professions, not because that profession condemns them to poverty, but because it dooms them to a sort of servitude. The American lawyer or physician is subject only to the judgment of his peers,— that is, to the well-established code of his profession. The American teacher, on the contrary, especially in the public schools, is not only subject to, he is often wholly at the mercy of, unsympathetic laymen.

This condition is inherent in the American system of education, and neither can nor should be wholly abrogated. The teacher serves the public (for even an endowed college is a public institution) and must rest, therefore, under some of a servant's disabilities. Yet, without impairing the proper powers of school or college trustees, it is possible to give teachers — or, rather, to restore to them — so much of authority, dignity and independence as shall raise teaching to the professional status of law, to a position, that is, where it will commend itself to the most ambitious and the best-trained youth.

The medieval universities were preëmently nurseries and citadels of intellectual freedom and political democracy. They were "essentially federated republics, the government of which pertained either to the whole body of the masters . . . or to the whole body of the students." Moreover, "what slight subordination did exist was, in the beginning, to the ecclesiastical and, later, to the civil power." The American universities, also, from the frontier college of Harvard, in 1636, to the latest frontier (if there now is any such place) college of the plains, have been strongholds of intellectual freedom; but in their administration they have been profoundly subordinate, in the early days to the ecclesiastical, and later — directly or indirectly, — to the civil power.

This subordination, under the stress of circumstances, has progressed until the American university has become an autocracy, wholly foreign in spirit and plan to our political ideals and little short of amazing. And this absolutism of the American university is not, as in the days of the scholastics, an autocracy of teachers and scholars; it is an autocracy of ecclesiastical or lay trustees. Whence has arisen this astonishing inversion? Why does the very fountain of our higher life present this paradox? Mainly, I think, because the European universities grew from within, while those of this country have been established from without. The old theocracy of New England, the younger democracies of her splendid daughters, created colleges to fit youth for service in church or commonwealth, and they placed over them men of notable authority. In the East, the hands of both church and state have been largely withdrawn; but in their place have appeared the dead or living hands of donors demanding that their gifts be safeguarded by stable and substantially irremovable trustees. College and public school funds are no less sacred than they are colossal; and those who administer them assume high legal as well as moral responsibility. But this large liability has been more than balanced by the gift of almost absolute powers,— powers surpassing, perhaps, those of any other bodies. In Massachusetts, for example, school boards are virtually despotic, far transcending in authority those sturdy democrats, their parent town meetings.

Excepting those strictly denominational, the balance of the extraordinary legal powers given to college trustees has gradually passed from the hands of the clergy into those of laymen chosen, as a rule, for their standing as financiers rather than as educators. From many aspects this has been a salutary change; but there has followed from it one signal disadvantage: that of putting the trustees more and more out of touch with the faculties whose members they appoint. Although the reverend gentlemen of those antique college boards could scarcely have distinguished a government bond from a wildcat stock, they were usually scholars by inclination and teachers by profession, and their relations with their faculties were close and sympathetic; while the modern financier who, by skillful investing, secures every possible penny of income for his college, generally finds its educational problems quite outside his range, and sees, therefore, less and less occasion for meeting, or even knowing, that faculty over which, legally, his power is of life and death.

This change in personnel, however, is not alone responsible for the progressive alienation between trustees and faculty. That estrangement has come about, no less, through the rapid growth of college curriculums and in college attendance. When educational institutions were small and their courses of study undifferentiated, it was possible for trustees, even though not trained as teachers, to acquire an admirable education (so far as concerned their own college) through intimate relations with the faculty and personal supervision of their work. But with the enormous development in numbers and complexity, this old-fashioned contact between trustees and teachers has become impossible and, at best, a trustee can now make himself familiar with only that department of the university which it is his duty (more honored in the breach than in the observance) to inspect. Therefore, the modern trustee has gradually withdrawn from the teaching side of the college to fix his attention upon those questions of revenue, housing and legislation which have multiplied even faster than the undergraduates.

But here again the size and complexity of the problem are appalling to men already overweighted with other responsibilities. These material questions, however, must be met and settled just as those on the educational side must be faced and solved. And both business and political experience have taught men of the world that the quickest and least troublesome way to solve administrative problems is to give as free a hand as possible to some man with brains, with tact, with power of initiative, of leadership and of persuasion — with, in short, those peculiar abilities which distinguish the generals of our intricate twentieth century enterprises.

Hence has arisen the modern college president, a being as different from the awe-inspiring clergymen of the eighteenth century or from such men as Josiah Quincy (who was given the presidency of Harvard as a sort of haven for his declining years) as it is possible to imagine. The modern executives have had thrust upon them powers which give their decrees the finality of an imperial ukase. They have assumed such sway, not from love of dominion, but because their task is so enormous that nothing short of practically plenary powers would permit of its being done at all. And it should be said to their honor that they have met the demands upon them as organizers and administrators so ably that, to-day, the leaders of the country are not, as formerly, the great statesmen and clergymen; they are these modern Cæsars, the heads of our principal colleges and universities.

These college presidents have their cabinets in the board of trustees, if that board be small, or in an executive committee selected from it if the board be large; they have their staff in the several administrative officers, such as deans and registrars; they have their field officers in the heads of departments or courses; and the work of the great machine, through committees, sub-committees, labor-saving devices and automatic methods of reporting, is as smooth-running (and sometimes, I fear, almost as impersonal) as a well-developed mercantile establishment. We have here a conspicuous example of the current tendency towards one-man power, towards that concentration of authority which makes, of course, for ease, rapidity and sureness of administration; but which, in politics, undermines manhood; in industrialism, destroys initiative; and in education tends to defeat the very object of teaching, which should be to develop and make the most of every man's individuality. If the goal of a college were the giving of mere instruction, nothing could be better than the present system of administration; but colleges should be fountains of true education, and the best part of education comes through the personal influence of the older governors and teachers upon adolescent, and therefore highly impressionable, youth.

Most modern colleges have expensive and excellent

material plants utilized substantially to their full capacity. They possess, also, admirable executives who, as already suggested, are used beyond their reasonable limits of endurance. But those colleges have also other educational forces which are not availed of to anything like their normal maximum. Those less used forces are: (1) The personal influence, as teachers and men (not as mere administrators) of the leaders of the faculty, an influence which should be exerted upon both students and trustees; (2) the personal influence, as men of power and broad human experience (not as mere moneyholders) of the trustees, an influence which should extend to students as well as faculty; and (3) the perennial and unselfish loyalty of the alumni, together with the unique experience given to those graduates in gauging their collegiate training by the tests of life. The third force is beyond the present scope; but let it not be inferred, therefore, that it is any less potent than the other two. Indeed, in the last analysis, the moral as well as the financial strength of a college must come from its own sons.

As one of the results of the complexity and autocracy of the American university the strongest men of the faculty—the men, therefore, whose personal influence upon the students would be of the highest value—have been converted into subordinate administrators harassed with details of department maintenance and committee attendance. As a further result, the teaching has been put largely into the hands of recently graduated youth, zealous but not always wise, untrained in the science and art of teaching, and quite incapable, of course, of giving to their classes the inspiration which comes from contact with men of wide experience. This throws the severest strain of the college upon the weakest part, and from it arises much of our educational ineffectiveness. Mere information, lesson-hearing, examinations, become paramount; scholarship and character are well-nigh forgotten, being impossible to register by even the most elaborate machinery.

The trustees, on the other hand, — excepting those who constitute the president's cabinet, — find less and less opportunity for usefulness in a machine so elaborate that any incursion into it, by those unfamiliar, may do infinite harm. Therefore most of them drift into the belief that their trust is discharged by attendance upon stated meetings and by, perhaps, an annual visit to that department which, nominally, is their special care. Yet the personal influence upon the students of men like college trustees would be second only, in educational value, to that of the leading members of the faculty. I am not prepared to suggest any plan by which the trustees can be brought into direct personal relations with the students; but I firmly believe that such a plan could be devised; and I know that nothing so vivifies a man of middle life and of large responsibilities, nothing so clears his brain and rejuvenates his heart, as comradeship with bubbling and eager undergraduates.

Whether or not trustees can broaden their powers and sweeten their responsibilities by thus meeting their students directly, it is clear that they can influence them indirectly by establishing closer relations with those young men's teachers. For their pupils' sakes and for their own advantage, the professors need the stimulus and the breadth of view which they would get from looking at the world through the eyes of such a man of affairs as the usual trustee; those trustees, on the other hand, need the insight into true education and into the difficulties of training youth which they would secure from intimate contact with the members of their faculty. The money conservatism of the trustee, hesitating to grant funds for new enterprises, needs to be enlightened by the vision which the teacher has of the demands and possibilities of higher education. *Per contra,* the academic conservatism of the scholar needs to be quickened by the hard world-experience of a man of more varied responsibilities. That purblind vision of the 'practical' man which exaggerates material success requires enlightenment through the opposite, but no less purblind, vision of the scholar which magnifies intellectual achievement. Each point of view is essential to the ends of true education, and unless each in authority can see and understand the other's outlook, the university will suffer and its youth will be defrauded of some of the best things in college.

At present — except for certain perfunctory visiting — almost the sole point of contact between trustees and faculty is their common sovereign, the president who, as a rule, has administrative duties and responsibilities beyond normal powers. Moreover, however conscientious he may be, his personal equation cannot but enter into his interpretations, so to speak, between two bodies of which he alone is a common factor. It is essential to his leadership that he should have large powers over the teaching staff, but the opinions of the most perfect of administrators as to the individuals under his benevolent despotism should have the salutary check of others' close and unbiased observations.

In order, therefore, that there may be many instead of only one channel of understanding between trustees and faculty (as well as for the more subtle reasons suggested earlier), I would advocate most earnestly the creation in every board of trustees of a new standing committee. This committee should be very carefully chosen, and its duty should be to confer, at stated and frequent intervals, with a like standing committee of the faculty, selected freely by that body itself. And I would advise, further, that this conference committee be distinct, if possible, from that executive committee which I have called the president's cabinet; and that no legislation of any consequence should be passed by the executive committee or by the trustees as a whole without the concurrence of this joint committee. And — at least so far as relates to questions having any educational bearing — I would have it understood that the joint committee should not concur until the proposed action had been submitted to the faculty as a whole, had been debated, if so desired, before the standing committee and the executive committee sitting in joint session, and had been approved by at least a majority of the teaching staff.

Such a general plan as this (the details of which, needless to say, would differ with each college) could not fail to increase the educational efficiency of a college to an extraordinary degree, by coördinating the views of those without and those within the daily routine of teaching; by establishing a clear understanding, in each body, of the other's problems; by relieving the legislative and administrative responsibility of the faculty; and, not least, by making that faculty — without adding to its legal powers — a body coördinate with, instead of subordinate to, the board of trustees. Unless American college teachers can be assured through some such change as this that they are no longer to be looked upon as mere employees paid to do the bidding of men who, however courteous or however eminent, have not the faculty's professional knowledge of the complicated problems of education, our universities will suffer increasingly from a dearth of strong men, and teaching will remain outside the pale of the really learned professions. The problem is not one of wages; for no university can ever become rich enough to buy the independence of any man who is really worth purchasing.

This plan of coöperation would not, however, except to a limited degree, bring the trustees as men into closer contact with the faculty as men. And the plan which I offer towards that second aim is put forward with much greater diffidence. The scheme of a joint standing committee would be productive, I feel certain, of most happy results; but of my minor proposition I am not so sure. This second plan is to make every member of the board of trustees an administrative officer in that branch of college work (so far as possible) which is most congenial to him, giving him no special individual powers over his assigned department, but increasing his responsibilities by making him — together with one or more of his colleagues — the direct and responsible channel of information between that department and the whole board of trustees. It is already customary in most colleges to create visiting committees with the duty of presenting annual reports; my suggestion would make substance out of what is now little more than shadow, by having it formally understood that in all matters relating to his department the trustee would be looked to for reliable information and responsible advice.

Difficulties, of course, stand thick in the way of such a project. Among them are the unwillingness of already busy trustees to accept further responsibilities, the danger of personal friction between the trustee and the department head and the natural fear on the part of the teacher that 'administration' might spell itself to the trustee as mere officiousness. It seems probable, however, that a short acquaintance with the minutiæ of a college department would show the trustee that the professor's as well as his own time is far too valuable to be given to details of administration, and that college funds could in no way be made more productive than by giving the heads of departments such clerks and underlings as would release them from much killing drudgery. There is no greater extravagance than to permit an expensively trained man to do ten-dollar-a-week work. And that same short acquaintance would, I believe, so interest the trustee and so increase his respect for what is being done and what is still to do, that officiousness or meddling would become impossible.

These two plans, if found practicable and if developed in a spirit of enthusiasm, would lead to many other points of helpful contact between trustees and faculty and would discover, I think, unsuspected avenues of mutual help. By these or some like methods trustees and faculties must be brought more closely together unless we wish to see the growing alienation of the administrative and teaching staffs develop into a real and fatal breach. Separation involves mutual misunderstanding and that, even among educated men, leads, as in industrial enterprises, to arrogance on the part of the employer, to suspicion and dislike on the side of the employed. If coöperation seems imperative to the solution of the problems of industrialism, how much more necessary is it if we are to solve the educational riddle. Coöperation would teach the trustees the antipodal difference between the problems of a university and those of a business corporation, and, at the same time, would show the faculty the importance of business methods and thorough organization. Coöperation would get things done without compelling universities to take refuge in an autocracy which, harmful in itself, is breeding a race of youth who scorn the slow methods of democracy. It would develop trustees who actually, instead of fictitiously, comprehend and apprehend their trust; it would unite faculties which, under the strain of departmental complexity, are fast disintegrating; it would double the educational efficiency of our colleges; and, most important of all, it would make our universities, as they ought to be, supreme conservers — instead of conspicuous destroyers — of that genuine spirit of democracy which, more than schools, more than churches, more than any other human agency, uplifts mankind and builds civilization.

SCIENCE AND THE UNIVERSITY

FORTUNATELY for the right progress of civilization, that part of education maintained by schools and colleges is a markedly conservative force. It acts as a balance-wheel to steady the social machinery when over-urged by material expansion or shaken by political disturbances. To do this it must obstinately cling to outworn systems of teaching, directly resisting, at times, the growth of human thought.

Through the discovery and utilization of natural forces, always existent but only gradually revealed, comes material progress. These new discoveries and uses, by changing man's habits and social relations, compel an unceasing readjustment of mankind; and from this continued change springs what we call civilization. So erratic, irregular and often revolutionary is this action that society would risk destruction by its own progress were its evolution not steadied by some strongly conservative, backward-reaching force, a force such as exists in school and college education.

To perform, however, this important function, even schools and colleges must continuously, though slowly, readjust themselves, often adopting temporary expedients and elaborate subterfuges rather than to surrender, at the call of new conditions, their outgrown forms and usages. Hence result those compromises in education which are the bane of both conservatives and radicals. Such, nevertheless, is the constitution of society that educational systems, like governments, apparently can never be rational, never a logical and economical means to a definite end. Rather must they be always makeshifts, clinging to the past and yielding only with protests to those innovations which will not be denied. "One of the greatest pains to human nature," says Bagehot,[1] "is the pain of a new idea." Remembering this, and conceding that social progress needs a steadying force, it is easier to bear with patience the bungling ways in which the old, useless husks of teaching are reluctantly discarded.

The process of educational adjustment has been hardest during the past century: first, because no previous hundred years has seen such enormous gains in material well-being; secondly, because the numbers admitted to mental training have been immeasurably increased; and, thirdly, because the means of and the causes for development have multiplied by leaps and bounds.

Whatever the dispute over the proper ends of secondary teaching, it will be generally conceded that the aim of the college and the university toward the minds of their students should be chiefly to discipline and leaven, not simply to inform. The range of human knowledge should therein be opened to young men, but in such a way and with so much of method as to create in them that desire for mental power, that habit of high think-

[1] Physics and Politics, V.

ing, that broad and always widening outlook upon life, which distinguish the really educated from the merely well-informed. In the words of Principal Caird,[1] "A university has for its function the cultivation of the scientific habit of mind,— the faculty of grasping the universal element in all human knowledge ... What lends distinctive significance to the name University is that it is an institution which teaches, or professes to teach, what is universal in all departments of knowledge, and each separate department in its relation to universal knowledge." The University of this definition includes the college; but for the present purpose the term will be used, more narrowly, with reference to those years of graduate study and of special research through which the bachelor becomes a doctor.

Not, broadly speaking, what the bachelor or doctor knows, but how he knows it and to what use he can put this knowledge measure his real education. Though he possess many tongues and philosophies and be yet intolerant, he is still uneducated; though his degree be *magna cum laude,* the praise of his generation will be proportioned — moral worth being assumed — to his breadth of thought and his hospitality to new ideas. "One of the benefits of a college education," declares Emerson,[2] "is to show the boy its little avail." The college degree, like the hall-mark upon silver, guarantees the genuineness, but not the perfection of finish or the usefulness of those that bear it. The living seal of a real education can be given only in a true college or university through

[1] University Addresses, 1898, p. 3.   [2] Culture.

the personal influence of genuine teachers upon men fitted by character and by earlier training to receive and nourish it. The degree, under such conditions, betokens, not the completion of a course of recitations, but thorough equipment for a notable career.

True colleges and universities, therefore, must give more than is literally implied in the studies prescribed for a degree, must demand more than is involved in attendance upon exercises and the passing of examinations. Were this not so, there would be little to distinguish them from those of China, where instruction and examination have been seemingly perfected. It is difficult to define this quality given by the real college and university to those ripe to receive it: "education" has too general a meaning, "culture" a too narrow one. Perhaps breadth is the best term, comprehending in a single word Doctor Caird's "faculty of grasping the universal element in all human knowledge."

The breadth of the college, however, is far less ample than that of the real university. As has been said, the college, fortunately, is conservative, anchored to solid foundations of accepted truth. Its body of teaching, therefore, must be that generally recognized, its educational spirit must be tranquil, its point of view sober, its tendency rather historical than speculative. Receiving young men at an age when mental and physical vigor is great, but judgment weak, when romance, enthusiasm, aspiration, have not yet been curbed and chastened, the task of the college is chiefly to impart to them some measure of human experience, through history and economics; to convince them of the supremacy of law, through mathematics and the physical sciences; to broaden their mental and spiritual vision, through language, literature and art. The college has, moreover, still two other duties: that of guiding the physical and moral development of its students — the first through proper gymnastics, the second through the character and ideals of its teachers — and that of helping the young man to find himself; that is, to determine so far as may be possible what inherited gifts and aptitudes are his.

This, and no broader, being the scope of the college, it is plain that its students must be held, though to an ever lessening degree, in tutelage. Were this not so, if youths of college age — which in this generation means from eighteen to twenty-two — did not need training of the general character outlined, why would it be necessary to send them to college at all, except for the purely utilitarian end of gaining a certain amount of information? If, as none will deny, the boy of eighteen does need to learn through human experience, to be persuaded of the inviolability of law, to be cultured through acquaintance with the ripest fruits of civilization, who is the best judge of how these weighty matters shall be opened to him, — the college faculty, or himself? Such a question can receive but one answer. Choice the youth should have; but not the aimless grasping of a child with a heap of toys. Only as he gains that wisdom and power which it is the province of the college to develop, ought the choosing to be more fully his; and never should it lie absolutely with him.

The general trend of his studies, after he shall have been at college long enough to have gained and given some knowledge of his capacities, must, indeed, be established by the youth himself; but having fixed his general direction, he is not then to be permitted to tack and veer, hither and yon, trying this and that subject as fancy or indolence may prompt; his course, a limited one at best, must be so far laid out for him, there must be such correlation in his lines of study, that in the short time of college residence he may be carried as far as possible out of irresponsible boyhood into well-balanced, broadminded, cultivated manhood. There is no contradiction in saying that a student's course should be narrowed in order to make him broad; but the restricting of his work and the resultant broadening of his life should be controlled, not by him, ignorant, but by those who through years of study, experience and teaching have "grasped the universal element in all human knowledge."

The breadth which comes from the university is widely different,—not in kind, but in degree. The college is designed to bring youth up to the mental level of his age, the university should carry him above it; the college fulfills its purpose in conserving present civilization, the university should build toward a higher intellectual and moral life; the college leaves its graduate measurably familiar with or able to familiarize himself with the sum of human knowledge, the university should graduate men able to make immediate addition to that sum; the college should make students, the university, scholars.

The spirit of the university, therefore, must be one of absolute freedom, yet of rigorous severity. Its students must not only be men,—such men as the genuine college breeds,—they must be treated like men and judged like men. Therein there should be neither ornament nor convention, neither excuses nor "conditions," but work of the most exact and exacting kind. The college must and may adapt itself to the average man; the university exists for the exceptional man. No flight of the imagination and no depth of research but the university should encourage and give scope to; but it must unflinchingly require imagination to be steadied by learning and sobered by hard work, it must demand that research set forth from established principles and follow rigorous methods to provable results. Whatever may have been its origin and however shamefully the word may have been abused, the time has come when, for the credit of scholarship and the sake of solid learning, a university should mean that place only in which are bred, through the highest scholarship and the fullest means of research, the intellectual leaders of the world.

How far from such a standard are most of the universities of to-day it is useless to point out; how completely such a standard can ever be realized it is idle to discuss; but toward this perfection all universities should strive, and in the light of it all pretenders to that title should be judged. Every college, moreover, without in the least attempting to inflate itself, should have such an ideal before it, closely affiliating with a university that will take its picked students and transform some few of them into scholars. It is not essential that the college and the university be associated under the same charter. Two or three institutions, indeed, the United States should have wherein is offered the entire range of collegiate and university work; the rest of them, especially the colleges, may well be widely scattered. But no college should rank as such which does not "hitch its wagon to the star" of some real university; and no university but should live in closest relation with one or many colleges.

As to the professional schools, — those of law, of medicine, of the other learned vocations, — their place in the scheme of education would seem to be a middle one between the college and the university, belonging, all of them, to the latter; but, from their special and restricted nature, partaking more fully of the methods of the former.

Four classes of students, therefore, would be found in a complete university. The first and largest class, that which finishes the college course alone; the second, and next in size, made up of those who pursue the college work, specialized more and more in the direction of their vocation, and follow it by a course in a professional school; thirdly, those who, aiming at no distinctive profession, supplement directly the work of the college with that of the university; and, finally, those who complete the full educational journey, equipping themselves in the highest possible degree for a life of professional research or of teaching.

In an attempt to provide for these four classes, let not the college puff itself into a seeming university either by assuming the name or, what is worse, by admitting boys of college age, who need — as never so much in their lives — mental discipline and oversight, to the freedom and self-direction of university methods. And, on the other hand, let there be no needless waste of time, no intellectual dawdling, but always a forelooking into the work ahead. Let the college anticipate, in the highest measure consonant with broad studentship, the special work of the professional school, and let the technical subjects of that school be ennobled as far as possible by the spirit and opportunity of original research distinctive of the university. The number of years spanned by a college-university is a matter of small consequence. The period may be as elastic as the extraordinary quickness of one student and the plodding thoroughness of another may make necessary.

The classical university of to-day has grown out of those of the Renaissance by slow accretion. Elaborate as is the modern curriculum, not a link is missing by which to trace it back to the few subjects of that earlier learning which found inspiration in the philosophy and linguistics of Greece, the oratory and jurisprudence of Rome, the theology of the Church and the disputations of scholasticism, — all of it subjective learning, centering in man himself as the ancient cosmogony centred in man's planet. This old body of thought found its authorization wholly in the custom of states, in the dogma of scholars, in the fiat of revelation. Because man had decided it thus, because God had revealed it so: these were the sole bases for believing. Arbitrariness was its only rule, custom its only visible foundation. And so aristocratic has remained this ancient learning, so absolute the entail upon its estates, and so unbroken the descent of its possessors that, despite the changed conditions of material and intellectual life, it retains to-day much of its earlier prestige. Like "My Lords and Bishops," who, politically almost superfluous, yet walk before the real determiners of Great Britain's policy; so the Humanities, with a pedigree centuries old, with fair estates of literature, with a great tenantry of students, demand precedence of the Sciences, those "mechanic" parvenues who humbly minister to universal comfort and meekly control the destinies of all mankind. It is devoutly to be hoped that a day of complete materialism, when the latter would inevitably supplant the former, may never come; but, for the good of civilization, the time must soon arrive when the new will have equal rank with the old in the world of education, when there will be no more prating of "learning for learning's sake," but only a universal desire to learn for the higher purpose of advancing civilization.

Because, in the very nature of things, this equal rank could not be given to science, in the last century, by the older universities, there arose independent schools or colleges of technology. Science in its many forms and applications is not now absent from any of the elder institutions of learning; but it is not fundamental to them; it has merely been added on — in some cases quite superficially — in obedience to pressure. Their science-courses have not sprung from the original trunk of college learning; they have not even been grafted upon that ancient stock; rather have they been used as props, put in perforce to save the tree from being rent asunder. There are to be found, indeed, very distinguished schools of science in connection with universities; but either they are really independent in everything except the legal sense, pursuing their rounded careers quite without regard to the colleges of arts, or they are subsidiary to those colleges, carrying out but partially the work of education and ranking, therefore, as professional schools, with those of medicine and dentistry.

This last position, it may be contended, is the proper one for a college of technology. In the eyes of many it should be a simple school for the training of engineers, architects, chemists and other "practical" men in the technical details of their professions. And this attitude would be justifiable were it a mere question of mechanic skill. Were the problem one simply of imparting professional secrets and peculiar knowledge, there is no reason why a boy from the secondary school should not be pushed through some sort of course corresponding to that of the so-called business college, and be sent thence to the office or the field for those finishing touches which only practical experience can give.

But this whole question is not one of technical skill; it is one of education. The aim of the day, the need of the day, is to produce not simply engineers, but engineers who are also educated men. And the best means of accomplishing this aim, of filling this need, is to provide for young men having a bent toward scientific study, a collegiate and, if you will, a university education. Such youths must not be content with mastering formulæ and acquiring information special to their vocations, — a thing which might readily be done in the office of a good practitioner, — they must acquire, if they would honor their professions, that quality which the college and university alone can give, that "faculty of grasping the universal element in all human knowledge" which is best called breadth. It is by balanced judgment, by far-seeing adaptation of means, by the modest yet persisting faith of real knowledge, by personal power to inspire confidence, by the irresistible force of the man who can, — in short it is by breadth of real education, that the engineer carries through those enormous undertakings which amaze and benefit his fellow men. The minutest acquaintance with formulæ, the most surprising "knacks," will not enable this stupendous work to be done by one who has not also breadth.

This being granted, where most directly and fully shall the young man who purposes to be a leader in some profession of applied science acquire this breadth? In the halls of an elder college, which has its roots deep down in the Renaissance humanities, which is builded upon an unalterable plan of linguistics and dialectics, to which such newer subjects as are gathered under the wide term, science, are but external and, in a measure, alien? Shall he best prepare himself for a profession whose methods must be almost purely inductive, whose results must be obtained by investigating phenomena, in colleges founded upon systems of thought largely subjective and knowing no other phenomena than those endorsed by Aristotle? Will he most profitably serve his apprenticeship to the master whose watchword is the absoluteness of natural law, in institutions whose foundation-studies are of purely human origin? Such training would not harm him. A college course of any kind is broadening, even though the subjects taught and the methods of teaching have a connection only most remote with the chosen vocation of the person taught. But the question here is how best to prepare the engineer, how most amply to broaden him for his intended career. With that in mind, it is clear that those colleges will most acceptably train young men for the professions of applied science which rest broadly upon inductive thought and methods and which prescribe from the beginning, as a chief source of education, the systematic and profound study of natural laws. It is a matter of small moment, though one not to be despised, that such a college presents subjects of immediate utility; but it is of immense moment that, at its most impressionable and active age, the mind of these young men should be steeped in an atmosphere of research, that, since every man must be a specialist, it should thus early be habituated to that essential tool of all scientific achievement, the inductive method.

It is true — so liberal and comprehensive are the leading American colleges — that a young engineer or chemist could easily select and follow in any one of them a course of study ample in preparation for the professional school of science; but the atmosphere essential to his best development would there be lacking. However earnest the student, however faithful the teachers, the spirit of the place, while not hostile, cannot be heartily sympathetic. The youth fails to receive, therefore, that immense and lasting impetus which is so vital to his future and which a college of some sort alone can give. That he should fail to receive this is not the fault of the classical colleges. They are designed to educate in a certain way to a well-defined end; and nobly are most of those of the present day fulfilling that design. The trouble lies in the fact that by tradition, by habit, by that very conservatism which makes them priceless to the community, they are unequal to the task of meeting fully certain conditions which arise and are rapidly expanding with the twentieth century. Startlingly as they have modified their curricula to keep pace with the progress of scientific discovery, there is still lacking in them that atmosphere of scientific method which the colleges of technology, unhampered by tradition, have received as a birthright and which is essential to the best education of an engineer.

Having maintained, then, that the young engineer or other student of science will be best trained in a college especially designed for him, a college resting, to speak broadly, upon objective rather than upon subjective study, it remains to show whether or not the new colleges arisen to meet this need are competent to their difficult and important office. In doing this, I hope to prove them not only, at least potentially, equal to this duty, but competent, as they slowly and legitimately grow, to provide the entire range of education of a college-university.

A college must be conservative, yet progressive; it must secure to its students breadth as well as information; it must convert irresponsible boys into well-poised men. To do this it must lead a lad gradually out of the complete supervision of the secondary school into the freedom of the university by paths of study that, while teaching him experience, impressing him with divine law, giving him culture, shall also conserve his physical and moral soundness and enable him to "find himself." For such a task as this has not the college of applied science unusual qualifications? What better field can there be for conservative progression than in a course of technology, where the measurably exact knowledge of yesterday is being steadily supplanted by the more exact knowledge of to-day, where the methods based upon earlier discoveries are always in process of modification through newer researches? By the very character of scientific investigation, which must be thorough, which must be honest, which must proceed from the student himself, the boy is led to an understanding of life, to a comprehension of and respect for law, to a self-knowledge, that of themselves would make a man of him. But, in addition, the "unity in variety" of such a college, the many professional courses emanating from a few fundamental sciences, permit of the gradual expansion of the student's mind, of his slow release from the supervision of the earlier work into the freedom of later researches, of an unfolding of himself, of a discovery of his weak and his strong points most broadening to him and most enlightening to his teachers and his friends. Such courses present the very ideal of conditions for the right application of the elective principle. And, by its nature, very much of what such a student does must be accomplished by laboratory methods, than which no better means has ever been devised, not only to develop self-reliance, but to bring student and teacher into close personal relations impossible in the lecture or recitation room. The physical effect, moreover, of laboratory work, of the strenuous and sustained endeavor inseparable from the pursuit of applied science, is, when properly supplemented by systematic exercise, most salutary. Finally, through all the work of the college of technology runs the incentive, by no means to be disregarded or disapproved, that what the student does is useful, that what he undertakes has results, that what he begins leads to a definite end. There is added, in short, to all his work that excellent butter to the bread of sustained labor, interest.

Granting all this, it may still be argued that a course in applied science fails to provide culture; that in this direction, if in no other, the classical college offers superior advantages. But in what way does culture differ from breadth? Does the possession of primitive learning give, of itself, greater culture than that of modern? If so, then folk-lore is superior to history, child-study to philosophy. There was wisdom, there was vigor of thought, there was purity of form, there was perfection of art, in the old days; but, even supposing that the college student of the classics absorbed, as he certainly does not, all this, would he not gain as much, or more, by an equal poring over modern learning? What has the world lost of all this old culture in its progress of centuries? On the other hand, what has it not gained by the bitter schooling of these more than two thousand years? Truly, as Bacon says, "These times are the ancient times, when the world is ancient;" and to-day's wisdom, not that of Greece, is the ancient wisdom, the wisdom acquired by generation after generation handing on the sum of experience, grown always greater and approaching ever more close to that eternal wisdom which is divine. The man of culture, it is true, should possess the largest measure possible of antique learning; but his well is but shallow if it does not draw also from the immense reservoir of modern scholarship. Culture, again, connotes the philosophic temper; but what is that but "the faculty of grasping the universal element in all human knowledge"? And will that faculty not come as surely from the study of Darwin as from that of Aristotle; from the thorough search into a problem of biology as from a digging for Greek roots?

Not the topic, but the spirit of the teacher and the taught, lies at the root of culture; and be they many or be they few, be they ancient or be they modern, the one requirement is that college courses should result in breadth. The sole study of biology, as, equally, the undiluted study of Greek roots, would result in insufferable narrowness and pedantry. Each must be modified by as many other human interests as possible, if we would produce that quality of mind and character called culture. But such a result will be just as fully and honorably reached by courses of applied science, relieved and broadened by history, economics and modern languages, as by courses of philosophy, relieved by ancient history, rhetoric and so-called classics. Intrinsically, therefore, the college of applied science is as potent for culture as the classical college.

That, however, the colleges of technology, in their few decades of existence, have yet reached their fullest development, none will maintain. They are attempting, at the present time, to fill the anomalous and well-nigh impossible rôle of giving an academic and professional education in the four-year period of the old college course. Since the immediate demand is for mere technical training, since that demand is greater than the supply, since the whole matter of applied science is so new that there is not yet a standard of technological culture, the performance in these colleges of the work of education must, perhaps for many years to come, be incomplete. But in acknowledging this incompleteness, in appreciating the fact that the work of seven years compressed into four cannot induce in graduates that breadth which should be the aim of higher education, let these colleges not agree that culture in the amplest meaning is not theirs to give when, by time, by public criticism, by repeated experimenting they shall have learned how best to enrich and amplify their courses. Already are they adding to and broadening the work in modern languages, in economics, in history; already are they widening the basis of their technical instruction so that it may rest more fully upon pure science and philosophy; already, as more scholarly leisure and greater wealth come to them, are they opening to their picked students the paths of higher research. And in time, as the greatness of their possibilities is perceived, as those large endowments needful for scientific research come to them, as the vast culture-power of modern learning dawns upon a conservative, classically educated public, the college of technology will grow into a complete college-university. Then will its earlier years be given to the development of boys into men through judicious courses of modern learning, its middle years be devoted more closely, though not exclusively, to professional training, its higher years be dedicated to research, most exact and thorough, into the stupendous problems of pure science.

These colleges of science are now on trial before the world. Their years of obscurity, of neglect, of almost abject poverty, are over; the public freely acknowledges that their work was needed and has been well done. But they cannot now stand still; neither can they longer follow the indefinite path permitted to experimenters. They must plainly indicate their future course. That course must be either backward or forward: backward into the comparatively easy position of a mere professional school, training engineers and others in the technicalities of their vocations; or forward over the long and difficult road of development, by traversing which they will become true college-universities fitted to lead young men, by paths of broadest culture, up to and through the most difficult researches of the highest education.

IV. IN RECONSTRUCTION

THE MAIN OBJECTIVES

THE war is ended, and for this fortunate outcome we owe endless debt to Belgium, who scorned to be bought, to France, who refused to be beaten, to Britain, who neither would, nor could, stand aloof. Even with their incredible sacrifice and valor, however, the decision hung in the balance until we of America, after almost fatal hesitation, finally comprehended what those steadfast nations and their allies were really fighting for, cast in our lot with righteousness and, having done so, threw our whole heart, backed by our vast resources and the incalculable strength of our superb young men, into the world conflict for democracy.

Because ours has been the final, and therefore the determining influence, because of President Wilson's remarkable state papers defining the true issues of the conflict, and because of the unique geographical and financial position of the United States, we have not only had a dominant voice at the peace-table, but also are looked to for leadership in the coming rehabilitation of the world. Needless to say, the problems of reconstruction are tremendous, involving such far-reaching matters as trade, finance, international relations, domestic readjustments, especially in the field of labor, the social control of public services and, in its widest meaning, education.

In that last broad field there is a section — originally a very small plot, but now of goodly acreage — which we try vainly to set apart under the unsatisfactory name of vocational education. It would be easy to maintain that all education, whether in or out of school, is in its ultimate effect vocational; but it is a mere juggling with terms to bring the training of the lawyer and that of the lathe-hand under the same educational umbrella. When we use, in these days, the term "vocational education," we employ it in a very special sense; and, in full recognition of this limitation, it is still safe to assert that the future of this country and, because of our new leadership, the future of the world, lies in a full and effective development of sound vocational education. And by "sound vocational education" is meant the bringing up of the child and youth in such a way that when he (and of course also she) arrives at majority, he will have such control of his mind and body and such mastery of his environment that he will be able, on the one hand, to earn a good living in a congenial way and, on the other, to make for himself such a place in the community as will assure the preservation and growth in him of that taproot of civilized existence, self-respect. Moreover, his education, far from concealing the fact that its major purpose is the earning of a good living, should stress that objective and should make it as clear as daylight to each boy (and girl), to each young man (and woman) that his chief business in life is to make himself a good citizen, and that no man can be such unless he has qualified himself to earn, through acquired skill, knowledge, or both, as good a living as the body, mind and general capacity that God gave him will permit. Having secured this firm foundation of ability to earn, a man may build thereupon such superstructures of learning, culture and erudition as he may choose, and the higher he builds the better for him and for the world; but whatever may be his intellectual ambitions, they will come to naught in themselves, they may even make him a curse to his kind, unless he is actively convinced that his first duty is to society, and that this duty can be fulfilled only through his making a contribution to the material welfare of society at least as great as has been its almost immeasurable contribution to his individual sustenance, education and general well-being.

The argument for vocational education has more, however, than this one corner-stone for its support. Indeed it has at least three others, each of them equally solid and all of them together holding vocational education " four-square." These three other corner-stones are: (1) the accepted doctrine of interest which finds in vocational education a stimulus almost wholly absent from so-called academic schooling; (2) the fact that vocational education enlists, as no other form of training can, the active coöperation of all the community forces; and (3) the further fact that this type of training arouses as few, if any, forms of abstract education do, that impulse towards service to society which is the life-blood of democratic organization and the fulfilling of which is the chief compensation for the more or less monotonous hardships of one's daily living.

Furthermore, vocational education directly ministers to democracy itself, which requires, for its perpetuation:

(1) a citizen body made up of men and women who, through their power of earning, are independent, self-respecting and with a substantial stake in the community;

(2) a citizen body so stimulated by the educational process as to be both receptive to new ideas and hostile to false political or social schemes;

(3) a citizen body habituated to working together and quick to understand the value of businesslike coöperation and effective team-play;

(4) a citizen body of which the dominant motive is unselfish service for the common weal.

The war has shown, as they never have been exhibited before, our weakness and our strength as a nation; and all the blood and treasure spent will have been in vain if the fact has not been emphasized that the essential foundations of enduring democracy are personal self-reliance, social common-sense, coöperative efficiency and a spirit of service dedicated to the common weal. Upon these were builded the New England town meeting; and the world, hereafter, if it is not to go war-mad again, must be carried on as the town meeting was, with every man free to speak his mind, to assert his individuality and to take his recognized, properly rewarded share in the joint work of the community.

Upon that town-meeting basis, educational systems

and educational methods must henceforth be squarely fixed. However pleasant it might be for the minority to continue to set itself apart as a race of gentlefolk educated, in ways of mystical erudition, above the common herd, the still unpunished crimes of the Junkers and their professorial supporters, the almost incredible blunders in diplomacy and strategy of those so educated as to be out of touch with democracy, have taught us, through bitter suffering, that no civilization can endure or can even exist which does not fully acknowledge the mental, social and moral rights of every least boy or girl, of every humblest man or woman.

To such town-meeting standards vocational education alone can fully measure up, for it touches every life at its fundamental point: that of working and earning, it can assure interest on the part of every pupil by linking itself up with the problem of his daily life, it can weld the whole community into a great common force for the promotion of the common training, it can make plain to every individual the fact that life is service and that he who learns most serves best.

Convinced of the soundness of these premises, I venture to draw from them certain conclusions as to what should be the main objectives not only of our schools and colleges, but of those many other social agents which take an active part in promoting sound education for life in a democracy.

Education, it is plain, is training for responsibility; and the chief responsibilities of a human being are: (1) towards himself; (2) towards his family; (3) towards the community; (4) towards the state and nation; and (5) towards the world as a whole. Since the sense of responsibility takes its rise in a state of mind rather than in a body of information, it is not easy to lay out courses of study covering those five fields, but it is possible to indicate some of the objectives towards which those courses should aspire. The war has emphasized those objectives and has quickened the general desire to make our educational processes function, as thus far they seldom have, in such a way as to produce healthy and competent men and women, sound home life, an intelligent and responsible citizenship, a people keenly alive to the necessity of coöperation not only within the nation itself, but also throughout the civilized world.

The first objective of education should be the securing of citizens stronger in body, wiser in matters of health and sanitation, more profoundly convinced that disease wilfully acquired — and most diseases, from that common ailment which we call a cold down to that equally common scourge which we do not call at all, are wilfully acquired — is a sin against ourselves, against society, against that Power which makes each of us for a lifetime the responsible guardian of a human body. Among other useful things, the draft demonstrated the folly of teaching boys the laws of Draco, while neglecting to teach them even the simplest principles of health.

A second educational objective should be a rational, definite preparation of every boy and girl for that vocation which practically every one of them is sure to follow: the vocation of being a father or mother or, at least, a member in some capacity of a family group. The one occupation: the creation, support and rearing of a family, which substantially every one of us is certain to follow, not only is sedulously ignored, but is so obscured by ignorant whisperings and obscene innuendoes, that most young men and women approach marriage and its responsibilities not only in lamentable but, too often, in evil ignorance. For the supreme vocation there is, as yet, no vocational training worthy of the name.

A third main objective should be the fitting of every individual, definitely and specifically, for some occupation through which he can make a real contribution to the material, mental or moral welfare of society. To spend billions in compelling boys and girls to go to school and then to turn them adrift with no definite capacity to earn and with no guide to the complex roads of industry, is as unfair to youth as it is harmful to society.

A fourth objective should be the arousing and teaching of every boy and girl, of every man and woman, both native and immigrant, to be an intelligently responsible citizen of the United States. Industrial exploitation without educational responsibility is no longer to be tolerated.

A fifth objective should be the creation in every American community of an intelligent attitude towards the rest of the world, a new feeling of obligation to those countries with so many of whom we have just been companions-in-arms and fellow-fighters for democracy. Provincialism and hatred of foreigners simply because they are foreign have no place in a country made up, as ours is, of immigrants and their descendants, in a country destined to be a leader, and perhaps the leader, of a league to maintain and, if need be, to enforce peace among the nations.

And, finally, through these five tangible objectives should run the golden thread of profound conviction that individuals, communities, states and nations are in the hands of forces as omnipotent as they are unseen, forces which have laid down as inexorably for Kaisers and Crœsuses as for plain John Smiths, the everlasting laws of right and the unescapable punishments of wrong. If the war has taught nothing else, it should have convinced mankind that education cannot ignore the great issues of morality.

With these fundamental objectives in view, education, now that the war is over, must embrace, if it is to meet the new demands, courses in right physical living, in homemaking, in civics, in economics, in politics, in foreign relations, in ethics and religion, simplified, if need be, to meet the needs of youthful or sluggish minds, of the native with scant opportunities and of the foreigner with handicaps. Substantially all such courses are in essence vocational, since the making of a home, the fulfilling of one's obligations as a citizen, the living of an effective life, are life-long vocations common to us all. But, in addition, every boy and girl, every young man and woman, should be given specific training in some industry, business or occupation, some art or other useful activity through which, because it makes a contribution to human well-being, he will be able, sooner or later, to gain, if he so choose, a livelihood. Whether or not he needs or intends to pursue this specific vocation, he should be required to fit himself for vocational service, for only in this way can he make return to society for what society has done for him. Millions of men for more than four years unselfishly mobilized themselves, as a matter of course, to face death, because only through such giving could the Allied nations, and civilization itself be preserved. But there is an equal obligation upon every citizen to give himself, with equal unselfishness, in times of peace; for the enemies of peace-time: enemies of health, enemies of the household, enemies of social order and progress, enemies of self-reliance, of self-respect, of all that makes uplifting civilization different from degrading barbarism, will be as real and portentous in the years to come as the field-gray hordes, the myriad munitions, the hideous engines and poisons of the Central Powers were from July, 1914 to November, 1918. And because, during this world struggle, most of the civilized world relapsed, some from evil design and some for self-protection, into a barbarism horrible to contemplate, there will be such need as never before to meet valiantly and unitedly those enemies of civilization against which sound education is the chief, if not indeed the only weapon. Those enemies are intangible, but the weapons of education to be used against them must be very tangible, very immediate, very up-to-date. Epidemics, social diseases, divorce, graft, chicanery, political incompetency, financial panics, "bread lines," trade hates, chauvinism, all the evil brood that lie in wait to overwhelm the ignorant, the slothful, the "penny-wise," the dishonest, can be met and overcome, not by a small group of superior persons educated in special and esoteric ways; they can be conquered only by a great democratic army made up of all the people, each of them able to make some specific contribution to the good of society, each of them with some stake in that society, each of them educated not in the wisdom of past centuries, whose problems are not their problems, but in the wisdom of the twentieth century, which has known and seen such things, which in the coming generations will experience such other things as make the wars of Persia, the niceties of Greek, the campaigns of Cæsar, the philosophies of the Renaissance, the intricacies of higher mathematics, even the speeches of Burke and the "Rime of the Ancient Mariner" appear but as the crackling of verbal thorns under an empty pot.

Vocational education cannot in itself or by itself solve the problem of that new world which has emerged from the fires of the great war; but unless it is utilized, expanded and made one of the chief instruments of human training we shall not have a world made "safe for democracy," we shall not have a truly democratic world at all. For the vocational motive, whether it be the vocation of making a home, the vocation of making a living or the vocation of securing leadership in the community, is the really dominant motive of each unit of the modern state. And each of these units should be brought face to face, in his impressionable and acquisitive years, with the fact that he is in the world not as a guest, not as a drone, not as a seeker of his own selfish ends; but that he is here to work out that dominant vocational motive as an integral element in the great engine of civilization, and that this engine will break down unless he performs, willingly and intelligently, his part as a homemaker, a community supporter, an effective contributor to the commonwealth, a genuine factor in the upbuilding of the nation and the world.

A NATIONAL SERVICE YEAR

To have seen daily in Washington and in so many other centres of the United States hundreds of magnificently well-set-up young soldiers; to have witnessed at the cantonments the almost magical transformation of the slouched hoodlum into the well-groomed, alert youth in uniform; to have followed the careers of even the rank and file, to say nothing of the officers, of the American soldiery in France, was to convert even a pacifist into belief in some form of universal discipline. Even those who have long believed that education in the United States has suffered grievously through lack of general, sound discipline, were astonished by what the War for Democracy has shown. The readiness to serve, the amenableness to authority, the alertness of mind and body under proper stimulus, and the seriousness of attitude towards the grave questions of international warfare were as marked among all types of American youth as the most enthusiastic patriot could desire. By the very act of mobilizing, the manhood power of the United States was raised to a degree that, measuring it in mere dollars and cents, was worth all the money cost. And those splendid youth who, in order that the Teuton menace might be forever laid, were called upon to give their lives in sacrifice, won a double victory: the destruction of autocracy and the redemption, as well as the vindication, of democracy.

They performed this second service through teaching this chief experimenter in democracy, the United States, that a republic cannot be maintained by occasional balloting, by voluminous legislation or by perfervid oratory; that it can be preserved only through organized service and intelligent self-sacrifice. What the present youth of the country so nobly rose to perform under the stimulus of threatening disaster, all the youth of all generations must do under the sober teachings of daily, peaceful living. In making such sacrifices and in rendering such service, those youth of the coming generations will be giving themselves, moreover, a strength of body and mind, a gravity of purpose and a breadth of education that were foreign to and, indeed, impossible in that time before the great war when the attitude of the average American was not, eagerly, "What can I give?" but, clamorously, "What am I to get?"

If, then, we are to make the sacrifices of the war worth while, if we are to emerge from this time of horror a stronger rather than a weaker nation, we must at once begin to plan for some system of universal service which will organize us into a real democracy, which will make us really prepared, not for the waging of aggressive war, but for the defense of international peace, and which will impress upon every man, woman and child in the United States what American citizenship actually means.

It would be presumptuous for any individual to attempt to lay down a comprehensive plan for the organization of the citizenship of the United States; but there are certain fundamental principles which must form the basis of any such organization. Those principles cannot be too early brought to the attention of the country, in order that they may have that full discussion which is an essential preliminary to federal or state legislation. However men may differ as to the manner of putting them into effect, the following principles seem fundamental to any plan of National Service which will be really effective in bringing about those ends concerning which all thoughtful citizens of the United States are in the main agreed.

Since this national service is for the purpose of teaching democracy and of making the country in fact, as well as in name, a republic, it must be truly universal, including every person, male and female, born in the United States, or coming to its shores before the period of actual old age.

With the exception of those foreigners who may be admitted to the country after their twenty-fifth year, this service should be exacted between the ages of sixteen and twenty-five. The lower limit is fixed by the fact that service under sixteen cannot be, as a rule, of much value; and the upper limit is determined by the necessity for getting this service out of the way before a man or woman settles down to his chief business in life: that of rearing a family and of making for himself and for them an effective career.

While, for the sake of physique, the training should

have a daily portion of drill of some kind, and while, for the sake of morale, it should include steady, definite and unrelenting discipline, the aim of this drill and discipline should be only indirectly military, and the object of the training should be, not occasional, feverish service in war, but daily, unending, humdrum service in peace. Emphasis in the training should be laid, therefore, not on its military aspects, but upon the mastery of some vocation, or avocation, which is of real use to the country. Not less than one, and not more than two hours daily might well be given to drill of some kind; but the major portion of at least an eight-hour day should be devoted to the organized, serious and intensive training of the youth in something which is acknowledged to be of real value to agriculture, to manufacturing, to commerce, to the professions or to the general well-being of society.

In order to make the training worth while, it should occupy at least an entire year. This may seem a large contribution of time to exact from every citizen; but it is a contribution that will yield manifold return to him as well as to society; and, even were it a pure gift to the state, it is a very small return to make for what every individual receives in general service, definite education and individual care from the community, to say nothing of that vast inheritance of civilization which has come to him as a matter of course. Moreover, the year of service can and should be woven in with his school and college training, if the youth is pursuing education beyond the sixteenth year; while, if he has gone to work, the training can be linked up with his daily duties through some plan of coöperation between school — or college — and industry in such a way that his career may not be interrupted, and that he may, if necessary, keep on earning money while fulfilling this obligation. In that case, the year of service might be extended over two, or even three, years of actual time. Furthermore, where the responsibilities of the youth are such as to require that his dependents have support while he is rendering national service, there should be devised some system along the lines of the War Risk Insurance Law, under which those dependents may be cared for while the service is being given. In such case, however, the aid from the government should be treated purely as an advance, to be eventually paid back and to be safeguarded by some plan of insurance upon the life of the worker.

What, roughly speaking, should be included in this year of training for national service? It should provide, in the first place, for a thorough overhauling of the citizen from the medical and hygienic point of view. He should have a comprehensive physical examination, should receive such surgical or medical treatment as may be necessary to bring him nearer to full physical efficiency, and should be given such general teaching in matters of hygiene, sanitation and physical welfare as all citizens should have, together with such special instruction as each particular case may require. Were nothing else than this physical "tuning up" accomplished in the national service year, the resulting increase in national well-being would more than cover the entire cost.

The service should include, in the second place, daily exercise of a military type designed to straighten the figure, develop alertness, quicken the circulation and teach men and women to act promptly and in concert for a common end. Much of the daily drill practised in the modern camp is admirably suited to these purposes, and most of it is as good for women as for men. Furthermore, it would probably be desirable to include in the service year at least three months' experience in the open, in properly organized camps, where, while pursuing in modified form his vocational training, the youth would be getting that bracing out-door experience (adapted, of course, to the greater age) that has been found to be of such service in the "Scout" training of boys and girls.

The service year should make provision, next, for the training of students in the fundamentals of ethics, of politics, of what it means to be a citizen of a genuine republic. Much of this teaching can be general, but some of it must be carefully individual, and, in many instances, there will be needed preliminary, or concurrent, teaching of the common school studies or even of English to recently-arriving foreigners.

As already stated, however, the major portion of each day of the service year should be given to serious and supervised training in some vocation which is of definite and recognized value to the common welfare. In most instances, it would be preferable to have this training cover some avocation, something perhaps quite disassociated from the vocation that he is pursuing or is planning to pursue. This is desirable, partly to emphasize the very special character of this service year, and mainly that the student may have another "string to his bow" in the working life that is ahead. Particularly is it important that those who are to follow "head" vocations should give a large part of this year to the training of the "hand," and that those who are likely to be workers with their hands, should give a major portion of the service year to the training of their heads. Not only will their outlook and their opportunities thus be greatly broadened, but they will learn to appreciate, as in no better way, the attitude of the "other man." A tolerance which has grown out of knowledge lies at the very heart of successful democratic living.

It goes without saying that the training suggested is to be provided mainly through public schools and colleges and that, while it must of necessity be under Federal supervision, the agencies to carry it out will be the state and local educational authorities, coöperating, of course, with those citizens, such as manufacturers, farmers, merchants, workmen, etc., and with those organizations, such as the labor unions, granges, women's clubs, parent-teacher associations, etc., that can be of direct assistance in carrying forward this common citizenship work.

When the boy or girl is able to remain in school or college beyond the sixteenth year, this work would be carried on therein, but not merely by calling one out of the years of the high school or college the service year. On the contrary, it must be a special year set apart for *service,* its training carried on in coöperation with industry, agriculture or commerce and with the whole outside community, and the work covering, as a rule, some line of activity other than that for which the high school or the college has set out to train the pupil. To excuse a youth from this service because he is fortunate enough to be following a higher training, or to make it merely incidental to that training, would be to defeat the main object of the service year: the emphasizing of the fact that, in a democracy, those who receive the most training must make the largest return. From the youth who takes this training as a part of his school or college career, there should be exacted higher standards of achievement than from those who are obliged to cease their formal education at an earlier age.

For the boy or girl who must give up regular schooling before the sixteenth year, arrangements will have to be made between the industry in which he is engaged and some school or college chosen to coöperate in the work of training him during his national service year. The simplest arrangement would probably be through some form of coöperative part-time training in which the boy or girl spends half his working time in a gainful occupation and the other half in school or college. This would involve, of course, spreading the national service "year" over twenty-four or even thirty-six or forty-eight months. Another method — practicable in industries sufficiently large — would be to carry the school into the industry, mobilizing each year all the youth of national service age who have not rendered that service, and utilizing every force possible inside and outside the industry, to make that training of the highest civic service. A third way would be to take the youth out of industry for a year, to subsidize him to such an extent as may be necessary to relieve the burden thus imposed upon his dependents and to exact from him eventual payment for such subsidy upon easy and long-extended terms.

One of the essentials to be emphasized, however, is that wherever and however this service year training be carried on, it must be serious, continuous, exacting and purposeful; that the youth must undertake it in a spirit similar to that in which our youth entered the great war; and that no possible way can be opened through which any person between sixteen and twenty-five possessed of any mind at all, can be relieved from it. To make any exceptions whatever would destroy the plan.

Furthermore, the obligation of service must not end with this single year. Every person who has been graduated from the full service year should, for at least ten years thereafter, give at least a week and possibly a longer time, annually, to the government. During that period he would be again physically examined and advised, would renew contact, if necessary, with the service year avocation, and would prove in various ways to those in authority not only that he is still able to render the special services comprehended in his year, but also other services in which, as time progresses, he is becoming ever more competent. In order to make this, as well as the original service year, possible, there must be established an efficient system of annual national registration.

The value of such registration in other directions can hardly be exaggerated. If it be objected to as an infringement upon personal liberty, a sufficient answer is that, as against the genuine promotion of the general welfare such as the keeping track of its citizenship unquestionably is, the citizen of a democracy has no individual rights.

What is the purpose of the national service year? Mainly to upbuild and to cement the structure of American democracy. Only that person or that thing to which one has given substantial service does one respect and love; and the millions of the people of the United States, of both long established and newly acquired citizenship, will never become true citizens until they have been brought face to face with the fact that the price of liberty is not merely eternal vigilance, but also unceasing service. The year will give them that essential experience; incidentally it will increase their physical and economic efficiency; and, whether or not they form, as Americans are so fond of doing, a "national service year society," they will in fact constitute an association of genuine patriots, who have proved their loyalty through something far better than words, something that has brought substantial good to the country of their citizenship. The "solidarity of service" that will bind these workers together will be one of the strongest forces in American democracy.

The more tangible purpose, however, of this service year will be that of national preparedness,—to maintain peace if possible, to wage war if necessary. The war will have been in vain if one of its certain results is not some strong association of the nations to prevent the recurrence of the needless horrors of the dire four and a third years. Membership of the United States in such a league will be futile, however, unless the country so organizes itself as to be able to enforce the decisions of the league should they be flouted by such outlaw nations as the Central Powers proved themselves to be.

The mere existence of such a potential citizen-army would make the United States so strong, however, that the decrees of a league of which it is a part would be in little danger of being set aside; while, on the other hand, the national service year would not be martial enough to build up a military caste eager to put its training to the test of actual war. Nevertheless, if war should come, the whole country would be organized and could be quickly trained for mobilization as a fighting force, as a force able to provide munitions of war, as a force competent to do at once what it took the United States more than a year just to begin to do.

In the event of a great calamity such as that of the San Francisco fire or the Messina earthquake,—even they seem small in contrast with the war—those who had passed through the national service year could at once be mobilized for effective service; and in the event of a lesser, comparatively local catastrophe, the national service men and women of that region could instantly be brought together in a corresponding way.

The war has made it plain that, if the United States is to take the place that should be hers in the family of nations and in the development of civilization, she can no longer pursue a *laissez-faire* policy in such vital matters as that of immigration, of illiteracy, of vocational efficiency and of the obligations of citizenship. She must sit down squarely before, and develop a policy regarding, the vast problem of democracy in general and of the important part which she must play, for good, in its working out. The lesson above all other lessons which the war has taught is the obligation of service on the part of those who aspire to political and economic freedom. That lesson cannot be left, for its learning, to chance or to the slow process of education through individual experience. It is a lesson which must be organized and taught until it becomes the political religion of substantially all the people of the United States and, indeed, of all democratic nations. One of the easiest and most effective ways of organizing it and of making it a factor in the life and in the thinking of every citizen is to establish a national service year through which every man and woman who wants the blessing of "life, liberty and the pursuit of happiness" under the Stars and Stripes must pay for it through a service that, while enormously strengthening the country, will at the same time vastly increase the physical welfare, the intellectual strength, the vocational competence, the sense of social solidarity and the moral well-being of every single citizen.

Following are, in essence, the fundamental principles which, it would seem, should underlie any system of national service:

It should be really universal, including every young person of both sexes.

It should be exacted between the ages of sixteen or possibly eighteen, and twenty-five.

It should be a combination of military and vocational (or avocational) service, with the emphasis strongly upon the vocational side.

As far as possible, it should be given as a part of school, college, shop, store or office training, but should always be under Federal supervision.

Service should be for the whole of at least one continuous year (or half of two continuous years) and for a certain part of a number of years thereafter.

The person who has rendered the year of service should give at least one or two weeks each year for perhaps ten years thereafter, to some sort of continued course, both military and vocational.

The year's service should include, for men, daily military exercises, and for women, organized calisthenics, gymnastics or a modified military drill. This should occupy not less than one hour or more than two hours per day.

The rest of the "National Service Year" should be given to the organized, serious and intensive following of some trade, occupation, vocation or avocation which is of distinct service to the country either: (1) in war, (2) in the support of war, (3) in the furthering of agriculture, industry or commerce, or (4) in the promotion of the general welfare.

Under the guidance of teachers and vocational advisors, the person to be trained should have wide latitude in his choice of national service.

He should be held, however, to strict performance and should be required to attain definite standards, varying, of course, with the service and with the capacity of the individual.

Where the service chosen does not require for its mastery the full year, the person so choosing should be required to take other work to round out the year.

There should be a recognized and permanent organization within the locality and throughout the country of those performing this national service so as to promote a feeling of national solidarity.

For those pursuing education beyond the sixteenth or eighteenth year, the service should be dove-tailed in with the high school, college or professional school training.

For those leaving school before the sixteenth or eighteenth year, the year of service should either be subsidized by the Federal Government, or there should be devised some plan of coöperative part-time work under which, possibly, the service might be spread over two years: the youth giving half his time during those two years to earning, and the other half to service.

Without making a calculation of the cost, it would seem best for this year of service to be subsidized, jointly, by the Federal Government, the State (or local) government, and the parent or guardian, — the last providing sustenance, and the first two sharing, between them, the cost of training.

In that case, the school, college or industry giving the training, would be subsidized by the Federal and State (or local) governments, jointly.

The National Service Year should include a thorough physical overhauling, and " bracing up," and there should be included as much out-door life as possible.

It might be desirable to arrange for spending the three summer months in the northern states and any three months in the southern or Pacific states, in properly arranged camps, with the teaching of much of the sort of thing now given to boy scouts.

The service to be rendered during this year by girls and women would include all the duties of the household, nursing, etc., as well as vocational work feasible for women.

A NATIONAL SERVICE YEAR 279

As an essential part of every course, there should be a substantial amount of teaching of ethics, civics and the duties of a citizen in a democracy.

Where necessary, there should be provision for teaching the public school elements; also English to foreigners.

Where there are dependents, making it impossible for the youth to give even half time to this service, there should be some form of family allowance by the government, on the same general plan as that of the War Risk Insurance Bureau. Such support, however, should be in the nature of an obligation to be repaid by the "National Service Soldier" in subsequent years.

Industries should be formally brought in, by requiring their coöperation in providing opportunities for training, in making coöperative part-time schemes possible, etc., etc.

Townships and other political divisions should be directly drawn in by requiring them to establish some form of local taxation to be directly applied to the supplementing of the Federal allowance.

In the event of war, the entire population which has been through this training should be mobilized, either for
- (1) war service,
- (2) munitions service,
- (3) maintenance of industries, including agriculture,
- (4) remedial service, such as nursing, etc.,
- (5) miscellaneous services called for by the dislocation of war.

In the case of a national calamity, other than war, such as a great flood, or crop failure, this same army should be mobilized for such short, or temporary, service as the occasion might require.

For a local catastrophe, the army of that particular region should be mobilized for similar service.

After having taken the year's service, the "National Service Soldier" should make at least an annual written report to the Federal Government, of such a character as to indicate that he or she is still competent for this special service, and showing also the additional service which, with the progress of time, the individual has fitted himself to render.

He should be ready, at all times, for such national, state or local service as his official training fits him to do. Usually, such service should be voluntary, but the State or the Federal Government should have authority to commandeer it.

SAVING HUMAN WASTE

We have just experienced the greatest waste and the greatest saving of all history. The contending nations paid daily for war purposes more than most wars have cost throughout. On the other hand, those same nations, some perforce and some of their own volition, saved more each day in food, fuel, clothes and even such incidentals as gasolene, than they ever proportionately saved before. The war spendings — except their legacy of debts — have, fortunately, ceased. The war savings will presumably go on, though in less degree, forever. Consequently, it is not extravagant to believe that the colossal outpourings of wealth which this orgy of war compelled will be redeemed, possibly in one generation, by the spirit of saving that, with many other hard and salutary lessons, the war taught.

Even though this view be too optimistic, the war, with frightful personal and national sorrow, brought home for all time one lesson that the United States above all other nations needed: the wickedness and the needlessness of waste. Under the brandishing of a certain Big Stick, we had begun to wake up to the evils of our material wastefulness; but when some of those predictions did not materialize, — when, for example, our hard-wood forests did not disappear within ten years, when we learned of a single range of mountains in the Southwest that will yield ten million tons of coal a year for at least three thousand years, when we began to tap the atmosphere for nitrates and to double the yield of each acre of corn or cotton, we were in danger of recovering from our national fright and of believing again that Providence has supplied this favored people with substantially unlimited resources. Fortunately, however, consideration of the waste of inanimate products had turned our attention to a far more important matter: the squandering, the mistreatment, the failure to make adequate use of that greatest of natural resources, men and women.

The war brought us face to face with the appalling fact that we were and we are wasting, like prodigals, these precious human beings, and in three chief ways: First, by killing and maiming them in battle, cutting off at the same time what would have been the high grade progeny of thousands of selected young men; second, by complacently permitting civilian conditions which not only kill off a frightful percentage of children and youth before they can render any service to the world, but keep the adult population in a state of low efficiency; and third, by failing to bring out, through proper training and subsequent effective utilization, the latent powers of creative work existing within almost every boy and girl.

The second form of waste — that due to bad hygiene and lack of sanitation — we are overcoming by sound and widespread teaching in the field of right living. The third form of waste — that due to failure to bring out the latent powers of boys and girls, and of men and women — we are beginning to remedy by wise, purposeful and individualistic education. The first and most wanton form of waste — that due to deliberate killing and maiming in war — we can, and please God we will, put an end to by covenanting the nations to root up war itself.

Meanwhile, however, we are fronted with the fact that, in a little over four years, the world murdered millions of men and caused at least equal millions to suffer physical or mental impairment through violence of war. For the dead we can do nothing; for the maimed living, we can and we ought to do everything that modern science, modern wisdom and modern appreciation of the hideous wickedness of waste can do. The character and magnitude of the responsibility laid upon this country by this handicapping of tens and perhaps hundreds of thousands of young men, should be brought home to every citizen of the United States. The federal government is fully awake to the situation, but its servants can do little unless behind their efforts stand the force of educated public opinion and the support of enlightened public help.

So long as war lasted this country ceased to be a huge group of individuals voluntarily associated for their common welfare. War fused that group into an autocratic war machine with all individual rights merged into the common necessity of overthrowing autocracy for all time. From the one hundred and ten millions of us, that war machine selected, by the process of the draft, such special millions and as many of those special millions as were needed for absolute, decisive victory; but, whether we were within or whether we were without that special group, every one of us was an atom in the war machine and upon each of us depended the final outcome of the war. As such units, we could function only through the war machine itself,—which, under the Constitution, is the federal government—and so far as concerned the war, all machinery of states and cities, all civilian organizations and all individual activities and rights absolutely disappeared until the one supreme end, that of winning the war, was attained. The facing of this inexorable logic of a state of war is one of the hardest things to induce a democracy to do; and the amazing thing in this war was not that the people of the United States were so slow in understanding it, but that when finally aroused, they faced it so quickly, so completely and with such total self-surrender.

The social and economic groups to which we belonged, the towns and states in which each of us had legal residence were, for the time being, merely the culture in which the organism of war was nourished, the reserve out of which had to come the material and moral sustenance of that fighting body of millions which constituted the actual fighting machine. Whatever was our personal relationship to any unit or units in that machine, whatever we, or those social and political organizations to which we belonged, did in connection with the war, we could not escape the higher demand of the war machine as a whole, we could not refuse, any more than the soldier could refuse, to obey its orders without question and without, at least audible, complaint.

While every one of us was a unit in the war machine, only males between eighteen and forty-five could be elements in the actual fighting machine; and, as a matter of fact, those who got to the front were within comparatively narrow limits of age. Moreover, while all of us had to sink our private wills into the public will of the war government, only those millions who constituted the actual fighting armies were required to surrender their bodies, as well as their wills, to the absolute dominion of that military General Staff which, under its civilian Commander-in-Chief, the President, determined the fate, from day to day, of individual men.

No government, however, and especially no democratic government, could assume such dictatorial powers without taking on, at the same time, equal responsibility. Not only was that military establishment bound, so far as the exigencies of war permitted, to conserve the life of every soldier, not only was it bound to see that, while fighting, he was fed, clothed, supplied with ammunition and, in a military sense, properly supported; it was bound also to look after his physical, mental and moral health, to make every provision for his rescue and rehabilitation should he be wounded or sick, and to return him, when the war should be over, or when he was unfit for further military service, to at least as good a position in the economic world as that from which, by military process, it inexorably took him because he happened, through youth, strength and comparative freedom from family responsibilities, to be fit for fighting rather than for supporting service in the all-inclusive war machine.

To argue, as some men do, that the work of getting these citizen soldiers disabled in national war back into the economic world is a task for the state from which they came, the community in which they lived, the churches which they attended, or even of such a world wide organization as the Red Cross, is not only to misinterpret the Constitution which, in war, places all power and all responsibility in the federal government, but to do violence to common sense. For the federal government to cease its responsibility for the disabled soldier or sailor at the moment he leaves the hospital, is as impossible to imagine as it would be that it should desert him at the moment of his wounding, refusing to send stretcher-bearers to bring him back or to provide hospitals and surgeons for his rehabilitation. It is no kindness to patch up a man's body, if that restored organism is to be thrown on the industrial scrap-heap. To mend a man just for the sake of mending him is to do him an ill service. The physical rehabilitation, far from being an end in itself, is simply the means for making him once more a normal being ready to take his place, alongside other normal beings, in the great business of daily work and daily life.

It is absurd even to imagine any country, least of all the United States, leaving its wounded uncared for on the battle field or untended behind the lines. But it is almost equally absurd to suppose that the federal government would abandon this task of surgery and medicine to the chance kindness of stray physicians, willing and competent though they might be. The work of functional restoration, we acknowledge without need of argument, is a task requiring complete organization by that power alone, the government at Washington, which can reach every man from every state and call to its assistance, if need be, every citizen of the United States. But what we have not seen, until this present war, is that this task of physical rehabilitation has its essential complement in that of vocational rehabilitation. Moreover, for this latter task, just as truly as for the former, is needed organization complete in itself and drawing its authority from that only source, the federal government, which can reach every state and, if need be, every man and woman in each state.

So strongly did this common-sense view of the situation appeal to Congress that, after due study and deliberation, it passed, unanimously in both Houses, in June of 1918, the Vocational Rehabilitation Act (known also as the Smith-Sears Act), placing as definitely upon a legally constituted federal board the responsibility for the retraining and placement of its injured soldiers and sailors as, by statute and by age-long custom, the responsibility for physical rehabilitation had been placed upon those far older federal bodies, the Office of the Surgeon General of the Army and the Bureau of Medicine and Surgery of the Navy.

Under this Vocational Rehabilitation Act, subsequently several times amended, the Federal Board for Vocational Education, made up, ex-officiis, of the Secretaries of Agriculture, Commerce and Labor and the Commissioner of Education, and of three other members appointed by the President, is charged with responsibility for the placing back in economic life and, if need be, for the training of every soldier and sailor so far disabled in military service as to be entitled to compensation under the War Risk Insurance Law. So long as that soldier or sailor needs daily hospital care, he is the sole ward, of course, of the medical military authorities; but from the moment that he is discharged from military service, he becomes automatically a ward of the Federal Board for Vocational Education and, as such ward, has established rights which he alone and by his own free choice can surrender.

The chief of these rights are two: (1) To claim the aid of the Federal Board in getting back into his old employment, or into such new employment as his capacities and his physical handicaps may make possible; and (2) to receive, through that board, such training for employment in agriculture, industry, transportation, commerce or the professions, as his wishes, modified by the reasoned views of the board as to his capacities and the opportunities in his special field of choice, may determine. Whether the board shall help to place him, whether it shall give him training before such placement, is wholly for the discharged soldier or sailor to decide; but, having elected to receive training, the Board assumes not only his support and that of his dependents, should he have any, during the process of training, but undertakes to follow him up, after placement, and to give him reasonable opportunity for further training should the first venture prove ill-suited to his capacities.

In order, as enjoined by the Vocational Rehabilitation Law, "to effect a continuous process of vocational training," the Federal Board will coöperate to such extent as it may be invited by the Surgeon General, in those vocational activities within the hospital which are believed to have also high curative value; and as soon as it is determined that a disabled man is destined for discharge, the Federal Board, through agents stationed in the reconstruction hospitals, advises with the patient, determines his wishes, aptitudes and best prospects for economic success, and makes plans, if he is vocationally handicapped, for such a course of training, be it one of months or of several years, as may seem necessary for him, under the conditions of his former lack of training and his present physical disability, to undertake.

When a course of training has been determined upon by the disabled soldier under advisement of the board, it is conducted, other things being equal, in or near his former home or future place of employment, and is carried on in that school or college (public or private), in that industrial or commercial plant, on that farm or in that mine, wherein, after proper investigation by the board, it seems likely that the disabled man will get the best training for the field of work which he purposes to follow. The board has not established schools of its own, believing that every consideration calls for the use of existing agencies; but the manner of teaching and the contents of the courses are determined by the board and, in most instances, since it is to meet the special needs of a particular man, are quite unlike the formal training given in the conventional school, or the somewhat haphazard training common in industrial enterprises.

Wherever the training may be given, it is paid for by the board, which is empowered also to provide, where necessary, special equipment and appliances. The time and extent of the teaching depend upon the needs and capacities of the disabled man; but the aim is always to make up, as far as may be, his earlier deficiencies and to fit him, if possible, for a better economic service than that performed by him before the war, or which he would have been rendering had the war not taken place.

As far as possible, the job into which the man is to go is determined before his training is begun, both that he may have the spur of a definite goal and that his training may be focussed upon a concrete opportunity. But he is not hurried in his training, neither is he allowed to dawdle, for the object of this process of preliminary education is quite as much to make the man ready for efficient general service in the world as it is for effective immediate service in the line of work which he has elected to follow. It is as far from the intention of the board to produce men having exaggerated notions as to the debt owed them by society, as it is to turn out half-baked workers to be tolerated simply because they are in some degree disabled. The jobs which these men undertake will be theirs because they are fitted to take them; they will hold them because they are ready to do a man's work; and while the board will see to it that they are not exploited, it will not ask any employer to keep a disabled soldier who cannot and does not "make good."

In this task of placement the board has the specific right, under the law, to ask the coöperation of the Department of Labor, and it has the general right, under the common debt which we owe to these disabled men, to seek the coöperation of every employer in every line of activity. There will arise many perplexing problems of wages, of employers' liability, of special equipment, of unusual conditions due to the man's handicap: each must be met as it arises, and all will be successfully wrought out if there is that same fine spirit of coöperation in solving the new problems brought forward by after-war conditions as has been shown in meeting the unprecedented difficulties of the war itself. The federal government will do its part by providing the money and the administrative machinery necessary to make every disabled soldier as effective in the economic field as he was effective on the field of battle; but the government can do little unless it has the hearty and intelligent backing of every school, every industry and every citizen upon whom it may call for aid in this great, complex task of fitting back into economic life the thousands of men who, taken out by the inexorable command of war and injured in the exercise of war, have been or are to be rehabilitated by the government. That government which had the right to summon them to the abnormal service of military duty, has no less right to call them back again to normal, life-long service upon the farm, in the shop or mine or counting-house, on the railroad, or in the several professions. Before it can exercise that right, however, it must have fulfilled, as it proposes to fulfill, its sacred obligation to make those men as efficient as possible, not only physically, but also vocationally in the widest possible field of effective economic service.

THE WAR'S CRIPPLED

Almost no problem in connection with the war makes an appeal so direct and so universal as that of the future status of those soldiers and sailors who, while they have not made the supreme sacrifice, have yet given to their country their eyesight, their hearing or one or more of their limbs, or who, having contracted disease in war, must go through life with diminished vitality and reduced earning capacity.

Because of this strong appeal, there is danger that so many organizations will undertake the work of amelioration that much confusion and overlapping of effort will result; that the important business of rehabilitating these stricken men will be approached from the angle of sentimentality rather than of common sense; and that, largely because of this, the work will fall too much into the hands of amateurs whose desire to be of help outruns their willingness carefully and painfully to prepare themselves for intelligent service.

The problem raised by the large number of crippled and otherwise handicapped men is both moral and industrial. It is supremely important that young men who have given so much to their nation should not be led, through unwise dealing with their cases, to sacrifice also their initiative, their self-reliance and even, possibly, their self-respect. It is to a less degree important that industry, which needs every resource in man power that it can muster, should not be deprived of the abilities, both mental and physical, that, diminished though they may be by the hurts of war, will still be available for many years of genuine contribution to the welfare of the state.

Whether a man injured in battle or by disease contracted in war is to continue to be an asset to society and to the industrial world, or is to degenerate into a burden not only to his family and to the country but also to himself, depends upon how this question of his rehabilitation is answered by the government which has been preserved through his sacrifices and those of his fellow soldiers and sailors. And the point at which it is determined whether he is to be the one thing or the other is the moment when, restored to life and to some measure of efficiency by surgical or other treatment at the base hospital, he realizes that he is to go back into the world in very different case from that in which, leaving the ordinary courses of his life, he became a part of the vast war machine. Beginning at that moment, everything possible should be done to make him believe that while he goes back with a different efficiency it is not necessarily a diminished efficiency, and that every force in the community stands ready to back him in his attempt to make himself a social and industrial unit just as effective as, if not indeed more effective than, he was before.

The problem, then, of the physical and vocational rehabilitation of the soldier or sailor injured in battle is a problem of the goal; and no argument for this or that course of surgical and medical treatment and for this or that subsequent education can be sound that does not keep constantly in mind the object for which that process of rehabilitation is to be carried on. If the work of the surgeon and teacher is to have no other result than that of re-creating a human body doomed to sit in idleness, or to be engaged in useless occupations for the remainder of its life, then that work is a real disservice, not only to society but to the man himself. Or if, skillful as the surgery and well-meaning as the education may be, these are looked upon as ends in themselves rather than as a means to the supreme end of turning back to the world as efficient a citizen as that maimed human being can become, then those efforts, no matter how imbued with learning and good-will, have been not only thrown away, but actually prostituted.

Since the goal is all-important in this matter of rehabilitation, it follows that the process of regeneration should be intelligently continuous, that it should always take into reckoning every pathway leading to that goal, and that it should be so broadly controlled as to permit of utilizing every force that may bear, in greater or less degree, upon that ultimate result. From this it follows that the rehabilitation of the soldier or sailor for whose handicapped condition the government is directly responsible, is a task that the government alone can carry out. Only the government has the comprehensive power to command, to organize and to make effective all the social forces which, sooner or later, must be focused upon the handicapped man in order to bring him to the desired social and industrial goal.

Important as may be the work of coöperation on the part of states and communities, necessary as it may prove to be to mobilize the forces of private philanthropy in this far-reaching work, all those minor elements and aids can be made effective only as they are tied into and made an integral part of the single process through which the government must undertake to restore to society in general, and to industry in particular, as effective and self-reliant a man as can be reconstructed out of the shattered thing for whose shattering the government was, of course, responsible.

In this process of reconstruction the fundamental necessities are continuity of action and definiteness of aim. The long and tedious process of physical healing and of industrial adaptation will wear down the spirit of the cheeriest patient unless there is kept clearly before him the reward of ultimate social efficiency. The methods of restoration will have not only no continuity, they will have no meaning, unless all those concerned in that restoration, from the stretcher-bearer through the surgeons, nurses and teachers of vocational therapy to those who are training the man for his old or for some new vocation, keep always before themselves, as well as before the patient, the fact that he is neither "victim" nor "derelict." He must be by direct argument persuaded that he is a normal member of society, handicapped for a time by his injury, but spurred by that handicap to make more of himself than would have been likely had he not gone through the virilizing process of service to his country and mankind.

The usual successive stages of this continuous process from the battlefield to the moment when the man reëstablishes himself, to all intents and purposes, as a normal factor in society, are, roughly, these: restoration to life through surgical or medical treatment, or both; bed convalescence, with such occupations as may be possible for keeping the mind of the patient diverted from himself; advanced convalescence, with such mechanical and other therapies as are essential to muscular and other restoration, and with such vocational therapy as will not only assist the other therapies but will keep the patient always headed towards industrial restoration; vocational training proper, in which either he is definitely retrained (under the conditions of his handicap) for his former vocation, is given advanced instruction in that vocation, or is fitted for an entirely new field of activity; placement, wherein, with the most careful regard not only to his present abilities but also to his future opportunities, he is so put back into industry as not to disrupt the normal industrial situation; and follow-up, through which those who have been responsible for restoring him to a place in the economic world see to it that, so long as he may really need guidance and moral support, he gets it, care being taken that nothing is done to weaken his self-reliance and his self-respect.

Fortunately, the machinery for this intelligent, continuous process of conducting the maimed soldier from the battlefield to the productive industry already exists and is, or has the promise of being, to a high degree efficient. The plans of the surgeon general's office for the care of the men immediately behind the line, in base hospitals, in general hospitals in Europe, and in distribution and special hospitals on this side of the Atlantic, were extensive, wisely made and under the supervision of the best surgical, medical and lay minds that the country, and indeed the world, can produce. The various therapies and other restorative measures, including vocational therapy, have been given unusual study during the past decade; and restorations that a few years ago would have been thought miraculous are now occurrences of every day.

Vocational education, a thing laughed at twenty years ago, has made extraordinary strides during the recent years; and its leaders, both inside and outside the schools, are competent to apply the now well-understood principles of that form of education to the special problems of the handicapped. The schools, the colleges, the professional schools not only stand ready, they are organized as never before, to give intelligent help both in restoring the maimed man to useful living and in lifting him to a position higher than that held by him before his injury. Large, well-organized and well-correlated bodies of employers and of employees are eager to do their part in putting these much-needed men back into the industries, to the mutual advantage of industry and of the mutilated man himself. Organized philanthropy is in such a position of preparedness as it never has been before to supplement the work of the government, both with money and with assistance in organizing those lines of social service in which governmental machinery is not usually effective. It is important to realize, too, that industry, partly through its own gradual enlightenment and mainly through the teaching of war, has come to recognize that the temporary problem of the crippled soldier finds its permanent counterpart in the unending problem of those maimed in every conceivable way by industry itself. For this reason it will be easy, as it will be imperative, to carry over into industry, to meet its normal demands, the same machinery that is being devised to fulfill the abnormal demands of war.

Excellent as all this existing machinery is, it will not function properly unless from the first to the last there is real, continuous, what one might call "flowing" coöperation by these agencies, and unless all their activities and all their coöperative measures have as their common aim the restoration of the man to his former place — or to a better place — as a genuine factor in the industrial, mercantile, agricultural or professional world. Having those two things in mind, continuity and singleness of aim, it is not without profit to consider some of the dangers that must be looked out for in carrying out, officially and unofficially, the truly sacred work of repairing, so far as it can be repaired, the manifold and cruel human damage to American citizenship that has resulted from the war.

An initial danger was that the beginning of the work of restoration might be delayed too long. It is obvious that the more quickly an injured man can be brought to the base hospital, there to be operated upon by the utmost skill obtainable, the better will be his chances of complete physical restoration. It is not, however, so generally recognized that every hour's delay in beginning, on the one hand, such treatment as may be necessary to prevent ankyloses, weaknesses, clumsiness and even tendency to undue fatigue in the injured parts, and, on the other hand, such mental and physical therapies as tend to restore hope, self-confidence and determination to live as normal a life as possible, diminishes in arithmetical if not in geometrical proportion, the man's chances of subsequent happiness and civic usefulness. The whole atmosphere surrounding the man fresh from the battlefield should be one of courage, of forward-looking, of confidence that the world still holds for him not only the old opportunities, but even better chances.

The invalid may come to be regarded and especially may come to regard himself, not as a man who has had a temporary "set-back" soon to be overcome, but as an interesting "case" to be worked upon and (in a proper sense) experimented with, to see what the surgical or medical results may be. Nothing is more fatal than for a sick man of any kind to take an interest in the invalid state and to view his treatment as an end in itself. So far as the patient is concerned, the means by which he is being restored should be treated as of the most minor consequence; the thing to be kept always prominent before his mind is the restoration, to which the treatment is merely the necessary avenue.

The soldier or sailor may become not only "hospitalized," but "feminized," by too much coddling both within and without the hospital. Hero worship is popular;

nurses are but human; thousands of well-meaning women have little to do and a large capacity for sentimentalism; the ease and comparative luxury of the hospital, after the hardships of the field, tend strongly to break down a man's morale; and he has larger opportunity probably than ever before for self-contemplation and, if it is not checked, self-pity. It is far healthier for the patient to regard the hospital period as a necessary nuisance temporarily barring his way towards active usefulness, than it is — as may happen if he be too much coddled — for him to look upon it as a sort of paradise between the hell of the battlefield and the nightmare of life out in the cold world with a leg, an arm or perhaps both eyes, gone.

The work of vocational training, which includes not only the work of fitting the patient to earn but also of teaching his shattered body to perform, through artificial aids, or through new dexterities, the work that the unmaimed body used to do, may be delayed so long that the man loses the habit of work and the impulse to achievement before the training for that work and achievement along the new lines begins. The danger in the "bedside occupation" lies not in the futility of it, but in the fact that it is not work, that a man could never be fooled into believing that it is, and that he may develop an appetite for "passing the time" rather than for doing genuine work that produces something real and leads at least a short step forward on the road to livelihood. It would seem most important to make a special study of "bedside occupations" with the view of ascertaining whether even they may not be made in some degree vocational.

The time of beginning vocational rehabilitation may be too long put off, again in deference to supposed surgical or medical demands. Nothing in the direction of vocational training should be permitted, of course, to interfere with the proper healing of the man's wounds, or with the restoration of his physical and mental poise; but there is always a possibility that the doctor, necessarily unfamiliar with industries and with processes of training, may exaggerate their danger from the surgical standpoint and very greatly minimize their value as a veritable aid to recovery. The surgeon cannot bring the vocational expert too early into counsel; and if each stands up as strongly as possible for his own point of view, while deferring as little as may be to the possible prejudices of the other, they are almost certain to reach a middle ground that will in most cases prove the safest for the welfare of the patient.

No connection, or little connection, may be set up between the vocational therapy of the hospital and the vocational training that, in most cases, the patient must have before he can be restored to industry. The results, in that case, are doubly evil: there is brought about an unfortunate, and often disastrous, break between the skill that the man attains in the hospital and that which he must attain outside, and there is thrown away a period that is valuable beyond reckoning in determining the fitness of the patient for his future occupation in general and for that special branch of it which, with his handicap, he is best suited to follow.

The whole question of vocational training, whether therapeutic or industrial, may be handled in too routine a fashion. Most of the men receiving hospital treatment are comparatively young. As a consequence, comparatively few had achieved a settled vocation before they went to war. Even those who have reached seeming equilibrium probably chose their vocation quite at haphazard. The experience of warfare has broadened their vision and may perhaps have stirred latent ambition. The early days of vocational training, therefore, are most fruitful in opportunity to relocate the young man industrially; to find out whether, even with his handicap, he may not greatly better his chances in the world; whether or not, with this exceptional opportunity, he may branch out into some quite new field of endeavor; whether or not he may have possibilities of achievement that had his life flowed in the old channels, would never have been discovered. But if this most valuable work of vocational exploration is to be undertaken, it is absolutely essential that the work of the surgeon and the doctor who must of necessity view the curative workshop from its therapeutic aspect, should be unceasingly supplemented by that of the real vocational expert who will know how to elicit from the patient's earliest vocational reactions, hints probably of the utmost value as to his latent possibilities, aptitudes and unexpressed ambitions.

Not only may the hospital feel inclined to hold on to the patient — especially if he be an interesting case — too long, but it may magnify an hour of needed massage or an occasional therapeutic exercise out of all proportion as compared with giving the man steady, purposeful and serious vocational training. Just as it is desirable, from the point of view of his future welfare as a citizen, to get the crippled soldier off the battlefield at the earliest moment, so it is equally important to get him out of bed as quickly as possible; and it is of still greater moment, from that same viewpoint, to get him out of the hospital and on the road to work at the very first hour that regard for his physical safety will allow. There is nothing so easy as relaxation; there is nothing so essential to abnormal as well as to normal men as the bracing tonic of real work. And there seems every reason to believe that such a "brace" is as valuable from the therapeutic as it is from the vocational standpoint.

There is danger, too, that the vocational training may itself be institutionalized rather than individualized. Even less than normal men can handicapped men and youth be treated by herd methods. Every crippled soldier is a problem in himself; and the very fact that he has been so long subjected, first in the army and then in the hospital, to disciplines that tend to crush individuality, make it doubly necessary that at the earliest moment his ego should be recognized and forced to assert itself in the opportunities for active decision inseparable from both the choice of and preparation for a real vocation. If there were no other arguments, this alone would prove the unwisdom of having his vocational training under army control.

The handicapped men may be trained for inferior and somewhat discredited vocations. Tradition seems to have set aside certain trades as belonging peculiarly to the handicapped and, almost without exception, those vocations are ill-paid, uncertain of patronage and verging on the field of beggary. Nothing could be more disastrous for the great experiment of putting handicapped men really on their feet than to continue to condemn them to these pariah jobs. On the contrary, the only hope of success is in training these men for, and securing their admission to, those dignified trades, occupations and professions to which normal men are proud to belong. There is no profession too occult, no occupation too complex, no trade too difficult for a handicapped man to aspire to, provided he have the ability to fill it and the grit to prepare himself to conquer it.

It may be attempted to meet this problem of vocational rehabilitation by methods of segregation, colonization, or by other schemes for putting the handicapped by themselves. It would seem almost superfluous to argue that one does not make an abnormal man normal by herding him with other abnormals, and that the action and reaction of a lot of handicapped men set apart by themselves would soon convert them all into physical and moral invalids with their lives given mainly to the comparison of symptoms and to multiple bewailing of their unjust lot. The salvation of a crippled man is to put him into as close contact as possible with whole men, who will give him not only actual help in his work, but the far greater assistance that comes to the abnormal from the breezy health and strength of those who are sound in wind and limb.

It may be attempted to undertake the work of placement for these handicapped men without proper consideration of such fundamental problems as those of general and of local labor demand; of the permanency of the proposed occupation; of the adjustment of wages, which in some cases will have to be on a lower level than that of the normal worker; of the relation of this particular problem to the larger question of industrial relations; of the legal and other difficulties involved in the conditions surrounding employers' liability insurance; of the circumstances under which the crippled men must work, etc. To make this mistake would be to nullify all that had been done in preparing the man for vocational efficiency; and the fact that such complex business problems as these stand at the end of the vocational road emphasizes anew the inadequacy of merely medical, or solely military, control for this far-reaching service.

It may be deemed sufficient to train the returned soldier or sailor, to find him a position and then to let him shift for himself. This, again, would be practically to nullify all that had gone before. With most cases, the hardest time will be that of adjustment, when the man, released from the supervision, first of the hospital and then of the educational process, finds himself, handicapped and probably in a new occupation, confronted with the rush and indifference of the competitive world. It is at this trying time that the man needs someone at his side to whom he may turn for advice, for courage, for help over the high hurdles of industrial adjustment. But, as has already been said, to coddle him at that time, to give him too much support, to treat him as a weakling, would be to do him the greatest of injuries. The work of " follow-up " will prove to be one of the most complicated in the whole series of big problems connected with rehabilitation; but it is a work that must be provided for as carefully as for any of the preceding steps. On no account, moreover, must this difficult service be put into the hands of amateurs. Here, of all places, are needed the experience, the wisdom, the clear common sense of men and women who have given years to preparing themselves for this most expert task of social adjustment.

These are a few of the dangers inherent in the work of rehabilitating the soldiers and sailors who gave of their youth and strength on our behalf. After that sad procession has been sorted out, after the hopeless cases have been sent to the asylums of one sort and another that this generous country will provide, after the slightly crippled have been easily put back into industry, and after the really handicapped have been, far less easily, helped to find their best places in the economic world, there will still remain, presumably forever, the equally sad procession of the industrially crippled, the men who, whether by their own fault or by that of industry itself, have been permanently maimed and who are, for society, a charge almost if not quite as sacred as that of men crippled by war. The bases of action and the fundamental dangers to be avoided are exactly the same with these industrial cripples as with the maimed soldiers and sailors. It would seem reasonable, therefore, that practically the same machinery should be utilized in the rehabilitation of these victims of economic, as in restoring those victims of military, necessity. Every step in the process of training, every need for coöperation, every obstacle to be avoided and overcome — above all, everything that concerns the ultimate goal of the rehabilitation — holds as exactly for one victim as for the other. And one of the ameliorations of the war will be found, it is practically certain, in the new and truly humane way in which society will in future view those industrial cripples, whom, heretofore, it has either ignored or condemned to mendicancy.

EMPLOYING THE HANDICAPPED

AMONG the many worries that rob the nightly rest of a manufacturer or other employer is the ceaseless fear of accidents which may injure one or perhaps many of his men. The continual and considerable cost of the problem, in the now usual form of liability insurance, is the least of the employer's troubles. What disturbs him is that his plant may be responsible for all the sorrow and economic loss which the killing or maiming of even one man or woman is certain to entail.

Moreover, a man with any decency of feeling (and most employers have a good deal more of this than they are given credit for) is always puzzled what to do with a maimed employee, especially if he has been long in service. The mischief of the thing has heretofore been that both employer and injured man have labored under the mistaken notion that a maimed workman is a " has been," whose only resource is either a pension paid straight out or a pension paid in the form of wages for some good-for-nothing job which the disabled employee holds down in order to preserve his self-respect. No one cares whether or not he really works and, as a rule, he could not work if he wanted to, for the employer will not trust him to do more than sit by a gate with a watchman's badge on his coat or occupy a chair near the time clock. Consequently industry, which needs at this time, and ought to need at all times, every man that it can muster for the carrying on of real men's jobs, is lumbered up with at least a quarter million of these derelicts thrown on the industrial scrap heap because everybody thought, and most people still think, that these 250,000 men are fit for nothing else.

If the federal government still clung to the fallacy that a man disabled is a man unable, the country would be facing the very serious problem of having to throw on this industrial scrap heap a new lot of derelicts injured not in promoting industry but in saving civilization. We at last did our national duty by going into the war, and we went into it fully and gloriously; but we must pay the price demanded, both in money and in men. We do not know even yet what the price will be, but we do know that for every million men we sent overseas a certain number will be permanently disabled. While surgery and medicine can do wonders, they can not restore lost limbs; they can not build up shattered nerves; they can not always overcome the effects of shrapnel wounds, of living in trenches, of lying for days in shell holes or out in No Man's Land. So there has come and still is coming back to the United States a stream of men injured in hundreds of ways by the unheeding hand of war.

Now that peace has come, with a quarter of a million men on the scrap heap already from industrial accidents, are these returned and returning fighters to be put there, too? What an economic waste and what an outrage to treat in this way men who have risked everything to keep this country safe, powerful and free! Pencil selling and other forms of camouflaged beggary may have been allowable when we knew no better, but they are not to be thought of for an instant in these more enlightened days. That is what Uncle Sam thinks; for he has put his war pensions on a proper basis as an insurance obligation, and has made extensive preparations for taking care of his disabled boys, not as beggars, but as self-respecting men.

The best return that the country can make for the service these injured men have rendered is to give them every opportunity to perform in the years after the war the same quality of fine national service that they rendered during the war itself. And the only way in which they can perform that continued service is as efficient workers in agriculture, industry, commerce or the professions. So the government is giving them that opportunity, under the best conditions, by making a federal body directly responsible for getting them back into civilian employment, for training them to render, taking account of their possible handicaps, the most effective service, and for seeing to it that when they are re-employed they secure a square deal.

The Surgeon General's Office, as it has always done, makes these men disabled in war as whole again physically as they can be made; but then, instead of turning them out to shift for themselves, the government has commissioned the Federal Board for Vocational Education to meet each one of these men, to offer to help him in getting his old or some new job, to provide any sort of training, at government expense, that he may need to secure that former or new position, and to support him and his dependents while he is getting trained. There is no compulsion in the matter. If the man, when he leaves the military service, does not want help of any kind it will not be forced upon him; but it is safe to predict that almost every fellow will be eager to receive the right kind of training needed, either to overcome his disability, or to develop him into a better worker than he was, or to make him competent in some new line of service.

The first question that a handicapped man offered this opportunity asks is, "What job will I get when I have finished this training stunt?" The trouble with most education is that the educatee — if one may coin the word — does not see whither the training leads. The law holds the boy to his task even when he can see no use in what he is being forced to do; but neither the law nor any talk as to the abstract value of training could in itself hold men like these who have been face to face with the very real and active task of dealing with the Hun. They will insist upon seeing where they are going; and they will usually waste no time in being educated for a job unless they can "spot" the opportunity itself and can be persuaded that the only right road to that goal is through a direct, concrete course of training such as those prescribed by the Federal Board invariably are. Therefore, to make its plans function the Board must be able to point the training toward a specific occupation waiting for the man when he is industrially fit, an occupation in which he will be kept not on a charity basis but because he can make good, and in which he will have the satisfaction of feeling that, handicapped though he may be in body, he is doing a man's work.

Consequently the keystone of this carefully considered plan of the government for salvaging the injured soldiers and sailors of its great military force is the hearty, intelligent and untiring coöperation of employers throughout the whole United States. The farmers must take back every farmer boy who wants to return to the land and as many more of the disabled soldiers and sailors as can be induced and can be adequately trained to take up this industry, so closely akin to that life in the open to which men of the Army and Navy are accustomed. The industries, large and small, must make a careful inventory to see where and how they can use properly trained, disabled men in real "man-sized" jobs. The merchants must reckon how far it is safe, from every point of view, for them to use in selling, buying and accounting men with this or that physical handicap. And especially must those professions and those occupations which are largely administrative in character make up their minds to give every proper chance to those disabled men who, through education secured before and after the war, are competent to undertake intellectual responsibilities. It is a truism, of course, that the more a man can use his head in earning a living the less will be the handicap due to a body more or less below par.

Scarcely an employer in the United States but will welcome the chance to show in a concrete way his appreciation of what these injured men have done for the country and for him as one of its citizens. But that grateful employer will do the injured man and society an ill service if he lets his heart run away with his head. He wants to be generous, of course; but he must not be so at the expense of his business, of his normal employees and of the general good. Above all, he must not try to get a reputation for public spirit by taking on handicapped men for whom he has no real opportunities that will keep real and dependable through bad times as well as good. Consequently, before any employer, in his natural desire to show his patriotism by giving these returning soldiers a helping hand, commits himself to a program for reëmploying his own disabled men or for taking on new men injured in the service, it is imperative that he look the thing squarely in the face and study this problem of using handicapped soldiers in his particular establishment in the clear light of questions such as these:

Is every job that I am offering one that a handicapped man can perform with real efficiency and without undue strain upon his reduced vitality?

Is the job one that, if he is properly trained and proves competent, the disabled man can hold even when it is necessary, through slack business, to lay off a part of the force?

If, as may happen in a few cases, I have to pay, because of reduced earning power, a lower wage to this handicapped man, are my relations to the unions or to my open-shop force such as to guard against friction when the inevitable hard times come?

Am I ready to provide, not only now but as long as he remains with me, such special appliances or such individual safeguards as the nature of this man's handicap may require?

Am I going to give this man a square deal all the way through, or am I going to let myself be influenced, when it comes to the matter of promotions, etc., by the fact that a handicapped employee is less able than a normal one to "hustle" for another job?

Is my willingness to give him a man's chance dictated by the desire to help, or have I a lurking feeling that if I employ a considerable number of handicapped men at a reduced wage I can get, under the guise of patriotism, a few inches ahead of my competitors?

And, finally, and most important of all, am I going into this scheme of employing handicapped men on the only basis upon which it can succeed: that of business "horse sense" which realizes that, by the full and wise utilization of handicapped labor on a footing that is as fair to business as it is to the injured man, industry as a whole will be a great gainer and a source of national strength that otherwise would be wasted is fully and steadily used?

Only after an employer has asked himself these questions and has answered them to the full satisfaction of himself and of those who are immediately concerned in getting the handicapped man back into the industrial, commercial or professional world is he really ready to consider the details as to just where the disabled soldier or sailor can be employed and just how much training or retraining a candidate for this or that particular line of activity ought to have.

It is on this sound basis of understanding and agreement that the Federal Board for Vocational Education is carrying forward its work of placement, and it hopes that every employer to whom its agents go, seeking chances for handicapped men, will look at the question from this broad viewpoint rather than from the somewhat hysterical attitude of indiscriminate philanthropy or the unthinking standpoint of those employers, fortunately growing few and fewer, who look no farther than to-morrow or the day after in their handling of that most vital of all business problems,—the employment question.

There are few men so handicapped by maiming or disease that, given proper training for a suitable occupation, they cannot make good. The federal government will provide the proper training; during its full period the man and his dependents will be adequately supported. No chance for work will be asked for on any ground except that of the man's efficiency. If he does not make good he will be taken away and, if possible, trained for something else. That is the government's side of the proposed plan of coöperation; the other side rests in the hands of the employing public; and the whole sensible scheme will fall to the ground unless every employer appreciates the fact that it is "up to him" to give these men who have been injured in his behalf a fair chance, a reasonable time to make good, a friendly "hand-up" and a square deal; that is to say, a foursquare deal in which the interests of the man, of the employer, of the labor market and of society in general all get full and equal consideration.

Printed in the United States of America.

THE NEW YORK PUBLIC LIBRARY
REFERENCE DEPARTMENT

This book is under no circumstances to be
taken from the Building

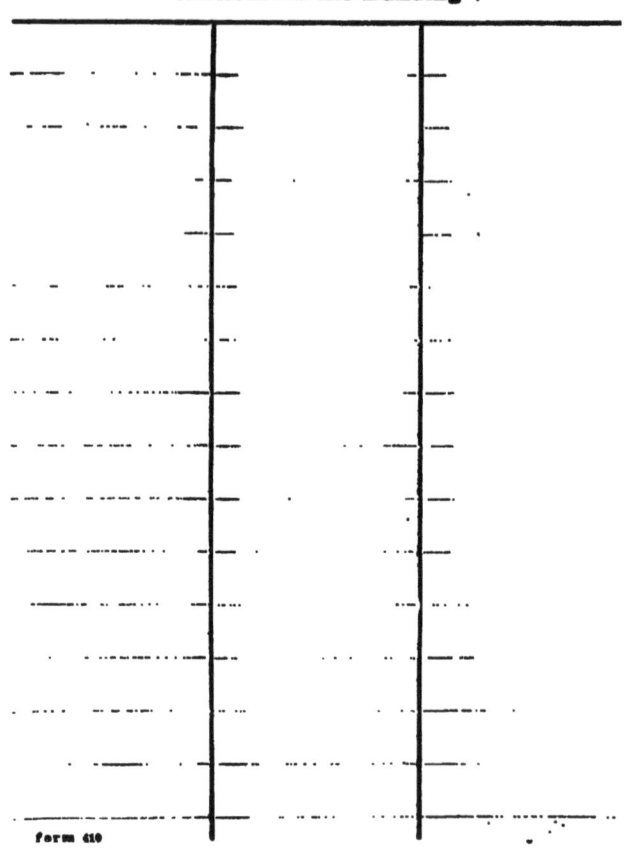

form 410

Lightning Source UK Ltd.
Milton Keynes UK
UKHW012045271218
334533UK00005B/421/P

1,000,000 Books

are available to read at

Forgotten Books

www.ForgottenBooks.com

Read online
Download PDF
Purchase in print

ISBN 978-1-330-53317-8
PIBN 10074912

This book is a reproduction of an important historical work. Forgotten Books uses state-of-the-art technology to digitally reconstruct the work, preserving the original format whilst repairing imperfections present in the aged copy. In rare cases, an imperfection in the original, such as a blemish or missing page, may be replicated in our edition. We do, however, repair the vast majority of imperfections successfully; any imperfections that remain are intentionally left to preserve the state of such historical works.

Forgotten Books is a registered trademark of FB &c Ltd.
Copyright © 2018 FB &c Ltd.
FB &c Ltd, Dalton House, 60 Windsor Avenue, London, SW19 2RR.
Company number 08720141. Registered in England and Wales.

For support please visit www.forgottenbooks.com